raphical User
terface Design and
/aluation (GUIDE)

A

Graphical User Interface Design and Evaluation (GUIDE)

A practical process

DAVID REDMOND-PYLE

Product Manager, LBMS

ALAN MOORE

Product Manager, LBMS

An imprint of **Pearson Education**

London · New York · San Francisco · Toronto · Sydney · Tokyo · Singapore ·
Hong Kong · Cape Town · Madrid · Paris · Milan · Munich · Amsterdam

PEARSON EDUCATION LIMITED

Head Office:
Edinburgh Gate
Harlow CM20 2JE
Tel: +44 (0)1279 623623
Fax: +44 (0)1279 431059
www.pearsoned.co.uk

First published in Great Britain 1995

Library of Congress Cataloging in Publication Data
Redmond-Pyle, David.
    Graphical user interface design and evaluation (guide) : a
practical process / David Redmond-Pyle, Alan Moore,
        p. cm.
    Includes bibliographical references (p.   ) and index.
    ISBN 0-13-315193-X (pbk.)
    1. Graphical user interfaces (Computer systems)   I. Moore, Alan.
II. Title.
QA76.9.U83R43   1995
005.1'2—dc20   94-42184
                                                             CIP

British Library Cataloguing in Publication Data
A CIP catalogue record for this book can be obtained from the British Library.

ISBN 0-13-315193-X

15 14 13 12
08 07 06 05 04

Typeset by MHL Typesetting Ltd, Coventry.
Printed and bound in Great Britain by CPI Bath

The publishers' policy is to use paper manufactured from sustainable forests.

Contents

Foreword

No one needs to be reminded today that graphical user interfaces are the dominant paradigm for exchanging information between computers and people. The amazing popularity of Microsoft Windows has made it clear to the software development profession that end users will not tolerate anything *but* a GUI for most applications.

Indeed, it often seems that the GUI is the *only* thing that matters in the systems we are building today. In the past, we devoted twenty per cent of our development resources to the (non-GUI) user interface, and eighty per cent to the business application where number-crunching took place; today, the opposite is true. At least, that is the way it seemed for the first generation of GUI-based applications: all of the energy was spent on designing the windows; once the user's input data was received through this medium, the actual computations and data manipulations were trivial.

We are also aware that this kind of application development is supported today by a wide range of visual programming tools, for example, Visual Basic, PowerBuilder, and several intriguing Smalltalk environments. The result is that many application developers operate on the assumption that (1) the application logic is so simple that it does not have to be formally analyzed or documented, and (2) the development tools support rapid prototyping so easily that one might as well begin prototyping on the first day of the project.

This was often successful in the early 1990s, when organizations were building their first modest client–server applications. But many organizations have now begun implementing GUI interfaces for *all* of their systems, and this haphazard process is beginning to break down. One of the big dangers is that the 'extemporaneous prototyping' approach has reversed the sequence in which critical issues need to be considered; the popular approach has been to say, 'I'll quickly prototype a window that the user finds pleasing to the eye; then I'll ask the user what bits and pieces of data should be displayed within that window'. As David Redmond-Pyle and Alan Moore point out in the following pages, a *much* better approach is to first model the tasks that the user proposes to carry out in the application, and then model the 'business objects' required to carry out those tasks; the user interface can be derived from that.

Even if the user tasks and business objects were intrinsically trivial, there is a growing danger associated with haphazard prototyping. For many of today's software systems, the user interface *itself* is a large, complex undertaking — and it must not only suffice for the software to which it is attached, it must also be compatible (in terms of 'look and feel', etc.) with a large variety of other software that the end-user operates on the same computer.

GUI design is thus no longer a 'quick and dirty' activity of prototyping a few screens in Visual Basic. It requires a thoughtful, organized approach — and for most software developers today, it requires the guidance of a guidebook in order to make certain that the proper steps are carried out in the proper order. Issues of aesthetics and psychology regarding user interfaces have been covered in numerous books in the past few years, but we have not had any books telling us how to 'connect' the traditional activities of business systems analysis and design; nor have we had a practical, straightforward 'cook-book' to lead us through the steps. David Redmond-Pyle and Alan Moore have done precisely that in *Graphical User Interface Design and Evaluation*, and I plan to begin using it immediately for my own projects; once you have seen their approach, I am confident that you will, too.

Edward Yourdon
New York City
March, 1995

Preface

Graphical user interfaces are dramatically changing the face of computing for millions of users. Over the last fifteen years the world has moved on from users having to know what commands and parameters to type at the ' – ' prompt, via tabbing and typing through data field boxes on a green form and pressing <Enter>, to clicking on windows and pull-down menus with a mouse, or pointing at a touch-screen. Well-designed systems with a graphical user interface (GUI) are more usable – they are easier to learn, more effective to use and more satisfying.

But easier for the user does not mean easier for the designer. GUIs are a very rich design medium, with an alarming variety of choices of color, metaphors, layout, patterns of interaction, structure. Among all these choices, there is so much scope for a designer to get it wrong and produce a mediocre or bad design, which confuses or frustrates the person using the system. Designing a good GUI is a difficult task.

Until very recently (about 1993) GUI design was a job largely reserved for specialists working in large specialist software houses – Apple, Microsoft, Sunsoft, Lotus, Hewlett-Packard, etc., supported by 'human factors' experts and 'usability laboratories'. But this is now changing very rapidly. During 1992–94 several affordable and usable GUI development tools have emerged, which make GUI design technically feasible for almost every organization which develops software.

Suddenly a whole generation of analysts, designers, programmers and managers need to know about how to design GUIs. Whether you work in a bank or a retail chain, in government or in a small software house, if you design application software someone will ask you to design a GUI for it. Using the powerful new GUI fourth-generation language (4GL) tools such as Visual Basic, Powerbuilder, SQL-Windows, CASE-W, Easel, etc., coding is no longer the hardest part. The most difficult task is to design a user interface which is easy to learn and effective for user tasks – in other words, 'usable'. End-users want and expect usable software; their expectations are set by professionally packaged GUI tools such as wordprocessors and spreadsheets. And software usability is often critical for achieving business benefits.

There are effective, proven techniques for achieving high usability, but many of these are not widely known outside the small elite community of 'human factors' experts who attend conferences on human–computer interaction. A few of these techniques require a deep theoretical background and substantial training before you can apply them, or take so long that they would never be cost-effective on a real project. But many of the techniques can be adopted and used effectively by practicing analysts and designers who are not human factors specialists.

The purpose of this book is to introduce you to the major techniques for achieving usability which are suitable for use by non-specialists in busy software project work. We have drawn together the essential concepts and techniques used by user interface design specialists, and combined them into a development process. Each technique and product is documented in a way that enables you to use it on a project immediately. The overall process emphasizes prototyping, evaluation and iterative redesign, and is sufficiently flexible to deal with most project situations.

We can say this with confidence because the GUIDE process has evolved out of real project work, both in LBMS where we work and with several of our consultancy clients.

WHAT IS THIS BOOK ABOUT?

This book describes a *process* for designing a *graphical user interface* (GUI) for a software system, which can be used by software developers in busy commercial environments. The process is called GUIDE: Graphical User Interface Design and Evaluation.

By 'process' we mean an organized set of activities, similar to a design method (or methodology). In designing a GUI system, there are lots of things to think about and lots of things to do. The purpose of the GUIDE process is to help you (the designer) know where to start, what to do and how to do it.

If you are uncertain what a GUI design process is, and whether (or why) you need one, please read the Introduction (Chapter 1).

Although the focus of the book is GUI design, some of the techniques and products are useful for other aspects of systems analysis and design. Task analysis is a general-purpose requirements analysis technique which helps you to identify required system functionality as well as to design the user interface. Similarly, user object modeling can contribute to system design as well as to user interface design.

WHO SHOULD READ THIS BOOK?

This book should be useful to the following people:

- Systems analysts, designers and analyst/programmers who want appropriate analysis and design techniques for GUI systems. Many of these people already have skills in specifying and designing systems with character-based user interfaces.

- GUI programmers who want to extend their range of skills from how to program windows to how to design a whole GUI system.

- Project managers who want to understand the new design products required and how to use a 'usability engineering' approach to controlling iterative design.

- Students of human—computer interaction or user interface design who want an example of a coherent practitioner-style design process. Note, however, that this book is not an academic textbook. It is highly selective — it does not intend or claim to offer comprehensive coverage of the literature. Neither does it seek to present comparisons of various alternative techniques and notations.

WHAT ENVIRONMENTS IS GUIDE APPLICABLE TO?

The GUIDE process is not limited to any specific GUI target environment. It is equally applicable to any of the main commercially used GUI environments, such as:

- Microsoft Windows
- Apple Macintosh
- IBM Presentation Manager (OS/2)
- OSF Motif
- Open Look
- Next Step

Some 'fine-grain' GUI design issues (such as when to use one type of control rather than another) are specific to the facilities and style of particular GUI environments. For details of this kind we suggest you refer to the standard style guide for your GUI environment (see Chapter 9).

GUIDE is less suitable for systems with a 'non-graphical' user interface, such as:

- full-screen character-based interfaces (e.g. IBM 3270 running under the CICS transaction processing monitor); or
- command-line prompt systems (e.g. MS-DOS).

WHAT TYPE OF SYSTEMS IS GUIDE APPLICABLE TO?

The GUIDE process is intended to design graphical user interfaces for:

- Management information systems (MIS)
- Data processing systems
- Office automation systems
- Decision support systems
- Executive information systems (EIS)

GUIDE is not focused on, but extends to design of various related types of system:

- Computer-aided design/manufacture (CAD/CAM)
- Geographical information systems (GIS)
- Multimedia information systems (see Appendix A)

Although many of the techniques are relevant, GUIDE as a whole is not recommended for designing user interfaces for real-time process control applications, where there are a number of special issues.

WHAT TOOLS OR EQUIPMENT DO YOU NEED?

You do not need any special tools or equipment to use the GUIDE process. All you require is the following:

- A GUI prototyping/development tool, with associated documentation. (It is possible but not recommended to design GUIs without a prototyping tool.) (See section 11.5.4 in Chapter 11 for discussion of some possible tools.)
- A 'style guide', this being a document which defines the 'look and feel' and standard interface components in the GUI environment you are developing for (e.g. Microsoft Windows). (See Further Reading section in Chapter 9 for references.)
- As many books and articles on the various aspects of GUI design and human–computer interaction as you have the money to buy and the time to read. There is lots of interesting and useful literature which can help you be a better informed and more effective designer. (See Further Reading sections throughout the book for notes on useful sources.)

Specifically, to use GUIDE you *do not need*: a CASE tool or a usability laboratory – although these may be useful if you do have them.

WILL IT TAKE TOO MUCH EFFORT?

If you develop software you are always under time pressure to deliver a finished product. You do not want to do anything that takes any more time or effort than absolutely necessary (and even if you want to, your project manager will not let you).

We encourage you to customize both the entire GUIDE process and its individual techniques, cutting them down to fit the requirements and time constraints of your project. See Chapter 1, section 1.4.8 'Customizing GUIDE', and Chapter 2, section 2.3.

WHAT IS THIS BOOK NOT ABOUT?

In order to achieve a clear focus and a manageable size book, the following topics are outside the scope of this book:

- The *implementation* of a GUI design in a multi-user client–server architecture, including issues such as client–server partitioning, concurrency, locking.

- The *programming* of a GUI design using a developer's toolkit.

- The production of *user documentation* for a computer system (e.g. user manuals, quick reference cards).

- The design of the *user's work environment*, such as computer hardware (e.g. screen size, type of pointing device), seating, lighting, etc. Usability problems in this area may, however, be identified during prototyping and evaluation.

- The *planning and management* of GUI design and development projects (e.g. estimating, scheduling, metrics, management of risk, quality control).

Acknowledgments

We are grateful to LBMS for allowing us to write and publish this book, which draws on LBMS experience and proprietary materials. We wish specifically to express our appreciation to our managers David Rodway and John Cameron, who encouraged us to produce a book and have supported us throughout.

GUIDE includes ideas suggested by many colleagues, and improvements as the result of critical review comments by a much wider group of people. We would like to thank all these people for their contributions, particularly John Cameron and Andy Higman who collaborated with us on developing the overall approach; Robin Heath of GUI Designers, who made several helpful suggestions on improving the application style guide chapter; Professor James Alty of the University of Loughborough and Jurek Kirakowski, Director of the Human Factors Research Group at University College, Cork for constructive review comments and suggestions; Julia Quine and Graham McConney for their detailed review comments; and all the consultants, lecturers and course delegates who have offered feedback on the LBMS GUI design method over the last few years.

Many people have assisted with producing the book. We would like to thank Tina Horan for much of the typing, and Chris Cook for the graphics. We are also grateful to our editor at Prentice Hall, Viki Williams, for her encouragement and support, and to Louise Wilson and other Prentice Hall staff for their professionalism.

Finally, we thank our partners Emma and Alison and our children Cara, Liam and Alexander for their patience during the many unsocial hours when we have been working on 'the book'.

The authors and publishers would like to thank the following for their kind permission to include material in this book.

Addison-Wesley for permission to reproduce 'Eight Golden Rules of Dialog Design' from Shneiderman, B. (1990) *Designing the User Interface: Strategies for effective human–computer interaction.*

IBM publications for permission to reproduce Figure 1.7 from IBM (1991) 'Systems Application Architecture: Common user access guide to user interface design' (document number SC34-4289-00).

International SSADM Users' Group for permission to reproduce Figure C.2

from *SSADM and GUI Design: A project manager's guide* (1993), HMSO, London.

Jakob Nielsen for permission to reproduce 'ten heuristics' for usability evaluation from his Discount Usability Engineering seminar papers.

Lawrence Earlbaum Associates for permission to reproduce Figures 3.1 and 3.2 from Norman, D. and Draper, S. (eds) (1986) *User-centered System Design: New perspectives on human—computer interaction.*

Prentice Hall for permission to reproduce material in Chapter 12 from Monk, A., Wright, P., Haber, J. and Davenport, L. (1993) *Improving Your Human—Computer Interface: A practical technique.*

TRADEMARKS

Apple Macintosh is a registered trademark Apple Computers, Inc.

Microsoft Office, Microsoft PowerPoint, Microsoft Excel, Microsoft Word, Microsoft Windows, Microsoft Visual Basic, Microsoft Visual C++ and Microsoft Access are registered trademarks of Microsoft Corporation.

Enterprise Developer is a registered trademark of Symantec Corporation.

SQLWindows is a registered trademark of Gupta Technologies, Inc.

PowerBuilder is a registered trademark of Powersoft Corporation.

Motif is a registered trademark of the Open Software Foundation Corporation.

HyperCard is a registered trademark of Claris Corp.

Presentation Manager is a registered trademark of International Business Machines, Inc.

SSADM is a registered trademark of International SSADM User Group.

ScreenCam and Notes are registered trademarks of Lotus Corporation.

AUTHORS' NOTE

The case study in this book refers to an entirely fictional company called UniSoft Inc. The authors are not aware of the existence of any real company of this name, and if such a company does exist, wish to emphasize that no material in this book should be regarded as referring to that company.

FURTHER INFORMATION AND COMMENTS

GUI design is a rapidly evolving field. If you are interested in further information about relevant seminars or support tools, please complete the business reply slip at the back of the book.

If you have any comments on GUIDE, suggestions for improvement, or experiences of using it on a project, we would be very interested to hear from you.

David Redmond-Pyle
Sunny Croft
Tarvin Road
Manley
Cheshire WA6 9EW
UK
Internet: david _ redmond-pyle@lbms.com

Alan Moore
LBMS Inc.
1800 West Loop South
Houston
TX 77027
USA
CompuServe 100345,366
Internet: alan _ moore@lbms.com

Introduction

1.1   OBJECTIVE OF USER INTERFACE DESIGN

The user interface is the part of a computer system which allows the human user to interact with the computer (Figure 1.1). In typical information systems and office systems the user interface includes the following:

- The parts of the computer hardware which the user can interact with, e.g. screen, keyboard, mouse, on/off switch, etc.
- The images which are visible on the screen, e.g. windows, menus, messages, help screens.
- User documentation such as manuals and reference cards.

The user has no access to the interior of the computer system except through the user interface.

The purpose of the user interface is to make the computer system *usable* by the user. In other words the most critical quality of a user interface is its 'usability'. Usability includes being easy to learn and effective to use. A fuller definition is discussed in the next section.

It is easy to recommend that a user interface should be usable, but this is often a difficult design objective to achieve. Usability involves adapting the computer system to the human beings who use it, which raises various complicated psychological issues of human memory, perception and conceptualization.

As usability is both:

- the most important quality of the user interface, and
- difficult to achieve,

we (as designers) need strong design techniques to help us.

Usability is the central design objective in the GUIDE process. As there is no single design technique which can guarantee usability, GUIDE uses a combination of complementary techniques integrated together into an overall framework.

One of the reasons why 'high-usability' GUI design is difficult for software designers is that it requires a deep change of perspective, seeing the world from a different orientation, almost like a religious conversion. The change of orientation involves

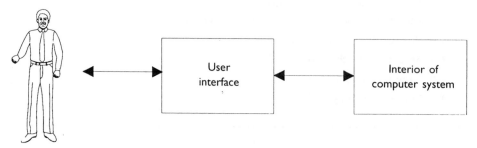

Fig. 1.1   The user interface, mediating between the user and the system

seeing the end-user and his or her purposes and beliefs as central and valid: if the system does not fit in with these, then the system has a usability problem.

If you want to experience this 'conversion', arrange to sit in on some usability evaluation sessions. The ideal scenario is to watch an experienced evaluator working with real end-users attempting to use a user interface you have yourself designed, and that you feel is quite satisfactory. As users make mistakes, cannot see what to do next and misunderstand the system, the intangible concept of a 'usability problem' comes alive before your eyes. From the perspective of a user who gets stuck and cannot work out what to do next due to a usability problem, the usability problem is just as serious and frustrating as being thwarted by a hardware malfunction or a software bug.

1.2   USABILITY

Some user interfaces are easy to learn and effective to use. Others are difficult to learn and confusing or tedious to use.

User interfaces which are easy and pleasant to use are often described as 'user-friendly', but this is a journalist's term which is not properly defined and is not measurable, so is not suitable as a design objective.

'Usability' is a clearer and more appropriate concept for describing the quality of a user interface. Usability is an abstract concept, but need not be vague. Over the last fifteen years researchers into human–computer interaction have reached a high degree of consensus on what usability means, and on approaches to measuring usability.

Usability has four main aspects (Shackel, 1990):

- Effectiveness: for a specified range of tasks and group of users in a particular environment, how effectively can the tasks be performed using the interface? This is sometimes referred to as 'productivity', as it includes how fast the user can perform tasks.

- Learnability: how much training time and how much practice do users require before they are effective with the system? If use is intermittent, how much relearning time do users require?

- Flexibility: to what extent is the interface still effective if there are changes in the task or environment?

- Attitude: do people experience using the system as tiring and frustrating, or do they find it rewarding to use, and feel a sense of satisfaction? Do users like the system?

A key point to note is that usability is defined in relation to specified users performing specified tasks. In other words you cannot answer the question: 'How usable is computer system X?' without first asking: 'By whom?' and: 'To perform what task(s)?'

For example, a PC system might have some primitive text-processing functions in its file management system. For experienced system administrators (the users) to annotate system files with brief comments (the task), the usability of these functions might be perfectly adequate. In contrast, for secretaries with little PC experience whose task is to prepare memos and reports, usability would be unacceptably low.

As well as having a clear concept of usability, it is important to be able to measure usability effectively. If we have two alternative designs, we want to be able to evaluate and compare how usable they are.

Two common approaches to measuring usability are the following:

- Performance tests, where users use the system to perform a task, and their effectiveness in terms of speed and accuracy (or errors) are measured.

- Attitude surveys, where user satisfaction and user perception of the software is captured using a questionnaire or interview.

Learnability can be assessed by measuring effectiveness after different lengths of training and practice. Flexibility is difficult to quantify, and in practice is not usually measured. Usability is discussed throughout this book, specifically in relation to the specification of usability requirements (Chapter 5) and evaluation of usability (Chapter 12).

Usability is frequently achieved by bringing the interface closer to the user's way of thinking and working, i.e. adapting the system to the user rather than asking the user to adapt to the system. This often means more work for the system developers:

- More work for GUI designer, as it takes more skill, effort and time to design a highly usable interface.

- More work for the GUI programmer, as making a GUI more usable often involves writing more code, e.g. alternative mechanisms for performing actions, more messages and warnings. Some of the extra code can be quite complex, e.g. undo facilities.

Extra work means extra time and cost to develop the system, and this must be weighed against the business benefits of greater usability.

Usability is the most important proprty of the user interface, but it is important for the whole system, not just the user interface. If a system does not provide suitable functionality to be useful for user tasks, it is unlikely to be highly usable, no matter how good the user interface. In addition to producing a GUI design, the GUIDE process assists with this deeper aspect of usefulness and usability.

1.2.1   Usability and business benefit

Usability is intrinsically desirable as a design objective. If you are designing a GUI system, you (and the people you are designing it for) want it to be easy to learn, effective for tasks and satisfying to use.

But this is not just a matter of aesthetic pleasure or professional pride. Software usability (or the lack of it) has enormous commercial significance.

The business climate of the 1990s is extremely competitive, and most organizations are seeking to improve their business performance, for example by implementing strategic programs of Total Quality Management or Business Process Re-engineering. For many organizations, improving the quality of customer service and increasing the productivity (or effectiveness) of office staff are among the critical business objectives. Software with high usability can make an important contribution to meeting these business objectives.

For the effectiveness aspect of usability this is obvious — usable software is software which assists the user to perform their work tasks productively. If we can increase usability, then staff can perform more work in a given time, i.e. an increase in productivity.

In addition to quantity of work, there is quality of work. A well-designed GUI can reduce the scope for user errors. Fewer errors means higher quality of service, and indirectly leads to an increase in productivity, as less time is spent on reconciliation or sorting out the consequences of errors.

High learnability reduces training time and training costs, which are often a significant proportion of the installation costs of a new system. In addition to this immediate benefit, it can have a wider commercial significance. Having systems which are easy to learn and easy to use can enable more flexible staffing practices, as staff moved from one system to another become effective more quickly. More radically, it may be possible for a single member of staff to use several systems, moving between them as required to perform all aspects of a complex task, where previously the work was fragmented between several people using different systems. In this way the learnability of a GUI can be critical to the success of a business process re-engineering initiative.

The flexibility of a user interface is also important for business. Most organizations experience ongoing change in their structure, products and operating procedures, and need software systems to be flexible to support users changing their business practices. Lack of flexibility either means a barrier to changes, or expenditure on regular amendments to the user interface to keep up with the business.

The user's attitude to a GUI system may seem very soft and subjective, but has serious implications. If people do not like using a system, if they feel frustrated or tense or anxious rather than confident and effective and satisfied, then they will tend to avoid using the system. Either extra training and management pressure will be required to force them to use the system, or people may ignore the system and perform their tasks in some other way, undermining whatever benefits the system was intended to bring.

Usability is important for any system but is especially crucial for GUIs, as their richness and potential complexity can be very confusing for the user, and designers can easily waste effort on inappropriate features and 'over-engineering' the interface.

1.3   USER-CENTERED DESIGN

The objective of usability discussed in the last two sections implies a particular approach to design.

Pursuing usability means designing the system so that it is intuitive and convenient for the user to use (i.e. adapting the system to the user), rather than developing what is convenient for the developer and the system, and then asking the user to adapt to the system.

Trying to achieve high usability for end-users has three important implications for the design process:

- The designer needs to understand in detail who the end-users will be, what tasks they will perform, and what their specific usability requirements will be. Without this information the GUI design cannot be organized around the users.

- End-users play an active role in the design team throughout the analysis and design process. It is not sufficient to interview some users at the beginning for their requirements, and to ask them to review the design once it is complete. The end user's perspective of 'how will I use this to do my job?' is an important contribution to every activity in the analysis and design process.

- The designer and end-users jointly evaluate the usability of a proposed design as early as possible, and modify the design (repeatedly) in the light of this feedback.

Together, the emphasis on users' tasks, user participation and user evaluation are referred to as a 'user-centered design' approach. The GUIDE process is strongly influenced by the principles of user-centered design.

1.3.1   Contrast with system-centered design

User-centered design may seem so obvious that it is simply 'motherhood and apple pie'. In fact, it contrasts sharply with the kind of 'system-centered design' currently practiced by most software developers. System-centered design works out from the heart of the system, and comes to the end-user last. The typical design sequence is as follows:

- Specify 'user' requirements (which are normally actually business requirements concerned with functionality, with little mention of the human beings who will be the end-users).
- Specify/design the heart of the system (often database data).
- Specify/design system functions.
- Design a user interface to put 'on top' of the system functions, to allow the user to invoke them, and to provide the input the system needs and to format system output.

Following this approach it is hardly surprising that user interfaces often provide fragmented support for user tasks, and are difficult for users to learn and use.

1.3.2   User-centered design not user design

It is important to distinguish user-centered design from design by users. We are not advocating that you just get the users to design the GUI, nor are we saying that the user's opinion of which design alternative is better is always right. Users know their tasks and know whether they find an interface easy to learn and pleasant to use, but they typically have even less understanding of and experience in GUI design than the software developers in the team. GUIDE provides a framework for user participation without the GUI designer abdicating responsibility and putting all responsibility for usability on the user.

1.4   EVOLUTION OF A GUI DESIGN PROCESS

The purpose of this book is to assist you to design usable GUIs.

The previous section discussed what is meant by usability, and approaches to conceptualizing it and measuring it. The problem is that even when you agree that high usability is the objective of GUI design, it is far from obvious how to achieve it.

The benefit of having a well-defined design process (or 'method') is that designers who are not GUI specialists can achieve acceptable levels of usability most of the time.

This section introduces the GUIDE process by discussing how the GUI design process has evolved. It starts with the simplest possible process, and discusses *why* extra elements may be needed to deal with various important concerns and problems.

The purpose of the section is to provide an introduction to the GUIDE process, and a rationale or explanation for it. An overview of GUIDE is presented in Chapter 2.

1.4.1   Naive GUI design

The simplest possible design process is just to have an activity to design the GUI. The product is a GUI design (Figure 1.2).

The problem is that the activity is, in general, too difficult to do in one pass and get right first time. GUI is a very rich design medium, and usability is a difficult objective.

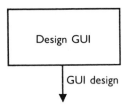

Fig. 1.2   Naive GUI design

1.4.2   Prototyping and iterative redesign

The universally agreed solution to this problem is to introduce a prototyping loop, as shown in Figure 1.3. You produce an initial design, prototype it, identify problems and potential improvements, revise the design, develop a second prototype, etc. This is a definite improvement. Indeed some writers suggest that prototyping is all you need.

However, prototyping is not a panacea — unless the scope and objectives are clearly defined, prototyping can easily lead to proliferation of features and losing sight of the original requirements. (Appendix D discusses this further and gives a real-life example.)

1.4.3   Usability engineering

In the 1980s a number of major computer vendors applied an engineering approach to this problem. Design and prototyping were incorporated into an outer control loop, which started with setting objectives (in this case usability requirements) and ended with evaluating the prototype against those objectives. This process is often referred to as 'usability engineering' (Figure 1.4). Its strength is that the design objectives are much more explicit. It forces the designer to ask the following questions:

- How usable does the GUI need to be?
- By whom?
- How do I measure usability, so I know when the design is usable enough?

This provides a rational exit criterion from the prototyping and iterative redesign loop. Usability takes time, effort and skill to achieve; in other words it costs money.

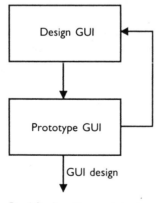

Fig. 1.3   Iterative prototyping

Usability engineering emphasizes that when a design is 'usable enough' to meet usability requirements, you can stop improving it.

You focus redesign work on the parts (or aspects) of the user interface that require improved usability.

1.4.4   Usability for tasks

The process in Figure 1.4 is strong on progressive improvement, but gives little guidance on how to achieve a reasonably usable initial design as a starting point for improvement.

To address this, let us return to the concept of usability. Usability means the GUI is usable to perform some tasks. Studying the tasks, their sequences of actions and their information requirements is an excellent preparation for designing a GUI to support the tasks. The revised process is shown in Figure 1.5, in which Design GUI, Prototype GUI and Evaluate GUI have been shown close together as in practice these activities overlap and sometimes merge into each other.

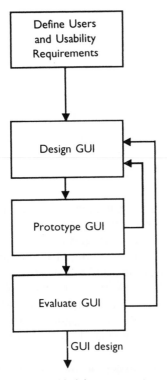

Fig. 1.4   Usability engineering

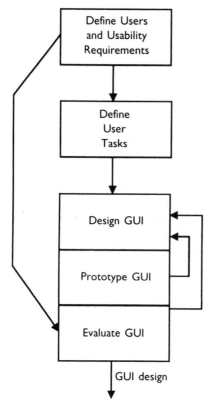

Fig. 1.5   Usability engineering with task modeling

1.4.5   Consistency through standards

In developing the discussion of prototyping and evaluation, we have not yet mentioned the importance of consistency for usability. It is an established fact that consistent 'look and feel' of a GUI makes it easier to learn and use.

Consistency is achieved by defining standards for the 'style' of interaction in a document usually known as an 'application style guide'. Individual elements of the GUI are designed to conform to the style guide. The application style guide is typically based on wider industry standards (or, if there is one, on the organization's general GUI style guide), but is specialized for this particular system. Figure 1.6 shows the design process including definition of a style guide. Note that the style guide should take into account the usability requirements.

Note that there is feedback from the evaluation process to the style guide. If a standard style does not meet usability requirements, it should be revised.

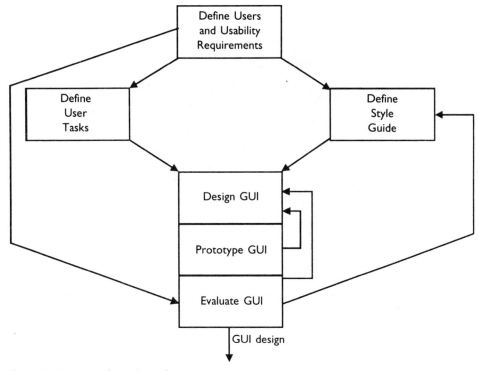

Fig. 1.6 Inclusion of a style guide

1.4.6 **Mental models for usability**

We have considered what the user is doing (i.e. the task context), but one area we have not discussed is what the user is thinking. You may ask whether this is really relevant, but research into human–computer interaction suggests that when people use computer systems (or other tools) they form a 'mental model' of what is in the system. This mental model helps them to use the system intelligently and effectively, and can have a profound effect on the usability of a system.

A computer system can be thought of as being like an iceberg – only a fraction of the iceberg is visible at the surface. The 'look and feel' is what is immediately visible, but beneath this there is a large structure of objects, relationships and behaviors. The mental model is concerned with the user's understanding of the submerged part of the iceberg. Figure 1.7 shows the three layers of the iceberg.

A designer's model includes object relationships, visual representations, and interaction techniques and mechanisms. Although the visual representations and interaction techniques are the most visible part of a user interface, the object relationships, which are based on a user's conceptual model, form the bulk of the interface. (IBM, CUA, 1991)

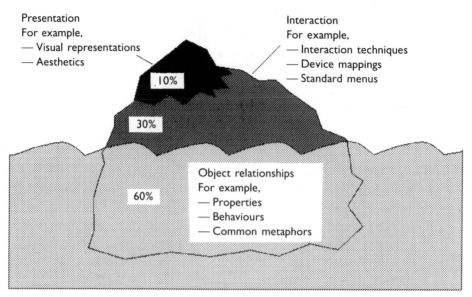

Presentation
For example,
— Visual representations
— Aesthetics

Interaction
For example,
— Interaction techniques
— Device mappings
— Standard menus

.10%

30%

Object relationships
For example,
— Properties
— Behaviours
— Common metaphors

60%

Fig. 1.7 The designer's model represented as an iceberg (reproduced with permission from the IBM CUA guide)

According to IBM, the structure and behavior of the underlying objects, and the way these are represented in the interface, makes the most significant contribution to a product's usability (accounting for as much as 60 percent).

The relationship between objects beneath the surface, mental models and usability involves a number of important concepts, and these concepts are discussed in Chapter 3. For this introduction it is sufficient to note that none of the design processes included in Figure 1.6 defines underlying objects, or facilitates a GUI design which helps the user to form an appropriate mental model.

The solution recommended in GUIDE is to create a 'user object model', a model of the objects the users think are in the system. This model ensures that the basis of a coherent users' mental model is built into the system (see Figure 1.8).

The diagram shows how user object modeling fits with the other activities. We identify user objects from the task models, and use them to validate and enrich the task models. As well as enhancing usability, the user object model assists in GUI design in a very practical way. We base initial windows on views of user objects, encouraging an 'object-based' interface.

1.4.7   The GUIDE process

Figure 1.8 shows the complete GUIDE process. See Chapter 2 for an overview of the process as a whole, and subsequent chapters for the techniques recommended to perform specific activities.

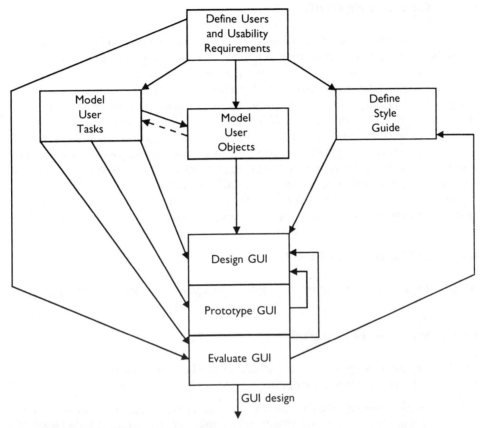

Fig. 1.8 Complete GUIDE process

In many respects, GUIDE merely summarizes what is accepted good practice among GUI design specialists. However, the GUIDE process has four key distinguishing features:

- It is integrated, combining techniques and perspectives which are usually described in isolation from each other, showing how the product of one technique is used as an input to another.
- It relates to objects, showing how object-oriented analysis is integrated with task analysis (which is usually procedural), and lead through to GUI design. (Much of the user interface design literature does not discuss objects at all.)
- It is geared to the practical requirements of software developers who are not specialist GUI designers or human factors experts.
- It provides a practical, usable technique for dealing with one of the most difficult and subtle areas of GUI design, that of enabling the user to form a coherent mental model (so that the system appears intuitive).

1.4.8   Customizing GUIDE

The overall GUIDE process is a rich process, addressing many dimensions of design for usability. We are not proposing that you have to perform every part of the process on every project. Performing an activity takes time and costs money. If an activity adds more cost to the project than it adds value, you are more effective if you leave it out, or if you cut it down and use it in a simplified or abbreviated form. The techniques in this book can be cut down in this way — if you cannot justify spending weeks on them, then squeeze as much value out of them as you can in days. If you do not have days, pick out the 'juiciest bits' of each technique that give you most benefit in least time and do them in hours. Each of these techniques can provide you with significant benefit from as little as a half-day workshop.

   To assist you in choosing techniques and how much effort to invest, each technique chapter starts with a section on objectives and benefits.

1.5   STYLE OF THIS BOOK

A few points about the content and style of this book are worth mentioning.

1.5.1   Selection of material

In selecting and writing material to include in this book we have used a number of principles. Each section is intended to be:

- *Useful to the practitioner*   Each section describes what to produce, why to produce it, and how, using realistic examples. We have only included material we think you will find useful in doing practical GUI design.

- *A single approach*   Where the literature offers five competing techniques or notations which partly overlap, we have simply selected the one that in our view is most suitable for the practitioner. We have not compared and contrasted the alternatives, as this would have made the book much longer and more complicated.

- *As simple as possible*   At each point we have attempted to keep GUIDE simple by defining the minimum set of techniques, concepts and terms which might be needed by the practitioner to do a good job on GUI design. We hope this makes the book readable and accessible. To achieve this, we accept that we have omitted material which might have been useful to some readers.

- *Realistic, everyday issues and examples*   We have avoided exotic examples, and concentrated on examples of very ordinary GUI designs, similar to those which many people will need to design in their everyday work.

- *Part of the whole*   GUIDE is an integrated design process, in which each part is compatible with and contributes to a coherent whole.

The book aims to give an overview of the entire GUI design process, and enough information and guidance for you to attempt each part of the process. Your initial understanding and skills can be developed in various ways:

- By attending training courses. GUI design is a subtle process involving abstract concepts, interaction with other people, and interaction with software. The most effective way of acquiring the relevant skills is in a structured face-to-face learning situation. We intend that courses in GUIDE will be available if required (see our contact details in the Preface, or the reply card at the back of the book).
- Through discussions with experienced designers or consultants.
- By reading published literature (see Further Reading sections).
- Through experience of actually doing GUI design.
- Through performing usability evaluations.

1.5.2   A cookbook?

It is *not* the intention of this book to suggest that GUI design can be reduced merely to following instructions in a cookbook.

Firstly, this is not achievable. A cookbook recipe produces a predefined result, whereas a great range of GUIs are required for a variety of different purposes. At the beginning of a project, no one knows what the GUI design should look like. Further, several alternative 'good' designs may be possible. Cookbooks simply are not applicable in these circumstances.

Secondly, it is not desirable. GUI design is a design activity, a creative act involving human intelligence, innovation and ingenuity. Even if GUI design could be made into a mindless routine (or fully automated), the result would generally be less usable than a GUI designed by a skilled human. The GUIDE process is intended to be applied with creativity and intelligence, not to be a substitute for them.

1.5.3   Experience and expertise

Designing a good GUI is difficult. Expert GUI designers draw on various kinds of expertise and on years of project experience. This depth and breadth of experience is of great value.

At the present time, the rapid growth in GUI technology means that many practitioners without this expertise or experience are being asked to design GUIs. The role of a GUI design process is not to create instant experts, but to help shorten the learning curve from being a novice without any sense of direction, to being a competent practitioner.

1.5.4 Relationship to other GUI design literature

The techniques in GUIDE are not new. They are described in various places in the academic and professional literature on human−computer interaction. Most of them are already widely used in practice.

What is new about GUIDE is the way that the techniques are integrated together into an overall process, showing exactly how the product of each technique contributes to the final GUI design. Also, from the reader's point of view, it is convenient to have a compatible set of techniques documented in one book, without having to search for obscure journal articles.

For GUIDE to cover the entire GUI design and evaluation process in a short book, some topics have only very brief coverage. If the readers want a more detailed discussion of a particular technique or product, each chapter has a Further Reading section with notes on recommended sources. There is also a general bibliography at the end of the book.

1.6   BACKGROUND TO GUIDE

GUIDE has its origins in work on GUI design at LBMS. LBMS is a multinational software company specializing in Computer-Aided Software Engineering (CASE) tools and software development methods. It specializes in methods and tools for client−server development, so has a strong interest in GUI design.

As a consultancy, LBMS advises client organizations on how to develop in-house application software. In response to client requests, LBMS defined a structured development method for GUI design as part of its Systems Engineering family of methods. This method combined internal expertise with a selection of the best available techniques from the human−computer interaction literature. The Systems Engineering GUI design method has been used on client projects and as the basis for training courses from 1992 onwards, being validated and enriched by feedback from practice. It currently forms part of the Process Engineer toolset library, which includes development processes and techniques for various types of software project.

In developing this GUI method, LBMS drew on its practical expertise as an early developer of GUI systems. In the late 1980s LBMS conducted a multi-million dollar project to design and develop a second-generation CASE tool (Systems Engineer). This tool was to run on PCs under Microsoft Windows, and at the time was one of the largest and most complex applications written for Windows. Much of the project was concerned with design and development of the GUI, as earlier experience had convinced the company that usability was critical to success. As part of this project, LBMS evolved a set of standards and practices for GUI design.

Another influence on GUIDE has been work to evolve a 'British Standard' approach to GUI design. The British government Structured Systems Analysis and Design Method (SSADM) was developed before GUIs were widely used and until recently had no techniques for GUI design. Through 1993 one of the authors was a member of a standards working group (SSADM/GUI working group) which met regularly to define a design process and a set of techniques for GUI design. This working group brought together leading UK experts from several different companies, seeking to establish an agreed framework for GUI design in the context of an SSADM project. The resulting document, *SSADM and GUI — A Project Manager's Guide*, is endorsed by the UK government and the International SSADM Users' Group as the recommended approach to GUI design. GUIDE is *not* specific to SSADM, but GUIDE is fully compatible with and complementary to the SSADM/GUI framework. For more details on using GUIDE in an SSADM context, see Appendix C.

In summary, GUIDE is loosely based upon the LBMS Systems Engineering GUI design method, but this has been adapted in various ways:

- To make GUIDE a self-contained process, which can be used with or without other development methods.
- To focus GUIDE on practitioner techniques and remove project management material.
- To incorporate useful techniques and guidance used by leading companies other than LBMS.
- To organize the material into a book format.
- To use industry-standard terminology wherever possible.

The GUIDE authors have been personally involved in all aspects of GUI design at LBMS, including the following:

- Developing the LBMS GUI design method.
- Playing an influential role in the SSADM/GUI working group.
- Contributing to GUI design for CASE tools and GUI design tools.
- Undertaking training and consulting.

1.7   STRUCTURE OF THIS BOOK

This introduction establishes the objective of user interface design (i.e. usability), and shows why each of the activities in the overall process is needed.

Chapter 2 (GUIDE overview) provides a summary of the GUIDE process, a summary of each of its constituent activities and products, and describes the standard chapter structure.

Chapter 3 briefly introduces a few key concepts for GUI design which we find are helpful to designers.

Chapter 4 discusses how GUI design is integrated with the design of business systems and other parts of the computer system. It includes a brief discussion of planning GUI design, introducing the concepts of incremental and iterative design. Finally, it contains the first section of the running case study, giving the background to the case study project. Chapters 5–12 are each illustrated by a section from this case study.

Chapter 5 describes how to analyze the users of the GUI, and how to identify and define the usability requirements that the GUI system must satisfy if it is to be successful.

Chapter 6 describes how to analyze and model the tasks which will be performed by the people who use the GUI.

Chapter 7 describes how to model the 'objects in the system' in a user object model. Users perform their tasks by interacting with these objects.

Chapter 8 describes an (optional) technique for modeling the dynamic behavior of objects in the system, using a special kind of state transition diagram.

Chapter 9 describes what an application style guide is, why you need one and how to produce it.

Chapter 10 describes how to design the GUI, using the task model, user object model and application style guide.

Chapter 11 describes how to prototype the GUI design.

Chapter 12 describes how to evaluate a GUI design to identify problems and confirm whether it satisfies usability requirements.

The Conclusion summarizes the main themes and offers some concluding remarks.

Appendix A discusses how GUIDE is applicable to the design of multimedia GUI systems.

Appendix B presents a 'metamodel' for the GUIDE concepts, for methodologists, academics and anyone else interested in the abstract structure of GUIDE.

Appendix C describes how GUIDE is used in the context of SSADM.

Appendix D addresses the issue of why prototyping alone is not sufficient. It uses a case study to discuss how an extensively prototyped GUI design can still have serious usability problems.

Appendix E describes a technique for evaluating usability using a specific package called SUMI (Software Usability Measurement Inventory).

1.8   HOW TO USE THIS BOOK

Different people may want to use this book in different ways. We have organized it in a modular way so that it is easy to 'dip into'. We suggest the following approaches to reading and using the book.

If you intend to use the GUIDE process on a project, we suggest you:

- Read through quickly in chapter sequence, to gain a feel for the process as a whole.
- Refer to Chapters 2 and 4 while planning the project.
- Refer to individual chapters during the project, as you are actually producing that product.

If you have time to read half the book, but are not sure which half, we suggest you read the following:

- This introduction for a general orientation to the issues and approach
- Chapter 2 GUIDE overview
- Chapter 5 on specifying usability requirements
- Chapter 6 on task analysis
- Chapter 7 on object modeling
- Chapter 10 on GUI design
- Chapter 12 on usability evaluation

From our own experience in the software industry we know that people are rarely given several days of 'professional development' time to study a book. Reading up on a new subject to keep up-to-date is something many software people do in snatched half-hours in planes, trains, airports and hotel rooms. We have tried to make the book clearly structured and readable so you can find relevant parts in short timeframes.

If you only have time to read selected parts of the book, we suggest you:

- Read this introduction for a general orientation to the issues and approach.
- Read the overview of GUIDE in Chapter 2.
- Use that to identify any other chapters of interest. Each chapter is as self-contained as possible.

1.9   FURTHER READING

Shackel, B. (1990) 'Human factors and usability', pp. 27–41 in Preece, J. and Keller, L. (eds), *Human–Computer Interaction*, Prentice Hall.
A very readable introductory discussion of what is meant by usability, why it is important and how it is measured.

Schneiderman, B. (1990) *Designing the User Interface: Strategies for effective human–computer interaction*, Addison-Wesley.
A good general text on human computer interaction and interface design.

Open University (1990) *A Guide to Usability.*
A general introduction to usability and user-centered design, produced as part of the Department of Trade and Industry's 'Usability Now' technology transfer program.

IBM (1991) *Systems Application Architecture: Common user access guide to user interface design* (document number SC34-4289-00), IBM Publications.
Gives a good introductory discussion of issues in practical interface design, and describes the process of interface design for CUA91. Of interest even if you are not designing specifically to IBM standards.

International SSADM Users' Group (1993) *SSADM and GUI Design: A project manager's guide*, HMSO, London.
The official report recommending how GUI design is integrated into an SSADM project. GUIDE provides practitioner-level techniques and examples which complement this management framework.

■ 2 ▬▬▬▬▬▬▬▬▬▬▬▬▬

GUIDE overview

2.1   THE GUIDE PROCESS

This chapter provides a high-level overview of the *process* of GUI design and evaluation. It describes how the overall GUIDE process is composed of several lower-level processes. Each process has a specific objective and produces a well-defined product.

The overview diagram shown in Figure 2.1 is an idealized representation of the processes and how they are related to each other. Boxes represent processes, and lines represent how products are produced by one process and input to another. To communicate the main ideas, the diagram has been kept as simple as possible. We recognize that real-world projects are almost always more complex.

Three main points should be noted about the 'shape' of the process:

- Various issues are considered *before* prototyping:
  - who the end-users will be;
  - usability requirements;

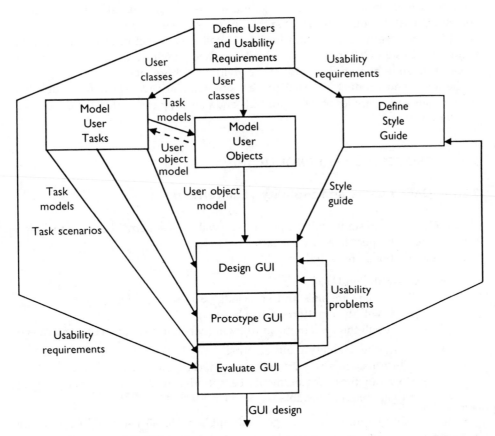

Fig. 2.1 Overview of GUIDE process

> — user tasks;
> — user objects;
> — style guide.

- The processes to Design GUI, Prototype GUI, Evaluate GUI overlap and in practice merge into each other.

- The latter process is profoundly iterative. The GUI design 'evolves' through an ongoing process of feedback from prototyping and evaluation. (In fact, Figure 2.1 under-emphasizes the extent of this feedback and iteration. All the earlier products — style guide, user objects, tasks, etc. — are liable to be revised as a result of feedback from prototyping and evaluation.)

While a schematic overview diagram helps with communication, it is important also to acknowledge its limitations.

Firstly, it is difficult to convey in a diagram the gradual emergence and evolution of a shared vision of the interface in the minds of the people in the design team.

Secondly, in a real-world project, the processes are human activities which do not have fixed boundaries. While investigating one issue, an analyst will often learn something useful about another issue that 'belongs in a different box', or a designer will have the creative ideas about how to visualize an object or streamline a task, before the 'Design GUI' process is officially reached. Having a design process is not a reason to stifle human flexibility or creativity with bureaucracy.

The focus and products of each process are summarized below. More detailed descriptions and examples of these products and how they are produced are provided in later chapters.

2.2   PROCESSES AND PRODUCTS

2.2.1   Define users and usability requirements

User-centered design starts with the people who will use a system. The aim is to design the GUI to fit the people and their tasks.

The key questions are as follows:

- Who are the end-users?
  - What characteristics and knowledge do the users have?
  - What will their pattern of use be?
  - What will the system mean to them (personal benefits, costs, motives)?
- What are the usability requirements?
  - Which usability requirements are critical to success?
  - How can these requirements be specified in a way that makes them measurable and testable?

Some usability requirements are general, applying to all users. Other usability requirements are specific to particular classes of user.

The products are as follows:

- User class descriptions, describing the different types of end-user.
- Usability requirements, each with one or more evaluation criteria and the level which the GUI must achieve to be acceptable.

For more details see Chapter 5, Users and Usability Specification.

2.2.2 Model user tasks

The initial aim is to understand what the users actually do and how they do it (in order to understand how the new system and its GUI can assist them).

The second aim is to design (at a suitably abstract level) how the tasks will be performed using the new system.

Task modeling ensures that GUI design, prototyping and evaluation emphasize the usability of the GUI for performing real user tasks (i.e. that the GUI is 'task-appropriate').

The key questions are as follows:

- What tasks do the users perform?
  - What are they trying to achieve (task goals)?
  - How frequently do they perform the tasks?
  - How can the task be analyzed to its component subtasks?
  - How critical is each subtask to achieving the overall goal?
- What are the representative scenarios for each task?
  - How are these scenarios achieved by actions on user objects?

The products are as follows:

- Task models. Agreeing what tasks a user will perform is a key prerequisite to GUI design (and indeed to system design as a whole). Note though that if there is a business process re-engineering exercise, the nature and scope of tasks may be subject to considerable debate and may change radically.
- Task scenarios (examples of individual instances of the task), which are suitable for prototyping. Task scenarios play an important role in the evaluation of usability requirements. They can be used to make abstract requirements like efficiency and learnability measurable.

For more details see Chapter 6, Task Analysis.

2.2.3 Model user objects

The aim is to enable the user to form a coherent and appropriate mental model of the 'objects in the system', by designing this into the GUI.

The key questions are as follows:

- What are the objects in the system?

- What actions can the user do to or with an object?
- What information does the user know about an object?
- How are the objects related to each other?

The products are as follows:

- One or more user object models. (Different communities of users may have different models of the objects in the system.)
- A glossary of user terms.

For a further discussion of what is meant by a mental model and the importance of the user's mental model in usability, see Chapter 3, Key Concepts for GUI design.

For details of the product and technique recommended, see Chapter 7, User Object Modeling.

Note that this technique is sometimes referred to as 'conceptual modeling', or 'user conceptual modeling'. Also, some writers regard it as being part of task analysis.

If the system has significant dynamic behavior, see also Chapter 8, Dynamic Modeling. This describes how to analyze and model the dynamic behavior of the 'objects in the system'.

2.2.4   Define style guide

The aim is for the GUI to have a consistent style (i.e. look and feel).

The key questions are as follows:

- What GUI environment will be used?
- What style will users be familiar with and expect?
- What will the windows look like?
- What standard menu items will be used?
- What types of 'window control' will be used (e.g. buttons, pull-down lists)?
- What standard patterns of interaction will be used?
- How will the help system be structured?

The product is:

- An application style guide, defining GUI standards to be used for the system.

For details, see Chapter 9, Style Guide Definition.

2.2.5   Design GUI

The aim is to design an initial GUI which:

- Supports user tasks.
- Presents the user's objects clearly.

- Conforms to the style guide.
- Meets usability requirements.

The key questions are as follows:

- What views of objects are required for tasks?
- How should these views be allocated to windows?
- What layout should be used for windows?
- How does the user navigate from one window to another?
- What menu items and other controls are required, and how do they behave?

The products are as follows:

- Window designs, including specification of interactive behavior.
- Window navigation design.

For details, see Chapter 10, GUI Design.

2.2.6 Prototype GUI

The aim is to investigate the usability (and feasibility) of the proposed GUI design and the validity of the task model, user object model and style guide.

The key questions are as follows:

- How can the user perform the task scenarios using the GUI?
- Are extra views of objects required?
- Should the windows be restructured to support the tasks better?
- Is the inter-window navigation adequate to support tasks?
- How can 'what the person does' be simplified and streamlined?
- What problems does the user encounter?
- What improvements does the user suggest?

The products are as follows:

- A working prototype GUI.
- Revisions to the GUI design.

For details, see Chapter 11, GUI Prototyping.
Appendix D discusses how prototyping alone is not sufficient.

2.2.7 Evaluate GUI

The aim is to evaluate the GUI to check whether it satisfies all usability requirements and adequately supports all tasks.

The key questions are as follows:

- How usable is the GUI by the end-users, in terms of the usability criteria previously specified?
- What usability problems do users encounter?
- Does the GUI provide adequate support to all types of users performing their full range of tasks?

The products are as follows:

- An evaluation of the usability of the GUI design and prototype.
- Usability problems.
- Proposed revisions to the GUI design.

For details, see Chapter 12, Usability Evaluation.

Appendix E also gives details of a usability measurement package.

2.3   STANDARD CHAPTER STRUCTURE

The chapters describing the lower-level processes (Chapters 5–12) are organized in a standard way. The aim is to help you to dip into the book and find the information you need quickly. Standard sections are as follows.

2.3.1   Introduction

For each process, the critical question is: 'Why do it?' This question is answered by two subsections:

- *Objective* – this states briefly what the process is trying to achieve.
- *Benefits* – this discusses the benefits of using the process, and (by implication) the costs or risks if it is omitted. As the overall objective is a usable GUI, the section considers how the product contributes to the usability of the GUI.

A third introductory subsection is *inputs/outputs*. This summarizes the inputs to the process and the outputs from it, reminding you of how this activity fits into the GUIDE process as a whole.

We suggest that each product in GUIDE is worth considering, and will be beneficial on most projects. If the objective and benefits of a product are not applicable or not important on a particular project, you should of course omit it (and the process which produces it). If a product may have some benefit, but not enough to justify the time and effort of doing it 'properly', use a shortcut or a simplified form.

2.3.2   Product(s)

The essence of a development process is that it produces something useful. This section answers the question: 'What product(s) does the process produce?'

Each product is described in four standard subsections:

- *What is it?* — what does the product consist of and tell you about?
- *Notation* — what diagrams or layouts does the product use?
- *Quality criteria* — how do you know when the product is complete, and whether it is good enough?
- *Where used* — where and how is the product subsequently used in the overall GUI design process?

We suggest that the product as defined here is (in general) sufficient to meet the objective and contribute towards GUI usability. You may prefer to substitute an alternative product that meets the same objective (and thus yields the same benefits), or to use an alternative notation for the product.

Appendix B describes a metamodel for GUIDE which shows how the different products are related to each other.

2.3.3   Process

This section answers the question: 'How do you produce the product?' It achieves this by describing a number of activities, and an approximate sequence in which they might be performed. We recognize that in reality there are many ways of producing something, depending on your experience, personal style, project circumstances, available information sources, etc.

The activity descriptions may appear prescriptive, but are intended to be a device for communicating ideas and illustrating how it might be done, not a procedure which has to be followed like a bureaucratic rulebook. In our experience people find detailed and concrete procedural guidance useful as an initial learning device, and during the first couple of times they perform a process. Once they are familiar with a product they produce it intuitively, and only glance at the guidance occasionally to see if it helps on some point of difficulty.

The objective of the process is to create products which satisfy their quality criteria, as a 'stepping stone' towards a usable GUI. If the process guidance helps you, then use it; otherwise don't bother.

2.3.4   Example

This section gives an example of the product, and of the process by which it has been produced. A substantial case study is developed throughout the book, running from one chapter to another.

The case study has been selected to meet a number of criteria:

- To be representative of the type of system which (we believe) many of you will need to design.
- To be small and familiar enough to include a reasonable proportion of it in the book.
- To be substantial enough to be non-trivial, and to provide examples of most processes and products.

The application used is a Helpdesk system, with a GUI and a small database system behind. It is smaller and simpler than the systems GUIDE is designed to be used for, but it is rich enough to illustrate the main points of the GUIDE process.

2.3.5   Practice tips

This section discusses miscellaneous hints and tips which we consider useful, but which do not fit naturally anywhere else, such as skill requirements for the process, and common risks and pitfalls encountered.

2.3.6   Summary

Each chapter has a brief section summarizing the main points introduced.

2.3.7   Further reading

This section suggests a small selection of sources from the literature for further reading on the process, the product(s) it produces, and/or the underlying theory. Each entry has some notes indicating why it might be useful to you.

3

Key concepts for GUI design

3.1 INTRODUCTION

Most of this book is practical rather than theoretical, and is devoted to products you produce, techniques you use and realistic examples. However, to design GUIs effectively, you need to have some conceptual framework for understanding the process of human–computer interaction. This chapter briefly introduces four key concepts from the study of human–computer interaction which are particularly valuable for practical GUI design:

- A theoretical model of how humans interact with computers.
- The concept of a 'user's mental model', and how this can be influenced by the design.
- The concept of 'views' of an object.
- Some implications of human cognitive abilities for GUI design.

We choose to discuss these particular concepts for two reasons:

- They can have a profound influence on the way designers think about and perform GUI design. In our experience these are highly useful concepts for practitioners.
- They help to convey the theoretical basis for GUIDE. Once you grasp these concepts you will understand how the GUIDE process works and be able to apply it more effectively.

The human–computer interaction literature contains many other interesting and useful concepts, but they are beyond the scope of this book. Some sources are identified in the Further Reading section of this chapter.

3.2 NORMAN'S THEORY OF ACTION

Our starting point in conceptualizing human–computer interaction is as follows:

- Human beings are conscious and purposive.
- Computer systems are just machines. They have capabilities but not intentions.
- Human–computer interaction consists of humans using computers as *tools* to achieve human goals.

There are alternative ways of thinking about human–computer interaction, but for the types of systems we are concerned with, this is both the most accurate and the most useful conceptualization.

It leads us to think of the human as taking the initiative – the human has a goal or intention, performs an action, and the system responds in some way. The person assesses whether the action had the intended effect, and performs another action.

In an influential paper on this topic, Donald Norman proposed that we must distinguish between the psychological aspects and the physical aspects of using a computer system to perform a task (Norman, 1986). The person starts with goals and intentions, which are psychological in nature. The computer system is physical, with physical mechanisms to be manipulated and a physical system state. Many of the central issues of human–computer interaction revolve around how the person translates their psychological intentions into physical instructions to the computer, using the interface mechanisms (e.g. keyboard or mouse).

An important transition is also required in the reverse direction. The system may produce some physical output at the user interface (e.g. a change in the images on the screen). The person perceives, interprets and evaluates this image, transforming it from a physical state of screen pixels to a psychological representation.

Norman suggested that we think of the gap between the person's psychological goals and the physical state of the system as 'gulfs' that must be bridged for the person to interact effectively with the system. The Gulf of Execution and the Gulf of Evaluation are shown in Figure 3.1.

- The Gulf of Execution goes from Goals to Physical System. (How are the person's psychological goals translated to physical interface actions?)
- The Gulf of Evaluation goes from the Physical System to Goals. (How is the physical state perceived, and its relation to goals evaluated?)

The gulf of execution is bridged by the user forming intentions, translating the intention into an action specification (a planned sequence of actions on the system), and then executing the actions on the physical interface mechanisms of the system (Figure 3.2).

The gulf of evaluation is bridged by the system displaying physical output which the user perceives, and the user interpreting the meaning of the output, and evaluating it against their goals.

These bridges over the gulfs can also be thought of as a cycle of user activities in performing a task:

1. Establishing the goal.
2. Forming the intention.
3. Specifying the action sequence.
4. Executing the action.
5. Perceiving the system state.

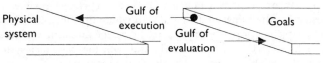

Fig. 3.1 Gulfs of Execution and Evaluation

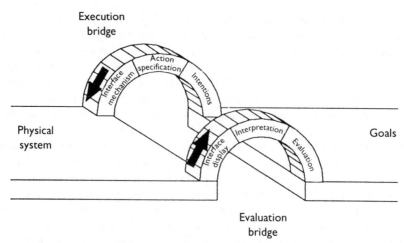

Fig. 3.2   Bridging the Gulfs of Execution and Evaluation

6. Interpreting the system state.

7. Evaluating the system state against their goals and intentions.

It is not suggested that these activities are separate (they merge into each other), or that they must always occur in sequence (some may be omitted). The power of the theoretical model is that it identifies the different kinds of user activity which an interface must support if it is to be usable. It draws attention to the extensive psychological activity in using a computer system.

Research by Norman and others indicates that users' 'mental models' play a key role in this psychological activity.

To translate a goal into a sequence of actions on the system, a user needs to have some understanding of the system, and of the meaning and effect of the actions they can perform on it. It is precisely this understanding we are referring to as a mental model. Similarly, to interpret what system output (e.g. pixels on a screen) actually mean, the user depends on having an understanding of the system (i.e. a mental model).

3.3   USER'S MENTAL MODEL

Norman describes mental models in the following terms:

Mental models seem a pervasive property of humans. I believe that people form internal, mental models of themselves and of the things and people with whom they interact. These models provide predictive and explanatory power for understanding the interaction. Mental models evolve naturally through interaction with the world and with the particular system under consideration. These models are highly affected by the nature of the interaction, coupled with the person's prior knowledge and understanding. The models are neither accurate nor complete, but nonetheless they function to guide much human behavior.   (Norman, 1986, p. 46)

Fig. 3.3 User with a mental model of what is in the system

We are particularly concerned here with the user's mental model of a computer system (Figure 3.3). Having an appropriate mental model enables a user to use a system effectively, because they can work out what to do in order to achieve their task goals, and can interpret information displayed on the screen correctly.

The following are familiar examples of mental models:

- *Schematic maps:* people often conceptualize the location of places, and routes to places, in terms of appropriate maps inside their head. Imagine you are asked the question 'How do you get from city A to town B?'

- *Analogies or metaphors,* such as the desktop metaphor in the Apple Macintosh, in which objects behave like documents in folders, and you can drag them around the desk and drop them in the trash can.

- *Floor plans:* in order to find their way around large office complexes or hotels, many people internalize a rough floor plan.

- *Organization charts:* in large organizations people often use a simplified internal organization chart as a mental model of where people 'fit in' (see Figure 3.4).

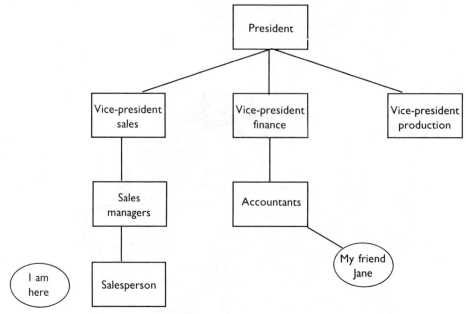

Fig. 3.4 Mental model of an organization

Mental models do not always involve visual images, indeed the majority do not. An example of a non-visual mental model is the concept of electricity flowing around a circuit. Using this concept we can understand (and predict) the behavior of objects in the circuit. For example, in the circuit in Figure 3.5 the concept of electrical current allows us to predict that if one light bulb fails or is removed, the other bulb will also go out.

3.3.1   Designing for a mental model

An important part of the interface designer's job is to assist the user in forming a suitable mental model of the system. The user's mental model will be influenced by the design of the user interface, by explanations in help text and system documentation, and by user training.

However, in developing a mental model of a computer system, users also draw on knowledge of other systems and mental models they already have of the everyday world, and this is a very important influence on usability. In particular, where a computer system relates to work tasks, the user will almost always attempt to under-stand the system using their existing mental model of the task and the objects which are relevant for it. Where this mental model is a good fit with the structure and behavior of the new system, the user has an advantage − they have less relearning to do, as they already have the basis of an effective mental model.

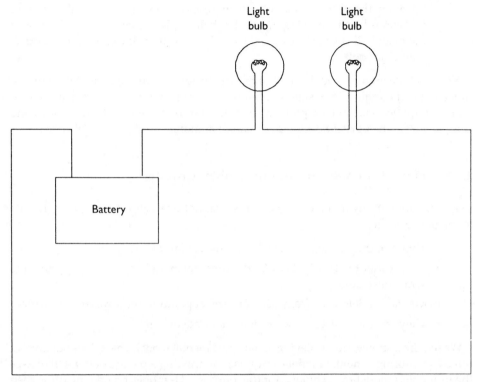

Fig. 3.5   Electrical circuit to illustrate mental model of electrical current

More importantly, if the objects in the system appear to be the same, but behave differently from the corresponding real-world objects, this will disrupt the user's mental model and will be an ongoing source of user confusion and usability problems. (The system will appear counter-intuitive.)

Therefore, the interface should be organized to support a mental model that:

- is clear and coherent;
- is as simple as possible; and
- fits with users' 'common-sense' knowledge of the real-world objects, relationships, actions and effects.

An interface can 'support' a particular mental model in several ways:

- By appearing and behaving in the way the user would expect from the mental model.
- By being consistent and avoiding behaviors which contradict the mental model. These confuse and weaken the model, and the user has to learn them as exceptions.

- By giving the user information which promotes the mental model (windows and controls named using the model, help explanations phrased in terms of the model, the user guide organized to help the user develop the appropriate mental model).

Note that the mental model need not be strictly accurate in implementation terms. Indeed one of our aims in designing for a users' mental model is to present the user with a simplified view which protects them from implementation technicalities and complexities. Analogies and metaphors are commonly used for this purpose.

3.3.2   Mental models and the user object model

The difficulty with mental models is that we cannot deal with them directly for the following reasons:

- They are intangible, existing inside users' minds.
- Users cannot normally describe their mental models precisely (they are only semi-conscious).
- Mental models vary from user to user depending on a variety of factors.
- They are difficult to draw or document adequately.

We require a strategy for achieving an effective mental model which does not involve directly capturing a mental model from a user or drawing a picture of it. GUIDE uses the user object modeling technique for this purpose. User object modeling (described in Chapter 7) is an object-oriented analysis technique for describing the objects in the system.

User object modeling assists a designer in the following ways to develop an interface that achieves an effective mental model:

- By having an explicit design for the mental model we intend our users to form (the user object model).
- By having a technique for creating a user object model, deriving it from analysis of user tasks (and optionally also from a data model).
- By having a technique for designing the interface windows, controls and menus, guided by the user object model.

This means the designer can work with a user object model, which is explicit, consistent, has a precise meaning, and can be represented in a diagram. This user object model is the agreed design for the users' mental model − it is a specification of the way we want the users to think of the objects in the system.

User object modeling also contributes to the usability of a GUI in other ways. The influential user interface theorist Ben Shneiderman (1992) proposes that to make an interface usable, it should represent task domain objects and actions, while minimizing the computer concepts and command syntax that the user needs to learn and remember. The GUIDE process of task analysis and user object modeling, followed by designing windows based on user objects, leads the GUI designer down this recommended route.

3.4   VIEWS

The concept of a user seeing a 'view' of an object is central to GUI design, and is worth some explanation and discussion here.

A view is a visual representation of an object (or some part or aspect of an object) in the user interface (e.g. in a window). There may be many views of a single object. A view may be textual; contain buttons, lists and other standard windows controls; be an icon; or have some other format such as a map, an image, a graph or a pressure gauge. In general, a view of an object often contains many windows controls, each control corresponding to an attribute of the viewed object.

A familiar example of the use of views in a graphical user interface is the views of a document in a wordprocessor. Wordprocessors vary, but most can offer at least four views:

- An icon view (when the document and word processor are minimized on the screen).
- An 'outline' view (showing the structure of sections, subsections, etc.).
- An edit view (for seeing and manipulating the text and format control characters).
- A 'print preview' view (for seeing how the document will appear on the page when printed).

Figure 3.6 illustrates the relationship between these four views and the document object.

In GUIDE we use the concept of 'view' in quite a precise sense. The document object on the left in Figure 3.6 is not just an object in a general sense, it is what we call a 'user object'. For each user object, we define a number of attributes (things you know about the object), and actions (things you can do to the object). Thus the attributes of a Document user object include its Name, Creation Date and Author; the actions you can perform on it include Print, Save, Delete, Create Section, Rename.

When we define a view of a user object we decide which attributes and actions are relevant for this view, and map the selected attributes and actions into suitable controls in which they can be visualized. For example, the name of the document may be visualized by a text display in the title bar in a window, while a Print action may be visualized by a menu item 'Print' or an iconic representation of a printer.

Views are defined to be useful for particular tasks the user will need to perform. In general, only those attributes necessary for performing a task will be displayed in the corresponding view (to avoid overloading the user with irrelevant detail). Inapplicable actions will be hidden or disabled.

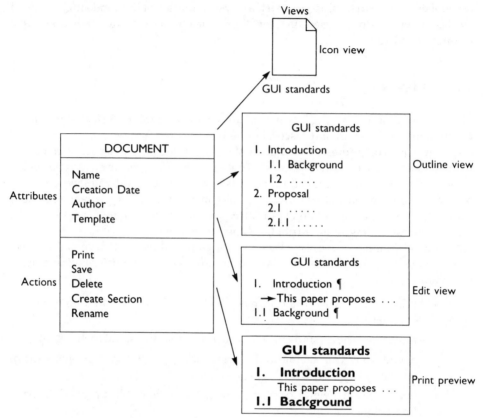

Fig. 3.6 A document object and four views

For example, in Figure 3.6 the edit view will show formatting control characters (such as the tab arrow) and enable editing actions because these are needed for the editing task. In contrast, the print preview view does not represent these attributes and actions. The outline view has some additional actions for rearranging the structure of sections, because reviewing and rearranging the structure is the task which the outline view is designed to support.

The use of views allows a GUI to maintain an illusion in the user's mind. The user acts on the representation of the object in the interface (i.e. the view) *as if they are acting directly on the object itself*. If the user changes some part of the view, they believe that the actual object will change in the same way. This illusion is like watching a film or theatrical play − we suspend disbelief, and see the actors as the people they represent. To be more precise, since the user is a participant in the interaction and not merely an audience, the illusion is like taking part in a role-playing exercise.

In the GUI context we 'believe' the screen image *is* the underlying user object. For example, on the Apple Macintosh, if we drag an icon of a folder across the screen and drop it over the trash can icon, we believe that the folder (and any files in it) are now in the trash can (i.e. that manipulating the interface images has manipulated the real objects in the same way).

3.5   IMPLICATIONS OF HUMAN COGNITION

An area of human–computer interaction in which there has been an immense amount of research is how human cognitive capabilities and limitations influence the way humans interact with computers. This research is too extensive to summarize here, but it is worth mentioning a few key issues which have direct relevance for GUI design.

3.5.1   Limited memory

It is well known that humans can only remember about seven unrelated items of information for short periods of time. If information has to be remembered for long periods of time, substantial effort is needed, and the information has to be transformed into some kind of meaningful code.

Don't make the user remember
It is the GUI designer's responsibility to anticipate what information the user will need at what points in each task, and to ensure that all the relevant information is displayed where the user can see it. Showing the user some information, and then asking them to remember what it was two windows later when they can no longer see it, places a memory burden on the user, and should be avoided wherever possible. Asking the user to remember things is a source of strain and errors.

Frequent task closure
When a user is halfway through a task, they have to remember what they are trying to do, what they have done so far, what they intend to do next, what they plan to do if this does not work, etc. This involves a memory load. When the system gives a user clear feedback that a task has been successfully completed, the user can feel a sense of achievement and relief; and clear out all the fragments of the task currently held in their memory. This is known as 'task closure'.

The limitations of memory indicate that designers should seek to achieve task closure frequently, minimizing the length of time and the amount to be remembered before the user gets their welcome relief. Where an overall task is big or complex, it should be divided into subtasks, each of which has a clear subgoal which can be a closure point.

Recognition rather than recall
Humans are much better at recognizing items of information which are presented to them, than at recalling the same items from memory when faced with a blank screen.

GUI systems should be designed to take account of this well-documented characteristic of human memory.

Some ways of doing this are obvious, e.g. the familiar drop-down list, where a user recognizes the value they want from a list rather than having to remember what the valid values are, how to spell them, etc.

However, there are also deeper implications. There is the whole question of whether the user, just by looking at a window or control, can recognize what they can do with it. For example, if you look at a push-button control, it is easy to recognize that you can push it. In contrast, many GUIs have functionality which is not visible, or where you would never guess from looking at it what action you can take on it.

Donald Norman introduced the useful term of 'affordances' to describe this phenomenon. Affordances are '... perceived and actual properties of the thing, primarily those fundamental properties that determine just how the thing should be used' (Norman, 1988). Norman describes the affordances of such everyday objects as door handles, where from just looking at a door you may be able to recognize whether to push or pull, and whether you have to turn the handle or not. Some doors are confusing because there is no visual cue, or because the visual cue is misleading.

Returning to GUI design, the more the user can recognize what actions are available and how to perform them just by looking at a window, the less they have to remember and the fewer errors they will make. Style guides are a way of codifying and summarizing commonly agreed affordances for a given GUI environment.

3.5.2 Humans make errors

Humans beings tend not to be consistently accurate, and frequently make errors. Rather than exhorting the user to try harder to concentrate, GUI designers should design the GUI so that it is suitable for use by error-prone users.

There are three main ways of doing this:

- Preventing the user from making errors.
- Intercepting errors with a helpful error message, which assists the user to perform what they intended or to recover from the error situation.
- Allowing the user to perform an action, see the results, and then change their mind and reverse or 'undo' what they have just done.

These are all common and important mechanisms in GUI design.

3.5.3 Capability for exploration

Having noted several cognitive weaknesses of human beings, we should also note a real strength. Human beings have a talent for exploration – for interacting with an unfamiliar object and 'working out' how to use it to achieve their purposes.

As well as designing GUIs to compensate for human weaknesses, we should design them to allow people to take advantage of what they are good at. This is done through encouraging the user to 'explore' the interface − literally to wander around it as if it were a strange place and find out what is in it and what it can do.

Many of the points discussed above contribute to encouraging exploration. It is important to make the user feel sufficiently safe and confident to explore. To achieve this the user must not be frightened of making mistakes − they must feel that either they will be prevented from making errors, or that errors will be easily reversible and not have catastrophic consequences.

Having recognizable objects and actions is vitally important. In exploring, the user wants to be able to open a new window and 'guess' by looking at it what it means and what it can do. And as they become familiar with more of the system, they need to be able to build up a mental model of what is in the system.

3.6   SUMMARY

This chapter describes selected concepts concerning human−computer interaction which are particularly useful for practical GUI design. These include the following:

- A theory of human action which regards people as purposive initiators, and computers (including the user interface) as tools that people use to achieve their purposes. The person acts; the system responds, giving feedback so that the person knows whether the system did what he or she intended.

- The concept of a 'user's mental model', this being a representation of a system inside a user's head. Having a suitable mental model assists a person to use a computer system effectively.

- The design strategy of producing a model of the objects in the system (a user object model), in order to 'build in' the basis of a suitable user's mental model into the GUI.

- The concept of windows containing 'views' of objects in the system. The user acts on the view, but behaves as if they are acting on the object itself.

- A brief mention of some human cognitive limitations and capabilities, and how these influence what you as a designer need to do to produce a usable GUI.

3.7   FURTHER READING

Norman, D. and Draper, S. (eds) (1986) *User-centered System Design: New perspectives on human−computer interaction*, Laurence Earlbaum.
   Chapter 3 'Cognitive Engineering' by Donald Norman describes the general approach to conceptualizing human−computer interaction which is adopted in GUIDE.

Potosnak, K. (1989) 'Mental models: helping users understand software', *IEEE Software*, September 1989.
Discusses what mental models are, how people build them, how to facilitate the process of building a mental model, and how to gain access to people's mental models.

Booth, P. (1990) *Introduction to Human—Computer Interaction*, Laurence Earlbaum.
A readable general introduction to the study of human—computer interaction.

Shneiderman, B. (1992) *Designing the User Interface: Strategies for effective human—computer interaction*, Addison-Wesley.
Chapter 2 discusses a powerful conceptual framework for human—computer interaction, distinguishing between purposive, semantic, syntactic and physical levels.

Open University (1990) *Human—Computer Interaction*, Unit 4 Knowledge and Action: Mental Models in HCI. Course PMT 607. Open University, Walton Hall, Milton Keynes, UK.
Part of material for master's degree course. Very good summary and discussion of the role of mental models in Norman's model of user action.

Norman, D. (1988) *The Psychology of Everyday Things*, Basic Books, New York.
A very readable book with excellent discussion of mental models and affordances.

IBM (1991) *Systems Application Architecture: Common user access guide to user interface design* (document number SC34-4289-00), IBM Publications.
Has a useful section discussing the relationship between the user's model of what is in the system, the designer's model and the GUI programmer's model.

Laurel, B. (ed.) *The Art of Human—Computer Interface Design*, Addison-Wesley, 1990.
A fascinating collection of contemporary short papers, including discussions of many important concepts such as metaphor, view and user illusion in a readable and practitioner-oriented format.

4

GUI design in project context

4.1   INTRODUCTION

The graphical user interface is frequently only part of what must be designed in a project. Although this book focuses on GUI design, it is important for practitioners to be aware of the linkage points where GUI design processes interact with other design processes. This chapter identifies and discusses these linkages.

In parallel with GUI design, there may be design work on a least two other kinds of system with which the GUI must interact:

- The business system which provides the context within which the GUI system is used. This consists of business processes, organization structures, roles and responsibilities, etc.

- The computer system to whose data and functionality the GUI is providing a user interface.

(GUIs may also be used for monitoring or controlling hardware devices − e.g. industrial machinery, weapons systems − in which case GUI system design has to be reconciled with hardware system design. This is beyond the scope of GUIDE.)

Linkages with these wider systems are discussed in section 4.2. Note that (i) some GUI design projects are not concerned with these issues; and (ii) GUIDE does not imply or depend upon any specific methodology being used for business system design or computer system design.

Two project management issues which are particularly important for GUI design are incremental development and iterative design. These are discussed in section 4.3.

The last part of this chapter introduces the Helpline case study, which is used as a running example through the remaining chapters of the book.

4.2   PROJECT CONTEXT DIAGRAM

To discuss the issue of project context let us consider how GUIDE fits into a broader systems development process. Figure 4.1 shows the GUIDE overview diagram located within a development process encompassing both business system design and computer system design. The diagram is loosely based upon the conventional information engineering style of development process, which is widely used in developing data-processing systems. The non-GUI aspects of the process are very schematic and simplified, but serve to identify key areas of interaction between system design and GUI design. These linkages are represented by the bold arrows in the diagram.

The four heavy arrows at the top of Figure 4.1 indicate how the design of the business system feeds into GUIDE and interacts with GUI design products. The three heavy arrows lower down in Figure 4.1 show how GUI design products feed into the design of the computer system. The wider system design processes and linkages are summarized in the following sections.

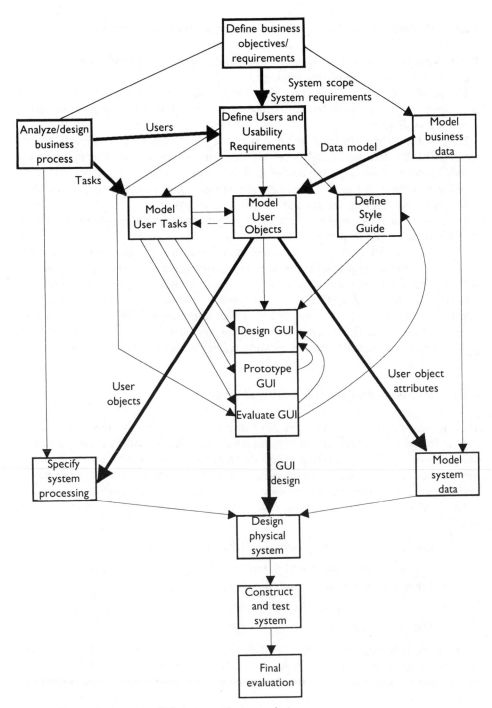

Fig. 4.1   Linkages between GUI design and system design

4.2.1   Define business objectives and system requirements

This process defines the objectives and scope of the project. Its starting point is usually business objectives or business strategy.

The product should include some definition of the scope of the project, e.g. a list of business processes or functions to consider, or an outline data flow diagram acting as a context diagram.

The product also includes a list of system requirements, such as a requirements catalog. This list defines the high-level requirements which the computer system must satisfy to meet the needs of the business. Before using techniques to design a usable GUI for the system, we need a document which establishes what the proposed system is for, and ensures that we are building the right system.

Techniques such as cost–benefit analysis may be used to assess whether a system development project is justifiable.

The link to GUIDE is that business objectives and system requirements are directly related to usability requirements. System requirements may already explicitly include some usability requirements, such as 'the system must enable the user to process ten cases per hour'. (Usability requirements are a subset of what are called 'non-functional requirements'.) Other usability requirements will be identified in user analysis as part of GUIDE, but it is important to show how these usability requirements produce business benefits, i.e. by relating them back to business objectives.

4.2.2   Analyze and design business process

This develops a model of the structure and functioning of the business system. It may include modeling the current business organization and proposing how it should be reorganized to make it more effective or efficient. A common theme in the 1990s is Business Process Re-engineering, i.e. rationalizing the business process by restructuring it, removing redundancy or reducing fragmentation.

The product is a model of how the revised business process will be organized. This may take the following forms:

- Organization structure, with roles and responsibilities
- Definition of management objectives and performance targets
- Process map (or workflow) diagrams
- Functional decomposition diagrams
- Data flow diagrams

There are two major links with GUIDE. Firstly, business process design defines who the people are who will use the system, their roles, responsibilities and organizational objectives. This feeds into the GUIDE identification and description of end-users.

Secondly, it must be possible to relate the business processes and functions to the tasks performed by individual users. The business process design is input to GUIDE task modeling, and typically a business process consists of several user tasks. Task modeling may reveal that the tasks are poorly structured, and indicate the need for revisions to the business process design.

4.2.3   Model business data

This produces a model of the data required to support the business processes. The product is typically a high-level logical data model, which is a subset of the 'corporate data model' or 'enterprise information model'.

The link to GUIDE is that this data model is an input to user object modeling. The major entities frequently become user objects.

4.2.4   Specify system processing

This process specifies the computer system processing required to support the business system. Some system requirements and functionality may be derived from the business process design, but most of the interactive functionality is identified from the GUI design.

The link with GUIDE is through user objects. Actions on user objects are the user's way of requesting system functionality — each user object action defines some processing required by the user. Also the attributes of user objects typically require enquiry functions to retrieve and derive the required information.

4.2.5   Model system data

This process combines the information requirements of the business with the data required to support user objects in the GUI. The process frequently involves data normalization, and produces a detailed logical data model which provides the basis for physical database design.

The link with GUIDE is through user object attributes. Part of the definition of a user object is a specification of how the user object attributes map onto entity attributes and relationships.

4.2.6   Design physical system

This process designs the physical components required to implement the GUI design, processing specifications and logical data model. The product is a design of the windows programs, physical processing components and physical database tables.

One of the main design objectives during physical design is to achieve acceptable performance, and so the process may include tuning the database or other parts of the design.

Systems with a GUI are often implemented in client–server architectures, and thus the process may involve deciding how to partition the processing components and data between the client and server.

Physical design is concerned with designing the system components and mechanisms which produce this behavior (e.g. GUI 4GL programs, messaging, remote procedure calls). The direct link from GUIDE is through the GUI design, which defines the appearance and user-visible behavior of the user interface. (There are also two indirect links from GUIDE, via the influence of user objects on the design of system processing and system data.) (It is beyond the scope of this book, but LBMS also has a client–server design method for designing the implementation of GUI systems in a client–server architecture.)

If evolutionary prototyping is being used, the GUI prototype may be used as a 'first-cut' physical design.

4.2.7 Construct and test the system

This process develops the program code in the physical design components. The components are compiled, unit tested, integrated and system tested.

If evolutionary prototyping is being used, the GUI prototype code is extended to evolve into the production code.

4.2.8 Final evaluation

A key part of the acceptance test of the completed system is to repeat the user evaluation process to ensure that usability requirements have not been compromised during physical design and construction.

4.3 PROJECT PLANNING CONCEPTS

GUIDE is not about project planning or project management, but it is important to understand two key concepts:

- Incremental development
- Iterative design

It is also worth discussing briefly the likely distribution of effort in a GUIDE project.

4.3.1 Incremental development

The classic systems development lifecycle is a waterfall model, consisting of performing all the Analysis, followed by all the Design, then all the Construction, etc. (see

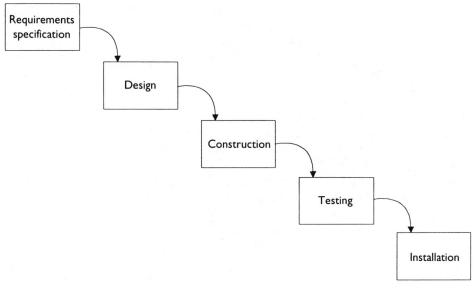

Fig. 4.2   Waterfall Lifecycle Model

Figure 4.2). This has numerous well-documented problems, notably the following:

- The user does not receive anything until the end.
- Requirements have to be frozen for a long period (during which the users' real requirements may change).
- There is little opportunity for problems encountered or experience gained during construction, testing or use to influence requirements or design.

An alternative model, which is highly suitable for GUI systems, is incremental development. In incremental development, the overall system functionality is partitioned into a number of increments (anything from two to fifty).

Each increment consists of a relatively self-contained unit of functionality which would provide the user with some real benefit. The increments are prioritized, either: (i) to give priority to the increments with the greatest business benefit and the least cost; or (ii) to give priority to increments with high technical risk on which other increments are dependent.

A small amount of requirements analysis, application design and technical architecture design is performed across the scope of the whole system to ensure that there is an appropriate high-level direction and framework.

The increments are then developed in priority order, with each increment progressing through analysis, design, construction, testing and installation.

Incremental development can be visualized as a multiple waterfall, as shown in Figure 4.3.

The benefits of incremental development and delivery include the following:

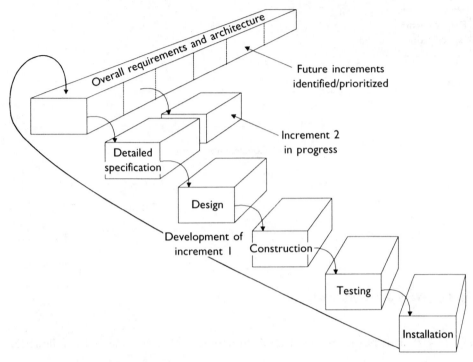

Fig. 4.3   Incremental development

- Some business benefits are received earlier.
- The elapse time between requirements analysis and delivery is much shorter, so requirements are less likely to have changed before implementation.
- The risk of failure is reduced (each increment is small and short).
- There is feedback from the construction, testing and use of the first increments into the specification and design of the subsequent increments. Indeed, even the overall requirements and the priorities for the next increment are re-evaluated at the end of each increment (as shown by the bottom loop).

4.3.2   Iterative design

Chapter 1 introduced the concept of usability engineering, with its cycle of specify requirements, design, evaluate, redesign, evaluate, etc.

GUI Design is an iterative process − the initial design is followed by successive revisions and redesigns until an acceptable design is produced. This iteration must be deliberately incorporated in the planning process.

Note that this is a quite different issue from incremental development. Each

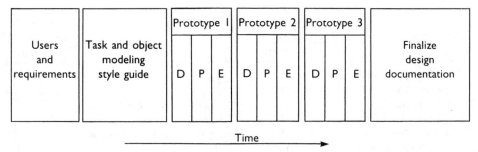

Fig. 4.4   Plan showing three iterations

increment is concerned with a different part of the system. In contrast, each iteration is concerned with redesigning or extending the same part of the system − having several passes at the same window design.

Planning for iteration involves making a judgment about the number of iterations that will be required. The minimum recommended number of major iterations is three. If the application area is unfamiliar, or the developers are inexperienced, or the usability requirements are particularly stringent, then plan for more − e.g. four or five.

A major iteration is where the whole design−prototype−evaluate cycle is performed. In addition there may be many brief localized iterations to solve a specific design problem.

A GUIDE plan allowing for these iterations is shown in Figure 4.4. Each prototyping cycle consists of three activities, (D)esign, (P)rototype, (E)valuate. After the third evaluation, some time is allowed to make any agreed changes to the design, and to ensure that the documentation is complete and consistent.

Control of prototyping is discussed in more detail in Chapter 11, GUI Prototyping.

4.3.3   Distribution of effort

The distribution of effort between the design activities varies greatly between projects, but an indication of possible proportions of effort is given in Figure 4.5. This is for a project where the estimated effort is 100 person-days of developer time (e.g. analyst, GUI designer and GUI programmer), planning for three iterations as in Figure 4.4. Possible effort from end-user members of the team is shown in the right-hand column. The figures and proportions are bound to vary substantially by project, but are sufficiently realistic to illustrate a few important points:

- Defining users and usability requirements is important, but takes relatively little time and effort.
- The big project management and estimating decision is how many iterations to plan for, and how much effort and elapse time to allow for each iteration.
- The balance of effort between the early activities and GUI Design, Prototyping

Activity	Developer effort (person-days)	Comments	User effort (person-days)
Define Users and Usability Requirements	1		2
Model User Tasks	10	Plus revisions during iterations	20
Model User Objects	5	Plus revisions during iterations	5
Define Style Guide	5	Plus revisions during iterations	2
Design GUI (iteration 1)	15 ⎫		
Prototype GUI (iteration 1)	10 ⎬	30 (iteration 1)	15
Evaluate GUI (iteration 1)	5 ⎭		
Design GUI (iteration 2)	5 ⎫		
Prototype GUI (iteration 2)	15 ⎬	25 (iteration 2)	15
Evaluate GUI (iteration 2)	5 ⎭		
Design GUI (iteration 3)	2 ⎫		
Prototype GUI (iteration 3)	8 ⎬	20 (iteration 3)	25
Evaluate GUI (iteration 3)	10 ⎭		
Finalize design documentation	4		2
Total	100 days		86 days

Fig. 4.5 Distribution of effort across project activities

and Evaluation is not what you would guess from the GUIDE overview diagram. You might infer that GUIDE recommends you spend more than half the effort on the activities before GUI design. In fact we suggest about 20 percent on the early activities, and about 80 percent in the design, prototyping and evaluation cycles.

- Within the design and prototyping iterations, the balance of effort progresses from an emphasis on GUI design, to effort on getting the prototype built, working and exercised, to effort on evaluation.

■ 4.4 INTRODUCTION TO CASE STUDY ■

An extended case study is used throughout this book to illustrate how the GUIDE process takes you through a number of intermediate products to a final GUI design.

The case study is based on the use of the GUIDE process in a real GUI design project conducted by the authors. We hope basing it on a real project makes it more authentic than an invented example, and that you will see how the GUI design emerges and evolves throughout the process.

This section introduces the case study, discussing aspects of the case study that illustrate the topics in this chapter, i.e. examples of inputs to GUIDE, and the planning of increments and iterations.

4.4.1   Customer support Helpline

The setting for the case study is the customer support group of a UniSoft Inc., a fictitious company which develops and markets software products. The software products are expensive and complex, and many customers have some queries or problems on which they need advice or assistance. The central element of UniSoft's customer support service is a telephone helpline, which is available twelve hours a day to provide assistance to any customer who requires it. The quality of this Helpline support is critical to maintaining customer confidence and satisfaction, which in turn is critical to the success of the overall business. (A high proportion of UniSoft product sales consist of additional sales to existing satisfied customers.)

To show how the GUIDE process is linked to wider system development projects, the background information on the case study is presented in the format of the project documents that might be given to the GUI designer. These documents are as follows:

- Business objectives and critical performance areas
- System requirements
- Workflow diagram showing the business process
- Data flow diagram showing project scope and the business functions
- Data model

These are not intended to be a definitive or recommended style of system specification, merely an illustration of the type of system documentation which is sometimes available as input to the GUIDE process.

It is possible to use GUIDE where there is no prior documentation defining scope and system requirements. However, in these circumstances it is advisable to produce and gain management agreement to some form of high-level document which identifies objectives, scope, high-level system requirements and expected business benefits.

4.4.2   Business objectives and critical performance areas

Figure 4.6 shows a very simple hierarchical model of the customer support business area, with the business area as a whole (customer support) at the top. The lower levels show 'critical performance areas' (CPAs), which are functions in which effective performance is critical in order to meet the business objective(s).

System requirements are specified in relation to these CPAs. Each system requirement must make a significant contribution towards the level of performance on one or more CPAs, and hence towards achieving the business objective.

4.4.3   System requirements

The agreed system requirements are listed below. Where relevant, requirements have been cross-referenced to the critical performance area they contribute to, e.g. CPA1.1.

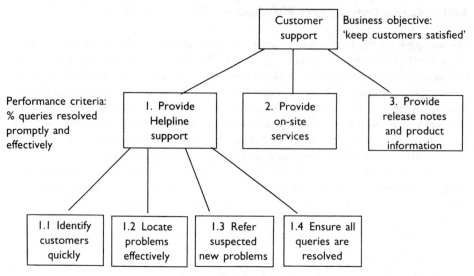

Fig. 4.6   Critical performance areas for customer support

R1 To enable Helpline staff to resolve customer problems more effectively and quickly. (CPA 1)

Required performance level: 60 percent of problems solved immediately (within 15 minutes, while the customer is on the phone); 80 percent solved within one hour of initial call.

R1.1 System performance for customer identification and entering queries must be fast (as fast as the customer can speak and the Helpline advisor can enter data). (CPA 1.1)

R1.2 System performance for retrieval of related problem information already in the system must be fast enough to perform while the customer is on the phone. (CPA 1.2)

R2 To improve the flow of relevant information from the Helpline to the sales and product development groups, without increasing the cost of information dissemination.

R3 To provide information to enable the customer support manager to monitor and control Helpline activities. (CPA 1)

R3.1 To provide information identifying problems requiring management intervention. (CPA 1.4)

R3.2 To provide an on-line history for each query and problem (who did what, when).

R3.3 To monitor the responses of second-line support to problems referred to them. (CPA 1.4)

R4 The system must have continuous availability for 100 percent of Helpline working hours.

R5 The system must support updating by up to twenty concurrent users without significant performance degradation.

R6 The system must allow flexible updating of product information and problem classification information. (CPA 1.2)

4.4.4   Workflow diagram showing business process

The workflow diagram shows how units of work move through the organization. Figure 4.7 shows how work is initiated by a Customer raising a Query with the Helpline. If the Helpline staff can resolve the Query, they do so and give the Customer a Solution, otherwise they identify a Problem and refer this to Second-line Support. Second-line Support reproduce and investigate the Problem. If it can be solved by advice, they refer it back to Helpline; if there is a software defect which requires a change to the software, they raise a Software Change Request, etc.

4.4.5   Data flow diagram showing business functions and scope

The data flow diagram in Figure 4.8 shows the scope of the Helpline system, and represents the various people and organizations who are sources or recipients of system information as ovals.

The business functions are identified as follows:

- *Capture query and respond:* answering the telephone, learning who the customer is and what their query is, and where possible identifying and resolving the underlying problem immediately over the telephone.
- *Reproduce problem and analyze:* where a problem cannot be identified immediately, it is reproduced and analyzed further until the problem is well understood.
- *Disseminate information:* relevant Helpline information on customers and their problems with products is distributed to many parts of the company.
- *Monitor Helpline:* the progress and status of queries is continuously monitored to identify any required management intervention.
- *Maintain customer and site information:* a record is maintained of customer site information (e.g. hardware configuration) from site visit installation reports and from the software licensing system.

The business process (e.g. 'provide customer service') is like a thread running through several of these functions. In this example, the business process itself is not being re-engineered.

The main store of data is Queries/Problems. This holds current and historic customer queries and all known system problems. A second store holds customer and site data.

4.4.6   Data model

The initial data model which was used to define the scope of the system is shown in Figure 4.9. (See Chapter 7 for details of the notation used, which is the same as the user object modeling notation.)

Reading from the top, 'Customer' represents an organization which buys and uses one of UniSoft's software products. 'Contact' represents the person who telephones the Helpline with a query (and works for the Customer organization). 'Call' is a telephone call to the Helpline. A Customer may have (zero, one or) many Contacts who may each make many Calls. A single call may consist of several Queries.

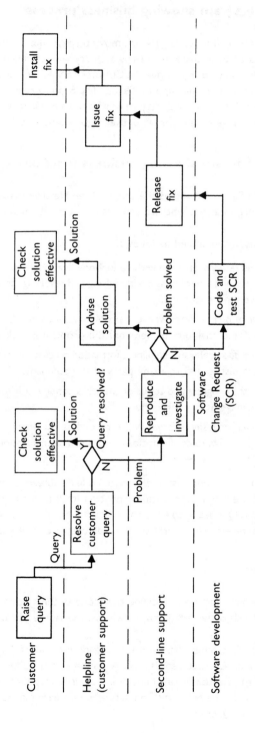

Fig. 4.7 Workflow diagram for Helpline

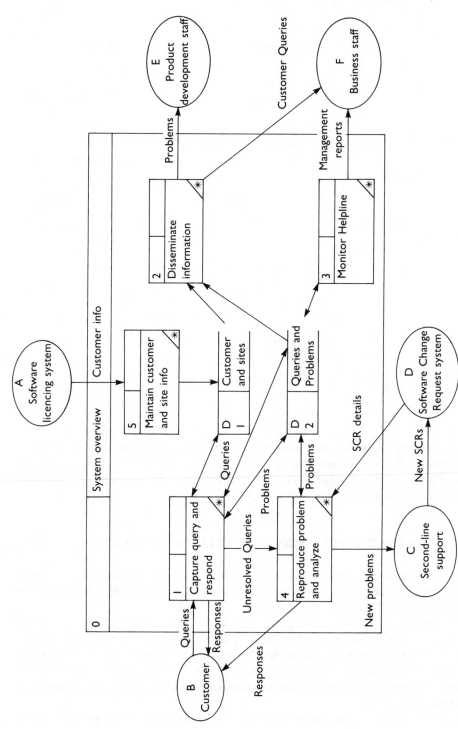

Fig. 4.8 Data flow diagram for Helpline system

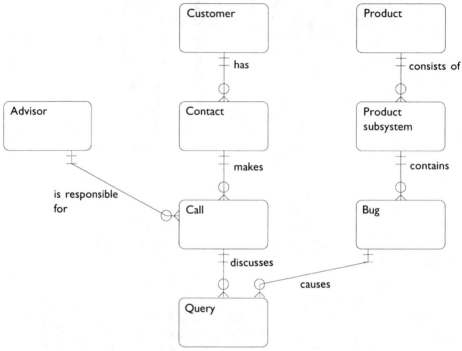

Fig. 4.9 Initial Data Model

The right-hand side consists of Product (the UniSoft product sold to the Customer), product Subsystem, and Bug, a known defect in the Product Subsystem. A Product may consist of several Product Subsystems, a Subsystem may contain many Bugs, and a Bug may cause many customer Queries. Some Queries may not relate to a Bug.

4.5   EXAMPLE – PLANNING THE HELPLINE PROJECT

This section describes the way that the Helpline case study project was planned, as an example of planning a GUI project. Although it is only a small system, it was decided to adopt an incremental delivery approach, shown in Figure 4.10.

The planning objective was to make the scope of the first increment as small as possible – it was the smallest subset of system functionality which could be installed and be useful to the users. In this project it was decided that the first increment of the new system had to provide all the essential functionality in the old system. (Note that this is frequently *not* the case. It is often possible for the first increment to build 'on top of' or 'on the side of' an existing system.)

Various features of the new system which were not essential on 'day 1' were deferred to

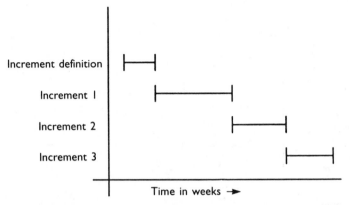

Fig. 4.10   Top-level schedule showing all increments

the second and third increment. (These tasks were handled manually until the subsequent increments were installed.)

The blocks of work in the incremental plan in Figure 4.10 are as follows:

- Increment definition
  - high-level scoping;
  - analysis of requirements;
  - prioritization and definition of increments;
  - definition of technical architecture.

- Increment 1. Minimum installable functionality
  - customer identification;
  - problem identification;
  - query logging;
  - advisor workload monitoring/allocation.

- Increment 2. Information dissemination
  - salesperson facilities;
  - software product group facilities.

- Increment 3. Integration with Software Change Request System

Each increment includes analysis/modeling, design/prototyping, construction, testing and installation of a subset of the system.

A more detailed plan and schedule is prepared for the first increment, as shown in Figure 4.11. This shows the use of prototyping cycles for iterative evaluation and redesign. We decide to plan for three prototyping cycles. The first prototype will be a paper prototype, while the second and third prototypes will be software prototypes. (In a more substantial project, we might have had a paper prototype and three software prototypes.)

We decide to use an evolutionary prototyping approach in which the prototype will evolve into the installed system. For this to be feasible, we have to select a GUI environment and development tool which has good prototyping facilities and is suitable (in terms of performance,

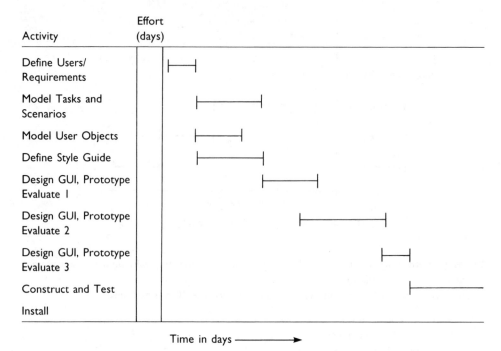

Fig. 4.11   Schedule for increment 1

robustness, maintainability, licence fees, etc.) for the delivered system. We selected Microsoft Visual Basic, but there are a wide range of GUI development tools which have similar facilities. (The case study includes examples of windows built in Visual Basic, but the GUIDE process is not specific to Visual Basic or even to Microsoft Windows.) GUI Prototyping is discussed further in Chapter 11.

4.6   SUMMARY

This chapter describes the context of a GUI design project. Major points include the following:

- How the design of the business system, and the design of the remainder of the computer system, are linked to the design of the user interface. Linkage points identify which earlier products feed into GUIDE, and how GUIDE products are useful inputs into later design activities.

- The importance of dividing a GUI design project into increments (whenever possible), and planning for a series of iterations for the design of each increment.

- Some discussion of the likely distribution of effort between the GUIDE activities.
- An introduction to the Helpline case study which is used as a running example throughout the book.

4.7   FURTHER READING

Gilb, T. (1988) *Principles of Software Engineering Management*, Addison-Wesley.
  This is the classic text on incremental software engineering. It also contains excellent material on specification and testing of non-functional requirements.

Ould, M.A. (1990) *Strategies for Software Engineering*, John Wiley.
  A readable recent text on the project management and quality management of systems development projects, which discusses incremental and iterative approaches to managing project risks.

5

Users and usability specification

5.1   INTRODUCTION

GUIDE recommends a philosophy of user-centered design (as discussed in Chapter 1). The GUI should be shaped to fit with the needs, preferences, skills and task requirements of the human beings who will use it. The process:

- starts with identifying the end-users and their usability requirements;
- continues with users' tasks and mental models;
- involves end-users participating in analysis, design and prototyping;
- concludes with end-user evaluation of the usability of GUI prototypes.

This chapter describes how end-users are identified and described, and how usability requirements are specified (see Figure 5.1).

Analyzing users and usability requirements is important because they are so diverse. Shneiderman sums it up well:

The remarkable diversity of human abilities, backgrounds, cognitive styles, and personalities challenges the interactive-system designer. A preschooler playing a graphic computer game is a long way from a reference librarian doing bibliographic searches for anxious and hurried patrons. Similarly a professional programmer using a new operating system is a long way from a highly trained and experienced air-traffic controller. Finally, a student learning a computer-assisted instruction session is a long way from a hotel reservations clerk serving customers for many hours per day.

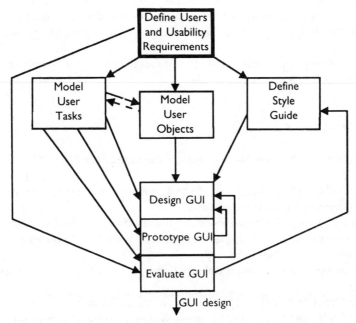

Fig. 5.1   GUIDE context of defining users and usability requirements

5.1.1   Objectives

- To identify who the end-users of the system will be.
- To understand the relevant characteristics of end-users.
- To specify usability requirements for the system.

5.1.2   Benefits

Identifying all the classes of end-user and their special characteristics is an essential prerequisite to specifying usability requirements.

Documenting end-user characteristics helps designers to be aware of whom they are designing for. Unless designers consciously hold in mind whom they are designing for, they are likely to design (unconsciously) for people like themselves. Most end-users are actually very different from GUI designers in their skills, task requirements, mental models and preferences.

Usability requirements specify the GUI design objective. It is very unlikely that usability objectives will be met unless they are explicitly specified, and used as the basis against which the GUI design is evaluated. The key benefit of usability requirements is that they enable usability engineering, where iterative redesign is controlled to meet usability targets.

Having explicit usability requirements helps designers throughout the design process to concentrate their efforts on the areas where usability is most critical.

Usability requirements provide a brief and comprehensible statement of requirements early in the design process, as a basis for senior management agreement and commitment.

Measurable usability requirements provide an excellent basis for acceptance testing of the final production version of the GUI.

5.1.3   Inputs/outputs

The products input to this process, and the products produced, are summarized in Figure 5.2.

Prior to the GUIDE project there needs to be agreement on the objectives and scope of the overall systems development project.

System scope defines the boundaries of the proposed system, for example in terms of a context diagram, data flow diagram and/or data model; or in terms of business functions or user tasks to be supported.

System requirements define the critical functional and non-functional requirements for the system.

User roles are frequently defined by the roles in the wider business system. If roles are changing (due to changes in the business system or computer system), it is the future roles we need as input.

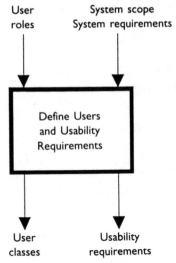

User roles   System scope
System requirements

Define Users
and Usability
Requirements

User classes   Usability requirements

Fig. 5.2 Inputs and outputs for define users and usability requirements

Other inputs include sources of information about users (e.g. personnel information, surveys).

5.2 PRODUCTS

5.2.1 User class

A 'user class' is a subset of the total population of end-users who are similar in terms of their system usage and relevant personal characteristics.

The users in one user class should be relatively similar in their pattern of use and usability requirements. For this reason, the people who perform one user role are often divided into two or more user classes.

For example, in a hotel room management system an important user role might be to maintain room bookings. We might identify three user classes:

- Reception desk staff, who are experienced and continuous users of the system.
- Management, who are experienced at taking bookings but intermittent users of the system.
- Trainees, who are inexperienced at taking bookings and unfamiliar with the computer system.

For each user class, the description should include information on the following:

- Type of user (direct/indirect/remote/support, etc.)

- Experience level of user (novice, intermediate, expert, transfer, intermittent)
- Frequency of use of system
- Mandatory/discretionary use
- Existing computer experience and skills
- Other systems that they use (or will use) concurrently
- Education/intellectual abilities
- Motivation for using the system and specific goals
- Number of users
- Tasks performed (cross-reference to task model)

If relevant, it may also include information on the following:

- General characteristics (age/sex)
- Differences between users
- Physical characteristics/capabilities
- Language issues
- Extent of task knowledge needed
- Training they receive on systems
- Learning style (i.e. preference for tutorial or trial and error)
- Organizational position
- How they are selected and promoted
- Ways of working

In principle it is possible for user classes to overlap, i.e. for one person to be a member of more than one user class. Note that a user class is not a 'class' in the object-oriented sense − it is just a collection of people with similar usability requirements.

Some of the terms and descriptive categories used above are explained below.

Type of user

'Direct users' use the system 'hands-on' to perform their own work. For example, a secretary using a wordprocessor.

'Indirect users' use the system by asking other people to use the system on their behalf. For example, a senior manager may ask their personal assistant to send an electronic mail message.

'Remote users' work at a different location from the system, but either depend on output from the system or prepare input to the system. For example, a customer of a telephone company receiving an itemized invoice showing their telephone calls is a remote user.

'Support users' use the system in order to help other users do their work effectively. For example, system administrators, helpline staff, trainers, maintenance staff.

Mandatory/discretionary user

A 'mandatory' user must use the system in order to do their job.

A 'discretionary' user can choose to perform their tasks without using the system. If initial learning is too difficult or takes too long, many discretionary users may opt never to use the system.

Existing computer experience and skills

Which hardware are people familiar with? (e.g. IBM PC, IBM 3270 terminal).

Have they used a GUI environment before? If so which? (e.g. Microsoft Windows, Apple Macintosh, OSF Motif).

What application software are they familiar with? (e.g. Lotus 1-2-3, Microsoft Word for Windows).

Motivation for using the system and specific goals

What are the personal costs/benefits to a person in this user class of using the system?
Does it increase/decrease their job satisfaction?
Does it increase/decrease their autonomy and control over their work?
Does it enhance their skills or involve deskilling?
Will it increase or decrease their status or prestige in the organization?

Notation

A textual description of each user class, plus a set of tables summarizing the characteristics of people in the various user classes (for an example, see Figure 5.4).

Where used

(i.e. subsequent activities in which the user class product is used)

Define Usability Requirements These are defined for each user class, related to their characteristics and key tasks.

Model User Objects Conceptualization and terminology depend on user background and pattern of use. Typically a number of user classes share a user object model.

Define Style Guide Appropriate styles of interaction depend on user characteristics such as frequency of use. Also, the style guide may be harmonized with the style of a previous system or a concurrently used system.

Design GUI Design may be harmonized with other systems used, or optimized to user characteristics.

Evaluate GUI To ensure representative members of each user class are involved in evaluation, and that the design is usable given their personal characteristics.

Quality criteria

- Is there sufficient information to guide analysis and design decisions?
- Within each user class, are the characteristics and usability requirements similar? (If the system is usable by a few members of the user class who participate in user testing, is it reasonable to infer that it will be usable by the others?)
- Have the numbers of users in each user class been identified?
- Have the benefits of using the system for people in each user class been identified?
- Have the implications for use been made explicit for each user class? (e.g. 'because staff turnover is 40 percent, the training time must be less than 2 hours'; or 'because half the staff can't read English well, all items must be recognizable by icons').

5.2.2 Usability requirement

A statement of a usability requirement that the GUI design must satisfy, including the following:

- What will be measured.
- How it will be measured.
- What level of the measure is required.

The concept of usability and the major aspects of usability are discussed in Chapter 1, section 1.2.

For each usability requirement the following information is recorded:

- *Usability attribute* What aspect of system usability is being specified, e.g. user task performance, user satisfaction, learnability, memorability?
- *Measuring instrument* What procedure or test will be used to measure this attribute? Often this is a task scenario, which would also specify how much training and previous experience the user should have before performing the test. Another common instrument is some form of questionnaire.
- *Value to be measured* What result does the measure produce? Common measures are: time to complete the task scenario; number of errors in completing the scenario; proportion of users able to complete a task successfully; questionnaire score (e.g. of user satisfaction).
- *Current level* The result produced by applying the measuring instrument to the current system. This is useful even if the current system is not precisely comparable.
- *Worst acceptable level* The worst level of the usability attribute at which the GUI system would be accepted and installed.

- *Planned target level*   The planned target level of the usability attribute, which the project is seeking to achieve.
- *Best possible level*   The best level which it is possible to achieve with a perfect system and an expert user.

(Note: some literature makes a distinction between a usability requirement − i.e. what is required − and a usability specification − i.e. how the requirement is specified and measured. The GUIDE approach treats the requirement and its specification as one product.)

Shneiderman (1992) recommends that five types of usability requirement are used:

- Time to learn
- Speed of performance
- Rate or errors by users
- Retention over time
- Subjective satisfaction

It is important to note that there are frequently trade-offs between usability requirements. For example, errors can often be reduced by having a low information density (only a few items on the screen) and using confirmation dialogs, but this reduces speed of performance. If lengthy learning is permitted, then the speed of task performance may be increased by asking users to learn special shortcuts or abbreviations. The relative priority of different usability requirements needs to be established early in the project.

Shneiderman gives an example of an early usability requirement for a programming workstation project: 'New professional programmers should be able to sign on, to create a short program, and to execute that program against a stored test data set, without assistance and within 10 minutes.'

Notation

A usability requirement specification table as shown in Figure 5.3.

Usability attribute	Measuring instrument	Value to be measured	Current level	Worst acceptable level	Planned target level	Best possible level	Observed results
Initial performance	Cancel order scenario 1	Time to complete	40 sec (old system)	40 sec	20 sec	10 sec	
User satisfaction	Questionnaire 3	Total score	30	35	60	73	

Fig. 5.3 Usability requirement specification table

Where used

Define Style Guide   Usability requirements influence the standard style adopted. For example, speed of data entry as a main requirement may lead to use of push buttons or shortcut keys in place of pull-down menus. Use by the public (without training) means that various controls whose behavior is not visually obvious should not be used.

Design GUI   Usability requirements influence the design of window layouts and interaction sequences.

Evaluate GUI   Usability requirements are the acceptance criteria against which the GUI design is evaluated.

Quality criteria

- Are these the most important usability requirements?
- Are the measuring instruments feasible to use with these users and the constraints of this project?
- Are the performance levels agreed as acceptance criteria for the usability of the GUI?

5.3   PROCESS

5.3.1   Identify user classes

Ask who will use the system. Be careful to identify all the less obvious groups of people who will use the system (indirect, remote and support users).

Group the people into classes according to their pattern of use and relevant personal characteristics.

5.3.2   Describe the users in each class

Gather relevant information about the people in each user class. It is important to meet the people face-to-face if possible, as it is difficult to gain an appreciation of people's point of view without meeting them, and we want to design the GUI to fit with their point of view. Find out how these people *feel* about the proposed system – what aspects can they engage with enthusiastically (e.g. reducing tedious verification or reconciliation) and what aspects are they concerned about (e.g. loss of autonomy or scope for personal style).

Write the user class descriptions and complete the tables of characteristics.

5.3.3   Identify critical usability requirements

Identify the areas of usability which are critical to the success of the GUI, such as the following:

- Rate of performance of high-volume tasks by continuous users (e.g. input a benefit claim).
- Learning time for a new discretionary user.
- Error rate for intermittent user (e.g. of a monthly timesheet system).

The key issue here is usually the benefit to the organization from a usability requirement:

- How can the GUI make a significant contribution to the effectiveness of the organization (e.g. increased productivity or lower error rates)?
- How can it reduce overheads (e.g. the non-productive training time for new staff)?
- How can it make information which is currently inaccessible available to a wider audience of users?

5.3.4 Specify measures and performance criteria

Identify tests or measuring instruments which will be used to measure the extent to which each usability requirement is met.

Common measuring instruments are as follows:

- Task scenarios, as described in Chapter 6.
- Questionnaire for user satisfaction or user perception of usability. A good starting point is to use a standard questionnaire such as SUMI (see Appendix E).

It is essential that the measures are feasible and realistic to administer, in terms of:

- Skills of project staff
- Special equipment or environment needed (e.g. usability lab)
- Capabilities of end-users
- Effort, time and cost

Decide what performance criteria to use. (Performance criteria are the variables which are measured by the test.)

One measuring instrument may yield several different kinds of result. For example, a task scenario could be used with one or more of the following criteria:

- Average time to complete scenario
- Average number of errors
- Proportion of users able to complete scenario successfully

Note that it is not usually feasible for performance tests using task scenarios to test the whole interface. This step involves selecting a sample of representative or important scenarios.

It may be difficult or impossible to measure every usability requirement for every design iteration. In particular, early prototypes may not be sufficiently realistic to support measurements of all aspects of usability. In this case, these measurements will only be made on later prototypes.

5.3.5 Define performance levels

Define the current performance level. Wherever possible this should be calculated by using the measuring instrument, even if the current system is a manual system or uses some different technology.

Define the best possible performance level when used under ideal conditions.

Define a target performance level which fulfils the following criteria:

- Is sufficient to bring substantial business benefits.
- Appears to be achievable (i.e. is not too close to the best possible).
- (Is usually a significant improvement over the current system level.)

Define a worst acceptable level.

5.3.6 Review and agree usability requirements specification

Review the usability requirement with end-users, human factors experts, user management and technical management.

Specifically consider the following points:

- Are these in fact the most important usability requirements?
- Are they achievable?
- Are the target levels high enough? Will users and management be satisfied if the system can meet these targets?
- Is the worst acceptable level correct? Above it the system should be just barely acceptable. Scoring below this level means that the GUI as a whole is unacceptable and should be returned for redesign.

■ 5.4 EXAMPLE

5.4.1 Identify user classes

This section develops the case study introduced in Chapter 4, section 4.4.

In the customer support Helpline system for UniSoft Inc., the following groups of people need to use the system.

- *Helpline advisor* — who takes telephone queries and tries to resolve them.

Example   73

- *Customer support manager* — who manages the Helpline staff and is responsible for service levels.
- *Second-line support* — to whom difficult problems and suspected product defects are referred for further investigation.
- *Salespersons* — who need to be able to monitor the problems their clients have been reporting.
- *Other UniSoft staff* — who occasionally need information on customer queries and problems. ,

Each of these groups of people is a candidate user class. Reviewing their usability requirements, we find that Helpline Advisor actually includes two different groups of users. UniSoft's US office has a team of full-time experienced advisors. However, UniSoft also has field support groups in several other countries who require the Helpline system. These people deal with a much smaller volume of queries and so are part-time or intermittent users of the system.

The Helpline Advisor role is therefore divided into two user classes — Expert Helpline Advisor and Intermittent Helpline Advisor.

All the user classes above are direct users. In the current system there are various groups of indirect users (salespersons, etc.) but one of the aims of the new system is to enable all these people to be direct users. This system has an important class of remote user:

- *Customer contact* — who telephones with a query.

System administration and training will be performed by Helpline Advisors themselves, so there is not a separate class of support users.

5.4.2   Describe users in each class

The table in Figure 5.4 describes the characteristics of Ex   : Helpline Advisors.

5.4.3   Identify critical usability requireme.its

The system requirements in the Helpline case study are described in Chapter 4. Let us revisit these requirements, highlighting issues of usability.

Although usability is not mentioned explicitly in the system requirements, it is in fact central to the reason a new system is needed. The existing system incorporates substantial functionality and (in the hands of an expert) is very fast and effective for some of the main task scenarios. However, it needs replacing because of very serious usability problems, specifically the following:

- The system is not usable effectively by all Helpline staff. To use it effectively you need a detailed understanding of its internal design. The system behaves in various ways that a new user would not expect.
- The system is not usable by the manager to monitor and manage the flow of work through the group. Some required status and responsibility information is not stored,

Expert Helpline Advisor	Notes on characteristic	Requirements implied
Type of user	Direct	
Frequency of use	Every day, 3–50 hours/week	Flexible, user in control, shortcuts
Mandatory/discretionary	Mandatory	
Computer experience	Extensive, PC with Microsoft Windows, database systems	Use PC with Microsoft Windows style
Education/intellectual abilities	Good communication and analytical skills	
Motivation/goals	Solve technical problems quickly, be seen as an expert	Support problem-solving
Number of users	6	
Task knowledge needed	Knowledge of products, known problems, problem-solving strategies	
Training on system	Several hours of in-service training	
Other systems used	Various Microsoft Windows applications, Microsoft Word, E-mail	
Ways of working	Variety of personal styles	Support variety of styles

Fig. 5.4 User characteristics table

and stored information cannot be displayed in ways which are required to support the manager's tasks.

- The system is not usable by other company staff to access Helpline information. The user interface is complicated, and takes too long to learn. Consequently when other staff need information they have to ask Helpline staff to retrieve the information for them. This wastes Helpline staff time, and inhibits other staff from asking for all the information they would like.

- The system is not flexible enough to be adapted to implement new quality procedures which are required to achieve quality certification.

The usability problems of the existing system provide an insight into how to achieve usability. They are discussed in Appendix D.

Let us return to the system requirements (reproduced here in italics) and make the usability requirements explicit.

R1 *To enable Helpline staff to resolve customer queries more effectively and quickly.*

The first usability requirement is:

UR1 Fast task performance on standard high-volume queries. This involves identifying the

Example   75

customer and finding a known problem which matches the query. The requirement will be tested by a task scenario measuring the time to complete.

We decide not to develop the scenario into detail now, just to note that we require a simple scenario for Resolve Customer Query where the query concerns a known problem recorded in the system. (The scenario is developed during task analysis — see section 6.4.6.1, scenario 1.)

A second usability requirement is:

UR2 The system should support a range of problem-solving strategies to allow for different types of problem and different users having different personal styles.

This is noted as a requirement for GUI design. It will be tested not by a measurement, but by a judgment by the customer support manager.

A third usability requirement is:

UR3 User satisfaction of Helpline staff. This will be measured using a questionnaire and must be an improvement on the existing system.

The second system requirement was:

R2 *To improve the flow of relevant information from the Helpline to the sales and product development groups, without increasing the cost of information dissemination.*

The usability requirement here is:

UR4 The system must be usable for enquiry by other UniSoft staff after minimal training. This will be tested by giving a brief training session (5 minutes) followed by a task scenario. The criteria is the length of time to complete the task.

Again, defining the detail of the scenario is postponed until task analysis. Section 6.4.6, Provide query status, gives a scenario which would be a suitable test for this requirement.

Most of the 'other staff' who use the system for enquiry will be intermittent users. A second usability requirement is:

UR5 Enquiry functions must be usable by intermittent users. A test is to ask the same individual to perform a second task scenario one week after the first, without any further training. Once again the criterion is the length of time to complete the task.

A third usability requirement is:

UR6 User satisfaction by other UniSoft staff.

Again this will be measured by a questionnaire.

Our third system requirement was:

R3 *To provide information to enable the customer support manager to monitor and control Helpline activities.*

We identify that the manager's central usability requirement is:

UR7 The manager must be able to obtain a clear overview of the current situation very quickly. This can be measured by a performance test, which identifies all the information the manager must check to be confident that he 'has a grip on the situation'. The criterion is time to complete the task.

An example of a suitable scenario is given in section 6.4.6, Monitor Advisor Workload, scenario 1.

Reviewing the usability problems of the current system, you can see that most are addressed explicitly by these requirements. One which is not is that the new system must be clearly structured, and have intuitive and predictable behavior. Although this is not measured directly (and is difficult to quantify), it will be assessed indirectly via the measures of user satisfaction, task performance by novice and intermittent users, and errors by novice users.

A second requirement derived from current problems is the need for future flexibility. This becomes an additional usability requirement.

UR8 The GUI design shall be flexible, so that its use can be adapted to accommodate changing task requirements.

It is very difficult to measure this. We agree that the Helpline manager will make a subjective assessment of this.

5.4.4 Specify measures and performance criteria

It is decided to measure user satisfaction with a usability questionnaire known as the Software Usability Measurement Inventory (SUMI). SUMI is chosen because it is easily usable by the evaluation team, coming ready-equipped with a data capture package, analysis facilities, and a database of past results for comparison. (See Appendix E for more details.)

As noted above, for the timed performance tests, we decide to use the task scenarios developed in task modeling as the basis for measurement. See Chapter 6 for identification and definition of task scenarios.

Various other usability measuring instruments are mentioned in Further Reading.

5.4.5 Define performance levels

Figure 5.5 summarizes the usability requirements and the performance levels for each requirement.

The current level for UR4 (enquiry by other staff) was calculated by telephoning customer support and asking for the information.

Note that the current system is so fast for some standard queries (UR1) that the target is only to achieve equal speed, and the worst acceptable level is to take 5 seconds longer.

Since we have not defined the task scenarios yet, the times are rough approximations. After defining the scenarios we will confirm (and if necessary revise) the times in the specification table.

Reqt ref	Usability attribute	Measuring instrument	Value to be measured	Current level	Worst acceptable level	Planned target level	Best possible level	Observed results
UR1	Expert performance	Resolve Query scenario 1	Time to complete	40 sec	45 sec	40 sec	30 sec	
UR2	Support various problem-solving strategies	Assessment by Helpline manager	Number of strategies	2	2	4	10?	
UR3	User satisfaction — helpline staff	Questionnaire (SUMI)	Total score	18	40	50	73	
UR4	Initial performance Other staff	Find Query Status scenario 1	Time to complete	120 sec	60 sec	30 sec	15 sec	
UR5	Memorability Other staff	Find Query Status scenario 2	Time to complete	NA	90 sec	40 sec	15 sec	
UR6	User satisfaction — other staff	Questionnaire (SUMI)	Total score	NA	40	50	73	
UR7	Expert performance, manager	Monitor Advisor Workload, scenario 1	Time to complete	NA	50 sec	35 sec	25 sec	
UR8	Flexibility	Assessment by Helpline manager	Yes/No	No	No	Yes	Yes	

Fig. 5.5   Usability requirement specification table

5.5   PRACTICE TIPS

5.5.1   Consequences of omission

Many user interfaces are designed without explicitly defining the different classes of user and their usability requirements. For an example of the difficulties this led to in one such system, see Appendix D.

5.5.2   Completeness

It is not usually possible to specify all the usability requirements, and even if you could specify 200 you would probably not have the resources to evaluate them all accurately. You are typically in a situation where you have to select a small set of usability requirements which you can realistically specify and evaluate, and the requirements (and more specifically the evaluation tests you can perform) are partial and incomplete.

Practical experience shows that this is not a fatal flaw. Specification of usability requirements and evaluation against specified requirements makes a positive contribution to usability, and the gaps in this are filled by complementary techniques (e.g. task analysis, prototyping, cooperative evaluation) described in later chapters.

5.5.3   Risks

The description of user classes is too long and detailed, so that the cost of producing it outweighs its contribution.

The description does not draw out the implications for usability requirements (and hence for GUI design).

Interviewing staff about their roles, motivation, etc., is politically sensitive with managers and personnel officers.

If the measures of usability attributes are too difficult or time-consuming, they will not be used in practice, and will certainly not be used several times (once per design iteration).

5.6   SUMMARY

This chapter discusses how to describe the end-users of the GUI, and how to identify and specify usability requirements. Major points include the following:

- GUI designers should identify end users and define their usability requirements at the very beginning of a design project.
- Well-defined and measurable usability requirements act as a target to aim for throughout analysis, design and prototyping.
- Two products are created:
  - a set of user classes (each with a user characteristics table);
  - a usability requirements specification table.
- The process is:
  - identify user classes;
  - describe users in each class;
  - identify critical usability requirements;
  - specify measures and performance criteria;
  - define performance levels;
  - review and agree the usability requirements specification.

5.7   FURTHER READING

Shneiderman, B. (1992) *Designing the User Interface: Strategies for effective human−computer interaction*, Addison-Wesley.
   A very readable and practical classic book on interface design. Good discussion of specifying usability requirements in Chapters 1 and 2.

Whiteside, J. (1991) 'Usability engineering: our experience and evolution', chapter 36 in Hellander, M. (ed.), *Handbook of Human−Computer Interaction*, North-Holland.
   An authoritative discussion of specification and measurement of usability requirements.

Hix, D. and Hartson, H.R. (1993) *Developing User Interfaces: Ensuring usability through product and process*, John Wiley.
Chapter 8 'Usability Specification Techniques' and Chapter 10 'Formative Evaluation' provide an excellent practitioner-oriented discussion of specification of usability requirements.

HUFIT Planning, Analysis and Specification Toolset (1990) HUSAT, University of Loughborough, UK.
The user mapping and user characteristics techniques provide clear guidance and examples of identifying user classes and relevant user characteristics. The usability specification for evaluation technique discusses the identification of measuring instruments, criteria and target levels.

Whitefield, A., Wilson, F. and Dowell, J. (1991) 'A framework for human factors evaluation', in *Behavior and Technology*, vol. 10, no. 1, pp. 65–79.
A readable and comprehensive discussion of current methods of usability evaluation and a warning about common pitfalls of usability evaluations.

Ravden, S. and Johnson, G. (1989) *Evaluating Usability of Human–Computer Interfaces*, Ellis Horwood.
A useful book on usability evaluation.

Task analysis

6.1   INTRODUCTION

This chapter is concerned with analysis and modeling of user tasks. Task analysis is important in user-centered design — it is a practical way of ensuring the user's perspective is adopted, and that the GUI is designed to support the user's actual work activities.

The primary style of task analysis described in this chapter is known as hierarchical task analysis (HTA), and is widely known and used.

In GUIDE, HTA is supplemented by the development of task scenarios, which are concrete examples of how tasks are performed. Task scenarios are a very productive practical approach to GUI design and prototyping — it is often easy to see whether a design works well for a concrete example, even if it is difficult to assess whether a design supports all the possible task variants implicit in a more abstract task model.

The task scenarios created here are used as scripts to drive prototyping, and form the basis of evaluation benchmarks (see Figure 6.1).

6.1.1   Objectives

- To understand what the user is trying to achieve (their 'task goal'), what the user actually does, and the environment within which the user works (task context).

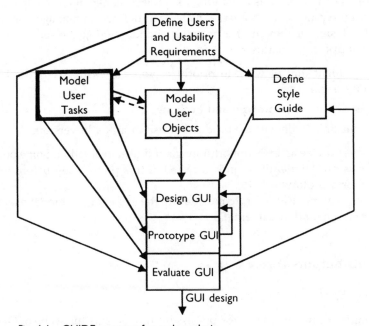

Fig. 6.1   GUIDE context for task analysis

- To produce task models.

- To create an abstract interaction design, concerned with how the user will perform the tasks using the objects in the system, but without details of the GUI design.

- To produce task scenarios which will be useful in GUI Design, Prototyping and Evaluation.

6.1.2　Benefits

Understanding the user's task goals and activities enables the interface designer to propose GUI designs that are appropriate to the tasks.

Analyzing user tasks helps the analyst to understand the world view of the user, in terms of identifying the objects in the system and the actions that people perform on these objects. Thus task analysis feeds the user object model (see Chapter 7), which in turn assists in the design of an easily comprehensible and intuitive system.

Task scenarios help to ground the development in reality. They provide concrete examples of how tasks will be performed, in a format that is easily usable by those involved in GUI design and prototyping. This improves communication between designers and end-users.

Task models and task scenarios are the main way of exercising and validating the GUI prototype.

Task scenarios can be used as a 'handle' for project management control of GUI design and prototyping. Once scenarios have been defined, a manager can define the scope of a design increment or a prototype by identifying the set of scenarios which it will support. Scenarios are:

- a convenient unit of work to prioritize (you can easily select the highest priority ones);

- a feasible unit to prototype and evaluate;

- a useful unit to deliver for production use in an early version.

Task scenarios provide an early opportunity for end-user evaluation. Some potential usability defects can be identified and corrected at this point, even before there is a GUI design or a prototype.

Task scenarios can be useful for demonstrating the system to potential users, and for training material and documentation.

6.1.3　Inputs/outputs (Figure 6.2)

Task modeling has two main inputs:

- Definition of required business processes (from outside the scope of GUIDE).

- User classes (who will use the system).

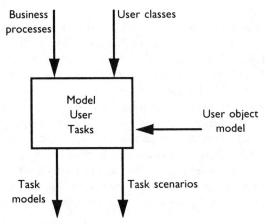

Fig. 6.2   Inputs and outputs

Task modeling is performed partly before, and partly in parallel with, user object modeling. The user object model is a late input. It allows tasks to be validated against objects, and scenarios to be expressed in terms of user object actions.

Task analysis creates two products:

- Task models, showing the generic hierarchical structure of each task.
- Task scenarios, which are concrete examples of individual tasks.

6.2   PRODUCTS

6.2.1   Task model

A task is a human activity designed to achieve some goal. A task model is an abstract model of the structure of a task, which shows the subtasks a person performs in order to achieve the overall task goal.

Task goals should be brief, and expressed in language which is independent of the computer system and user interface. Examples of task goals are: to reserve an airline seat; to prepare a letter; to transfer money from one bank account to another.

Each task is modeled as a hierarchy of subtasks, with decomposition continued as far as is required. Sometimes it is helpful to think of higher-level subtasks as subgoals – i.e. not as something you do, but as an intermediate goal you are trying to achieve.

Relevant information about each task includes the following:

- Who performs it.
- Frequency (how often it is performed, e.g. ten times per day).
- Average time to perform.
- Frequency of user errors (e.g. 1 in 50 using current system).
- Notes about the context in which the task is performed.

Notation

A hierarchy diagram as shown in Figure 6.3. Tasks are shown as boxes, with lines showing how the task above is broken down to a set of subtasks. Thus Task X consists of the subtasks 1, 2 and 3, and subtask 1 consists of lower-level subtasks 1.1 and 1.2.

A second line under the box indicates that there is no further decomposition of the task (see subtasks 1.1, 1.2 and 3 in Figure 6.3).

The diagram may be split into segments to make it easier to read. Subtask 2 shows the notation for a subtask which is further decomposed on a separate diagram.

The diagram notation does not show the sequence in which the subtasks are performed, or the logic of how the subtasks are combined to perform the task. If this level of detail is required, it is recorded in a 'plan' for each box which indicates the circumstances in which its subtasks are performed and their sequencing or repetition. The plan may include alternatives (see Figure 6.3), or text defining the conditions in which subtasks are performed.

A hierarchic numbering system is used, with the task being 0, each immediate subtask being 1, 2, 3, etc., next level subtasks of 2 being 2.1, 2.2, 2.3, etc.

The diagram shows the structure of the task, but it is often not convenient for the diagram to contain all the detailed textual description of how the task is performed. Sometimes the diagram structure is all that is required, but where detailed text is appropriate this may be recorded separately from the diagram. The subtask reference numbers and names are used to relate the additional text to the diagram.

An alternative notational format that is often useful is provided by wordprocessor outliner facilities, with the task structure represented as a multilevel document outline (see Figure 6.9).

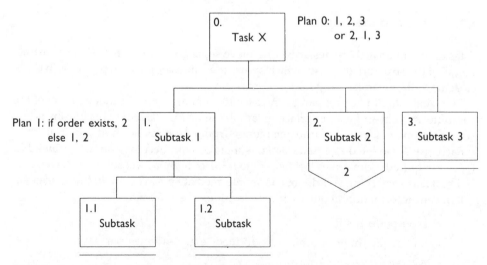

Fig. 6.3 Example of task hierarchy diagram notation

Task context notes

Associated with the task model are notes about the context in which the task is performed.

These may describe the following:

- The physical task environment (e.g. own office or open plan, relevant office equipment such as phone, fax, cabinets).
- The social/interpersonal task context (e.g. interruptions, nature of interactions).
- Constraints or pressures on the person performing the task (e.g. time pressure).
- Which tasks (or aspects of a task) are perceived as difficult.
- Task problems which are encountered in practice.
- Errors made by the user.
- Any other aspect of the task context which is likely to be relevant for GUI design.

Each 'task context note' is a free-text description, and together these notes allow the analyst to record a richer picture of the task than could be expressed in the task hierarchy diagram alone. The notes are recorded on the diagram, or with the detailed task text (if this exists). Selectivity and caution are needed to avoid the designer being overloaded with too much descriptive text here.

Task context notes should not describe characteristics of users, as this information is best recorded in the user class description.

Where used

Task models are used to identify the required 'objects in the system' during user object modeling. They are also used to identify views of objects in the first part of GUI Design.

Finally, they are used to review the completeness of the task support provided by the GUI design.

Quality criteria

- Is the set of task models complete? (i.e. are there any significant user activities within the scope of analysis which have not been modeled?)
- Do the people who perform the task think each model is a realistic representation of their task?
- Do the task models include all significant task variants and deal with any contingencies that might occur?
- Have the task models been validated and evaluated by users other than those who provided them?

6.2.2 Task scenario

A task scenario is an example of a task. A task model is an abstract structure showing many possible variants and subtasks. In contrast, a task scenario is a single concrete instance of a task, with specific initial circumstances, input and subtasks performed. The scenario includes typical data, and may include exceptions.

A task scenario can be thought of as a test case for a task. It is useful to note whether a scenario represents a typical task occurrence, or an exceptional set of circumstances.

A task scenario has two aspects:

- A *situation* or *set of circumstances* for a task, described in terms of any input and the prior state of the system (and the world). For example, 'Withdraw $50 from the ATM from account 123987, where the account exists and has the necessary funds available.' Or in a wordprocessing application, 'Change "dollr" to "dollar".'

- A *script* describing *how* a user performs the task on this occasion. The scenario is expressed in terms of a sequence of user object actions (i.e. actions that the user can perform on objects in the user object model). This script is an abstract interaction design − it defines how the user interacts with the objects in the system, without referring to the design of the user interface.

The second aspect is more detailed and more related to system design. Scenarios are usually defined initially as situations, and subsequently extended to be expressed as scripts of user object actions.

Each scenario is documented from the user's point of view, and includes actions that do not involve the system, such as making a mental decision or talking on the telephone.

Notation

A textual description of the scenario, in terms of its input, any background, and how the subtasks are performed.

Non-system actions are distinguished from system actions by using italics.

For actions involving the system the description is annotated with the name of the object on which the action is performed (and where applicable the user object action) in square brackets. For an example of the notation see Figure 6.4.

Where used

Model User Tasks   to validate the task model.

Design GUI   to provide a task context for defining views of objects; to indicate where the user moves attention from one object to another, which influences window navigation design; to provide a task context for defining window actions.

Prototype GUI   as scripts providing sample input data.

Evaluate GUI   as benchmarks for the formal evaluation of usability, measuring time to complete, error rates, etc.

Make Ticket Booking: Scenario I — customer has account, seats available

Answer phone.

Customer: 'I'd like three balcony tickets for Hamlet at the Barbican Theatre on 27th September.'

Select Barbican   *[Theatre]*
Select 27 September   *[Date]*
Check performance details, availability and price   *[Performance]*

Operator: 'The performance starts at 7.30 p.m. We have tickets available at $25 or $20.'

etc.

Fig. 6.4   Example of task scenario notation

Quality criteria

- Are the scenarios representative of the real tasks commonly performed by users?

- Are the task scenarios usable? Regarding the scripts as interaction designs, would they meet the usability requirements?

- Is there sufficient information to be useful for GUI design, prototyping and evaluation?

- Are the task scenarios consistent with the task model (i.e. is each scenario a concrete instance of a task?)

- Are all actions involving the system expressed in terms of user object actions which are defined in the user object model?

- Do the scripts refer to a particular user interface design? (They should not.)

6.3   PROCESS

The process described below produces one set of task models, describing the intended future structure of the tasks (though without going into details of how the new user interface is used).

An alternative process is to produce two sets of task models, the first being 'current task models' representing the way the tasks are currently performed; and the second being 'required task models', describing the intended future task structure. This process is more thorough, but takes more time and effort. The additional effort may be worthwhile if creating the current task models increases the design team's understanding of the tasks, and helps to ensure that the required task models are complete and stable. A danger of documenting the current task model is that the required task model may be influenced more than it should by the assumptions and practices of the current system.

6.3.1   Identify tasks

The tasks to be analyzed are identified from various sources, including the following:

- Observation of users at work, and discussion to classify user activities into tasks.
- Interviews or workshop discussions with users.
- Analysis of the proposed 'business system' (discussed in Chapter 4). Each business process is divided into a set of tasks, each with a well-defined goal.
- Analysis of business events. It is common for a task to consist of the human activities required to deal with a business event, such as the arrival of an order, or reaching the end of the month.

Define the task goal for each task.

6.3.2   Select task scenarios

It is often possible to 'sample' or 'harvest' task scenarios from the real business process. For example, if the task involves answering customers' orders or letters of complaint, take copies of all the orders/letters received in one day as a sample. If the task involves answering telephone enquiries, record a hundred enquiries on tape.

Ask expert users to classify the sample into recognizable 'types' of scenario for the task. Then select one representative case from each type, and use this as a typical task scenario. (It may be necessary to remove identifying information to make the scenario anonymous.) It is valuable to include some scenarios in which user errors are common.

Using scenarios sampled from the real world can have two benefits:

- The scenarios are more representative of real tasks.
- It makes prototyping more realistic and authentic.

6.3.3   Analyze and model tasks

Collect relevant information about each task (frequency, duration, errors, etc.).

Identify which tasks (and task scenarios) are most important to focus on in analysis and design work. Usually these are tasks which are:

- very high volume; and/or;
- are time critical (i.e. must be performed fast) and/or;
- where user errors are very significant (either because errors are common, or because even one error is dangerous or expensive).

Analyze each task into its constituent subtasks. Each subtask should have a well-defined endpoint.

Develop the task hierarchy diagram.

There is an issue about how far to continue subdividing the subtasks. Continuing too far greatly increases the size and complexity of the task hierarchy, and is not an effective use of time. Stopping too soon can mean that important task requirements may not be identified.

As the purpose of the task analysis is to aid the design of a new user interface, it is sufficient to go to the level of logical actions on objects in the system (e.g. find the order, create a new customer, change the invoice status to 'paid'). It is not useful to model the details of the user interface of the current computer system. For example, 'Tab down to the fourth field, type in "MXV", and press <Enter>', is not useful documentation.

Although it is often the current task structures which are being analyzed, the aim is to abstract away from the current procedures and to model the 'essential' activities required to achieve the task goal.

Decide whether any of the subtasks require a textual description in addition to the diagram. This is only recommended where the subtask is non-trivial, and where the added detail is likely to influence GUI design.

As soon as the task hierarchy seems stable, add the plan logic.

Enrich the task model by considering the contingencies which may arise while the user is performing the task. For example:

- What happens if some input information is missing or incorrect?
- What happens if someone else has borrowed the folder?
- Is the task ever interrupted to perform some other more urgent task?
- What happens if the user makes an error?

For each contingency consider whether additional subtasks are required. Extend the task plans to deal with contingencies.

Analysis of contingencies is important in teasing out the complexity of real-world tasks. Often our 'first-cut' task models are oversimplified and idealized. They describe the way things are supposed to happen when there are no complications. If the GUI supported this simplified ideal but did not support dealing with contingencies, it would not be usable.

6.3.4   Describe task context

While identifying and analyzing tasks, collect brief notes on the task context. The richest source of context information is observation of users performing their tasks in their normal work environment, interspersed with informal discussion of the tasks and environment.

The analyst needs to put themselves in the place of the person performing the task, and note down any issues which should be 'borne in mind' during GUI design.

It is particularly important to note errors that are made by the user, so that the new GUI design can attempt to prevent these.

6.3.5   Identify subtasks requiring computer support

Examine each task model and consider how the computer system will be involved in each subtask.

There are three possibilities:

- The subtask will be entirely manual, in other words it will be performed by the person without any interaction with the computer system. An example is a person explaining company policy to a customer on the telephone.

- The subtask will be performed by the person, but with some interaction with the computer system. This will require specification of the system functionality and the user interface. An example is a person identifying a required product using an interactive search facility, or entering an order to an order-processing system.

- The subtask will be performed by the computer. It may be actively requested by the person using the system (e.g. a benefit calculation), in which case it will require specification of the system functionality and the user interface for the request. Alternatively it may happen without user action or knowledge (e.g. logging a transaction in an audit trail), in which case the system functionality must be specified but there is no user interface.

The general principle to follow is that people should perform the parts of the task that human beings are better at (e.g. making judgments, dealing with novel situations); while the computer should perform the subtasks and aspects of tasks that machines do well (e.g. storing information, performing calculations). Issues to consider in deciding computer system support include the following:

- Can the computer assist significantly with the subtask (e.g. in reducing the time taken or human effort, reducing the frequency of errors, or enabling less skilled staff to perform the task)? In other words, what is the benefit of computerization?

- How does the benefit of computer assistance compare with the cost of developing, installing and operating the computer system? In other words, perform an informal cost–benefit analysis for providing support.

6.3.6   Express scenarios as actions on user objects

The activities so far are performed before modeling user objects, and are a major input to user object modeling. After the user object model has been produced, the task model is refined and integrated with the user object model by expressing each task scenario as actions on user objects.

For each task scenario, consider how the user needs to interact with objects in the system in order to perform the task most effectively. At what points in the task does the user require information (i.e. the attributes of objects), and at what points does the user perform some action on an object (i.e. a user object action). Where possible, use existing user object actions defined in the user object model. Where suitable actions are not available, define new user object actions. (It will often be found that each bottom-level subtask can be expressed as a user object action.)

Where there are alternative sequences of actions for the scenario, organize the actions into the sequence which seems shortest, simplest and most natural to the user.

The task scenario now consists of a script of what the user does (both system actions and non-system actions). The system actions are annotated to show how they relate to user object actions and attributes. This validates the task model against the user object model, and makes the task scenarios more precise and useful for GUI design.

As well as showing what the user does, ensure that the script shows all the user's information requirements at each point in the task. What information does the user need, both to make judgments or decisions, and to perform their actions. Where this information is available in the system, annotate the script with the user object attributes that represent the required information.

6.3.7   Validate task models and scenarios

The task models should be validated in various ways:

- By checking with the task performers who helped produce it.
- By checking with other people who perform the same task.
- By observing additional task scenarios being performed, and checking that they map onto the task model.
- By checking with relevant managers that they want the business to operate in the way described by the task models.

Each task scenario should be validated to assess whether it is the simplest possible interaction design.

Examine the script for likely usability problems:

- Is this a scenario which people find difficult to complete successfully?
- Do users frequently make errors in this task?
- Is the user having to hold too much information in their memory at once?
- Does the script for the scenario provide a suitable basis for meeting agreed usability requirements?

Consider ways in which the scenario could be simplified for the user, for example:

- by rationalizing the task (e.g. omitting some operations or logic);
- by automating more of the processing (allocating work to the system);
- by acting on different user objects.

Revise the task scenario, task model and user object model as necessary to improve usability.

■■ 6.4 EXAMPLE ■■■■■■■■■■■■■■■■■■■■■■■■■■■■■■■■■■■■

The project team includes Helpline advisors who have a detailed understanding of the current tasks, so we decide to proceed directly to required task models. (As is often the case, there would not be sufficient benefit from producing current task models.)

6.4.1   Identify tasks

In the Helpline case study, tasks were identified in a workshop session with Helpline advisors and the customer support manager. The data flow diagram showing the main business processes was used as input to this discussion (see Chapter 4, Figure 4.8).

The following tasks were identified:

- *Resolve customer query*   Identify the customer, listen to their query, attempt to resolve it and record details of the query.

- *Provide query status*   Respond to a customer telephone enquiry about the current status of an unresolved query.

- *Reproduce problem*   Recreate the circumstances in which a customer query arose, and analyze to identify the problem.

- *Update known problem*   Document a new 'known problem' or update the information on an existing problem.

- *Provide customer information*   Respond to an internal request for information on the queries raised by a particular customer.

- *Provide problem information*   Respond to an internal request for information on all known problems associated with a specific software subsystem.

- *Monitor advisor workload*   Check how many queries each advisor is currently dealing with and their urgency and reallocate if necessary.

- *Monitor unresolved queries*   View all queries which have not been resolved to determine the action required to resolve.

- *Resolve 'management action' queries*   View all queries referred to customer support manager and take required action on them.

Advisors were observed at work, and frequently asked 'What are you doing now?' This confirmed that the identified tasks accounted for almost all their advisor work activity.

6.4.2   Select task scenarios

A random sample of the telephone calls received in one day was tape-recorded. Three representative scenarios were picked for 'Resolve Customer Query' (a complex task), and two for 'Provide Query Status' (a simple task).

Example   93

Two scenarios were also created for 'Monitor Advisor Workload'.

At this point the input and/or background to each scenario was recorded in detail, and the main features of how it was handled were briefly summarized.

6.4.2.1 Resolve customer query

Scenario 1 — resolve using system

Customer: 'I'm trying to upgrade from version 4 to version 5 of your DesignAid tool, and the installation program is crashing. It's giving a message ERROR SSDB8 FILE MISSING, and then INSTALLATION FAILED.'

Background: Known problem recorded in system under database error code.

Task: Use system to identify cause of problem. Advise Customer.

Scenario 2 — need further information

Customer: 'Good afternoon, I'm phoning from the University of San Antonio. We are a user of your PACER product. I have been trying to restore a backup database and the system has crashed with a database error. I've checked the error log, and the last entry is Error Code 453.'

Task: Look up error code and advise; request customer sends in copy of backup database for investigation.

Scenario 3 — resolve without system

Customer: 'I'd like your advice on what to do. We had a power cut while the database server was operating and now it's giving warning messages about possible lack of integrity.'

Background: Common query, familiar to advisor.

Task: Advise customer how to run database integrity check. Just use system to log query.

6.4.2.2 Provide query status

Scenario 1 — by customer name

Customer: 'Good afternoon, my name is Sandra Black from Provincial Insurance. I called you yesterday over difficulties with report printing, and someone said they would ring me back.'

Background: Query in system has updated information for customer.

Task: Apologize for delay, trace the Query by the Customer, date and topic, and inform the Customer of the current status, which is that Mark will phone them back by 2 p.m.

Scenario 2 — by query reference

Customer: 'Good morning, I'm ringing to enquire what progress you have made on a problem I reported to you last week, your reference number 3146. I posted in the corrupt database two days ago as agreed. Have you received it safely and have you sorted out what's wrong?'

Task: Retrieve the Query using the reference number, check the latest information on it and who is currently dealing with it (Suzie). Advise the Customer.

6.4.2.3   *Monitor advisor workload*

Scenario 1 — reallocate a query

Background: John has two urgent queries, Suzie has several queries but they are all low priority. Mark is on leave.

Task: Check the advisors' workloads and transfer one of John's queries to Suzie.

Scenario 2 — check but no action

Background: Suzie has one urgent (but not overdue) query. John has three routine queries. Mark has two routine queries.

Task: Check the advisors' workloads but take no action.

6.4.3   **Analyze and model tasks**

6.4.3.1   *Resolve customer query*

Consider the central Helpline task, Resolve Customer Query. (It is often a good idea to start by investigating the most critical tasks.)

There are four different parts to the task:

- Finding out who the customer is, and whether they have paid for Helpline support.
- Identifying what problem is at the root of the customer query.
- Advising the customer on the solution, or on what information is required for further investigation.
- Documenting the query, including its current status, priority and responsibility for future action.

Each of these is a subtask, and is further decomposed as shown in Figures 6.5 and 6.6.

6.4.3.2   *Provide query status*

The task model for Provide Query Status is shown in Figure 6.7. The first part of the task is to identify which previous query the customer is interested in, either from the query reference

Example   95

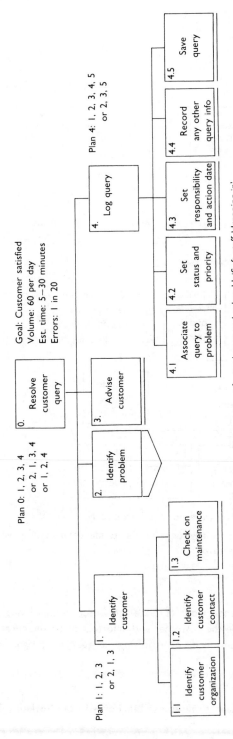

Plan 0: 1, 2, 3, 4
or 2, 1, 3, 4
or 1, 2, 4

Goal: Customer satisfied
Volume: 60 per day
Est. time: 5–30 minutes
Errors: 1 in 20

Plan 1: 1, 2, 3
or 2, 1, 3

Plan 4: 1, 2, 3, 4, 5
or 2, 3, 5

Busy open-plan office, each advisor has two workstations, lots of interruptions from phones and other UniSoft staff 'dropping in'

There is pressure on the advisor from the customer (who is on the telephone), peers and the manager to resolve queries quickly

In most cases the query is due to a customer error or a known problem — the skill is in identifying which problem quickly

Fig. 6.5 Resolve customer query task model

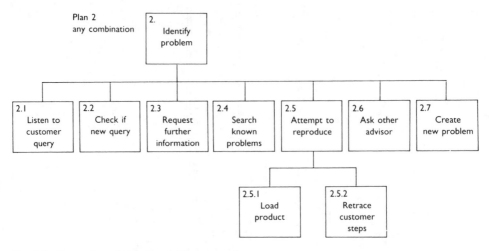

Fig. 6.6   Expansion of identify problem subtask

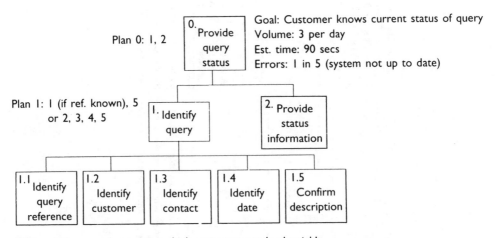

This only happens for queries which were not resolved quickly

Important for customer confidence for advisor to be able to identify query, say what progress has been made and what is happening now

Fig. 6.7   Provide query status

or by other information (Customer, Contact, Date and Description). Having pinpointed the query, the second part is provide the customer with information on the current status, such as whether any progress has been made on resolving the query (see Figure 6.7).

6.4.3.3   *Monitor advisor workload*

One of the customer support manager's tasks is to Monitor Advisor Workload. The task model for this is shown in Figure 6.8.

Example   97

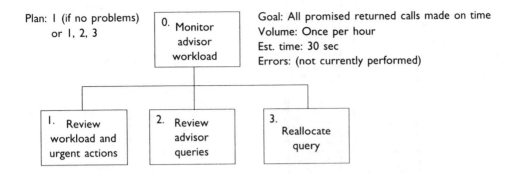

Plan: I (if no problems)
or 1, 2, 3

0. Monitor advisor workload

Goal: All promised returned calls made on time
Volume: Once per hour
Est. time: 30 sec
Errors: (not currently performed)

I. Review workload and urgent actions

2. Review advisor queries

3. Reallocate query

Problem: advisors take queries, promise to call back by specified time, and are then delayed or distracted by subsequent queries and fail to call back

Manager needs a quick way of checking the current position without interrupting advisors

Fig. 6.8   Monitor advisor workload

⇧ **Monitor Advisor Workload**
    ▫ **Review Workload and Urgent Actions**
    ▫ **Review Advisor Queries**
    ▫ **Reallocate Query**

Fig. 6.9   Task model in wordprocessor outline format

An alternative way of showing the same task hierarchy information is to use the 'outline' facilities in a wordprocessor. Figure 6.9 shows the Monitor Advisor Workload task in this format.

6.4.4   Describe task context

Some task context notes are shown on the task hierarchy diagrams in Figures 6.5, 6.7 and 6.8.

6.4.5   Identify subtasks requiring computer support

6.4.5.1   Resolve customer queries

The task model is reproduced in Figure 6.10, with the subtasks requiring computer support shown with a bold outline.

All the subtasks of 'Identify Customer' will require interaction with the computer systems to check that the customer is registered, has paid for Helpline support, and what recent queries they have raised.

The subtask where computer support is most essential is 'Search for Known Problem'. There are hundreds of known problems, and the computer can help to identify the relevant one from the symptoms and clues provided by the customer.

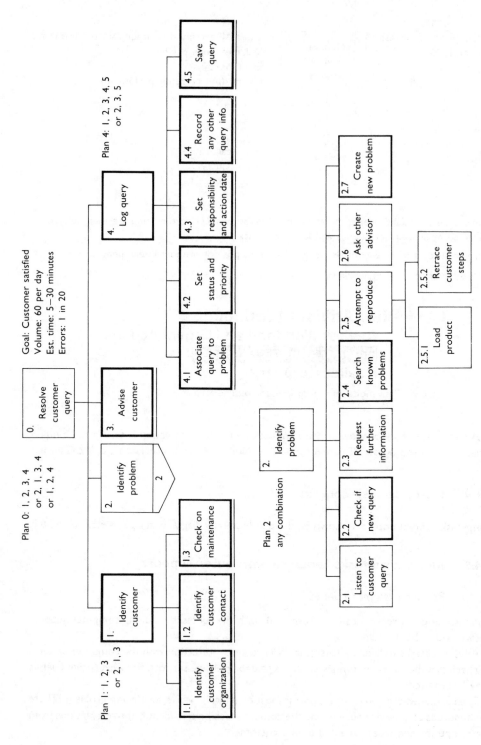

Fig. 6.10 Task models showing planned computer support

Example   99

'Attempt to Reproduce' does actually involve using a computer, but not the Helpline system, so it is not shaded. (The advisor loads a copy of the software product being used by the computer onto his or her second workstation and attempts to reproduce the error.)

In 'Advise Solution', the advisor reads the solution advice from the system.

Finally, details of the Query are logged into the system to manage follow-up actions and maintain a history of customer queries.

6.4.6   Express scenarios as actions on user objects

This activity is performed after the user object model has been created. (You may wish to come back to this subsection after reading Chapter 7, and specifically section 7.4 which discusses the user object model for the Helpline system.)

The task scenarios selected earlier are expanded into more detailed scripts of how they will be performed, based on the agreed task models and on how they will interact with user objects. User object actions are noted on the right-hand side.

6.4.6.1   *Resolve customer query*

Scenario 1 — resolve using system

Customer: 'I'm trying to upgrade from version 4 to version 5 of your DesignAid tool, and the installation program is crashing. It's giving a message ERROR SSDB8 FILE MISSING, and then INSTALLATION FAILED.'

Background: Known problem recorded in system.

Advisor: 'Can you give me your name and organization please?'

Customer: 'Yes, I'm John Smith from NickelCo in Ontario.'

Advisor: 'Can you wait a moment while I see whether anyone has had this problem before.'

    Find NickelCo (Ontario)   **[Customer.Open]**

    Open a new query   **[Customer.Add Query]**

    Search through problems in system. Try keyword 'Install — Upgrade' or a free-text search on the error code string 'SSDB8'.   **[Problem.Search]**

    Find candidate problem which looks likely to be the cause. Read details of problem and solution.   **[Problem]**

Advisor: 'We do have a record of a similar problem. Can you confirm for me exactly which software you were running before the upgrade?'

Customer: 'DesignAid version 4.0.'

Advisor: 'And can you read out to me the details on the installation disk that is failing?'

Customer: 'DesignAid Plus Version 5.0.'

Advisor: 'The reason you're having difficulty is that DesignAid Plus is not just a different version from DesignAid, it is actually a different product. I will arrange for a set of disks for DesignAid version 5 to be sent to you first class today, you should receive them tomorrow morning.'

Customer: 'Thank you. Good-bye.'

Advisor: Log query by associating query to problem,   **[Query.Associate]**

setting query status to closed,   **[Query.ChangeStatus]**

and saving the query.   **[Query.Save]**

         Scenario 2 — need further information

Customer: 'Good afternoon, I'm phoning from the University of San Antonio. We are a user of your PACER product. I have been trying to restore a backup database and the system has crashed with a database error. I've checked the error log, and the last entry is Error Code 453.'

Advisor: Find University of San Antonio   **[Customer.Open]**

'Ah yes, University of San Antonio.'

Create new query.   **[Customer.Add query]**

'I'll see what we have on that error code.'

Look up code in database manual.

'Error 453 means "Data is not a date value". At the point where it crashed, the system is expecting a date, but the data in your backup file is not a date. Do you know if the backup file could have been corrupted?'

Customer: 'Not as far as I know.'

Advisor: 'It's impossible for us to be sure without examining it. Can you send us the backup database disks and we'll get our technical staff to analyze it as soon as we receive them.'

Check query reference from system.   **[Query (Ref)]**

'Please mark them clearly with query reference number 3146, and quote that number if you phone to us again.'

Customer: 'Thank you. I'll send them today. Good-bye.'

Type in query description 'Database restore error. Failed with error code 453'
                                                           [Query.Edit Description]

Set query status to 'Waiting for Info'   **[Query.ChangeStatus]**

Save query   **[Query.Save]**

6.4.6.2   Provide query status

         Scenario 1 — by customer name

Customer: 'Good afternoon, my name is Sandra Black from Provincial Insurance. I called you yesterday over difficulties with report printing, and someone said they would ring me back.'

Example   101

Advisor: 'I do apologize if that has happened. It was very busy yesterday, we had over 100 calls. If you hold on one moment, I'll see what the position is.'

Find Provincial Insurance   **[Customer]**

Examine recent queries from Provincial Insurance **[Customer (Queries)]**

Find query with Sandra Black and yesterday's date. Check query short description.
[Query (Contact, Date, BriefDescription)]

Advisor: 'Let's see. You reported that numeric data imported from a Lotus 1-2-3 spreadsheet was being truncated. Is that right?'

Customer: 'Yes, that is correct.'

Advisor: Examine query status, description, responsibility and action date/time
[Query (details)]

'That is Query reference 3792. We are currently attempting to reproduce the problem on our software here. The person working on it is called Mark, and he will phone you back before 2.00 p.m. today.'

6.4.6.3   *Monitor advisor workload*

Scenario 1 — reallocate a query

Background: John has two urgent queries, Suzie has several queries but they are all low priority. Mark is on leave.

Examine workload   **[All Advisors]**

Note John overloaded

Examine John's current Queries   **[Advisor (Queries)]**

Examine Suzie's current Queries   **[Advisor (Queries)]**

Discuss with advisors

Manager: 'John, I'm worried that you've got two hot cases there, do you think it would be a good idea if Suzie dealt with one of them?'

John: 'OK, Suzie, can you take the Saudi Oil query?'

Transfer Saudi Oil query from John to Suzie
[Query.ChangeResponsibility]

6.4.7   **Validate task models and scenarios**

Task models and task scenarios are checked by all the Helpline advisors and the customer support manager. Minor revisions are incorporated.

Having defined the scenarios in detail, we now return to the usability requirement specification table (Chapter 5, Figure 5.5). We reassess and revise our earlier estimated times for the current level, worst acceptable level, planned level and best possible level for each of the scenarios we are using as benchmarks for performance tests.

6.5   PRACTICE TIPS

6.5.1   Task closure

In analyzing and modeling tasks, you need to think about how the person performing the task makes the task manageable in terms of its complexity and the amount to remember. An important issue here is how subtasks are related to subgoals.

When a person performs a complex task, they typically subdivide the overall goal into several subgoals, each of which can be dealt with separately. The first subgoal is worked on and brought to a conclusion before the second is considered. Doing this reduces the amount the task performer has to hold in their memory at any one point of time − they can forget information relating to subtask one, freeing their mind to concentrate on subtask two.

For example, in a telephone sales order task, the subgoals may be the following:

- Find out what the Customer wants to buy.
- Check that it is available from stock and what the price is.
- Obtain account or credit card information and check it is valid.

In trying to achieve closure on the first subgoal, the credit card information is not necessary, so it would be a poor task structure to expect the salesperson to obtain this information first.

The general rule is that each task (or subtask) should have a set of subtasks which are necessary and sufficient to achieve the (sub)task goal. If some subtasks relate to a different subgoal, they should be placed under that subgoal.

6.5.2   Reducing the effort

This chapter presents hierarchical task models and task scenarios as complementary techniques, and shows how they can be used in combination. You will see that there is some overlap between the techniques. There may be situations where the most cost-effective approach is to select either hierarchic task models or task scenarios. Because of the way task scenarios guide GUI design, and are used in prototyping and evaluation, we would normally prefer to retain scenarios even if we had to omit hierarchical task models.

Of course the choice depends on what you are trying to achieve. Hierarchic task analysis is a more powerful technique for analyzing, thinking about, and restructuring tasks, paying attention to the way subtasks should be organized around subgoals.

6.6   SUMMARY

This chapter describes how to model user tasks. Major points include the following:

- Before designing a GUI, we must understand what it will be used for. This means identifying the task goals that users are trying to achieve, and the subtasks they perform as part of the task. Most measures of usability relate to how well a system supports user tasks.

- A task model shows all the possible subtasks which may be performed during a task, arranged in a hierarchy. It also has any relevant 'context' information in the form of task context notes.

- A task scenario documents a single concrete example of a task.

- The task analysis process involves:
  - identifying tasks;
  - selecting task scenarios;
  - analyzing and modeling tasks;
  - describing task context;
  - identifying subtasks requiring computer support;
  - expressing task scenarios as actions on user objects;
  - validating task models and scenarios.

- Task models are used in defining views and assembling windows in GUI design.

- Task scenarios are used to drive prototyping, and as scripts for usability evaluation.

6.7   FURTHER READING

Diaper, D. (1989) *Task Analysis for Human–Computer Interaction*, Ellis Horwood.
  The GUIDE task analysis technique uses the 'classical' hierarchical task analysis developed by Annett and Duncan and described by Shepherd in Chapter 1. The book also contains descriptions of various 'richer' forms of task analysis which represent the users conceptualization of the task. In GUIDE the issue of the user's conceptual model is addressed using user object modeling.

Browne, D. (1994) *Structured User-interface Design for Interaction Optimisation (STUDIO)*, Prentice Hall.
  STUDIO uses a rather different task modeling notation, but it contains some good discussion of the task analysis process and a number of examples of task models for GUI design.

Gould, J.D., Boies, J.J., Levy, S., Richards, J.T. and Schoonard, J. (1990) 'The 1984 Olympic Message System: a test of behavioural principles of system design', in Preece, H. and Keller, L. (eds), *Human–Computer Interaction*, Prentice Hall.
  There is relatively little literature on the development of scripts of task scenarios. This case study describes how abstract interaction scripts were designed and evaluated first, and used to drive the design of a major system.

Hix, D. and Hartson, H.R. (1993) *Developing User Interfaces: Ensuring usability through product and process*, John Wiley.

The chapter on evaluation gives examples of using benchmarking scripts to explore the effectiveness of a GUI design for performing task scenarios.

Rubinstein, R. and Hersh, H. (1984) *The Human Factor*, Digital Press.

Chapter 3 'Task Analysis and Use Models' gives a basic overview of task modeling and some general guidelines. Easy to read.

User object modeling

7.1 INTRODUCTION

This chapter describes the user object modeling technique, which is concerned with ensuring that system behavior is comprehensible and intuitive to the user. The key to this is how the user conceptualizes the 'objects' in the system.

    The theoretical human–computer interaction literature has many references to the importance of the 'user's conceptual model' (see Chapter 3), but much of the material is too abstract or complex to be directly used by practitioners. To address this issue effectively on a project, a practitioner needs a technique and a notation. GUIDE recommends user object modeling as a practical technique for creating and documenting the user's conceptual model (see Figure 7.1).

    The user object modeling technique and notation are derived from mainstream work in object-oriented analysis, notably the work of James Rumbaugh and his colleagues on the object modeling technique (OMT) (Rumbaugh, 1992). As user object modeling may be less familiar than some of the other techniques used in GUIDE, the product and processes are described in more detail.

    User object modeling uses some 'object-oriented' ideas. However, this does not mean that the interface designer needs to have a deep understanding of object-orientation, nor does it imply that object-oriented technology is required to implement the interface. The technique produces designs which can be implemented using a wide range of alternative technologies, such as GUI development tools and database management systems.

7.1.1 Objectives

- To understand and define the users' concepts of the objects in the system.
- To express required system behavior in terms of business objects in the system, and actions that the user can perform on them.

7.1.2 Benefits

Producing a user object model promotes the usability of a GUI by ensuring that serious thought is given to how the end-user will conceptualize and comprehend the objects in the system. It provides a design for the end-user's mental model.

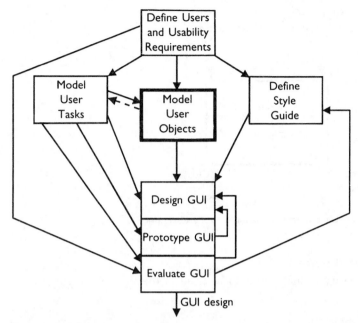

Fig. 7.1   GUIDE context for user object modeling

The user object model provides a useful basis for the initial definition of windows, and promotes an object-action style of user interface.

The user object model is the basis of an object-based GUI design. If you do not produce a user object model, you are less likely to arrive at a flexible, intuitive, object-based interface.

Defining user objects tends to encourage the design of a separable user interface, where the appearance and behavior of interface components is only loosely coupled to underlying system functionality. This yields benefits in system construction, maintenance and enhancement.

7.1.3   Inputs/outputs

Inputs to user object modeling (Figure 7.2) are as follows:

- Task models and task scenarios, from which the objects, attributes and actions required to support tasks are identified.

- A data model (if available). Objects may be identified from data model entities.

- User classes. Different user classes may require different mental models of the objects in the system.

Outputs are as follows:

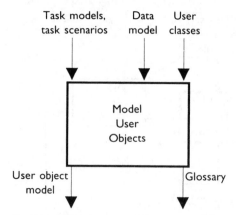

Fig. 7.2   User object modeling inputs and outputs

- The user object model.
- A glossary of user terms to be used in the interface.

7.2   PRODUCTS

7.2.1   User object model

A user object model is a model of the business objects which end-users believe they interact with in a GUI system. The model includes the following:

- What types of objects there are (user objects).
- What information the user can know about an object of a particular type (user object attributes).
- What actions the user can perform on (or with) an object of a particular type (user object actions).
- How objects may be related to other objects (relationships).
- Object types having 'subtypes' which have additional specialized actions or attributes.

User object
The key modeling construct in the user object model is the user object. A user object is something thought of by the user as an object, commonly:

- A business system object (e.g. customer, invoice).
- A computer system object or device (e.g. printer). (Note, though, that many computer objects are not represented in the interface, but hidden behind some metaphor which is familiar to the user).
- A container (e.g. a folder, list or directory containing other objects).

User objects can:

- contain other user objects;
- have relationships with other user objects;
- be specialized to user object subtypes;
- have attributes; and
- have user object actions.

In some ways a user object is similar to an entity in a data model, but there are some important differences. Unlike data model entities, user objects:

- include behavior, in the form of user object actions;
- may have no database data (e.g. a printer);
- are not 'normalized' (e.g. their attributes may include lists or repeating groups).

Container objects

Users frequently need to identify and manipulate collections of objects. Rather than having to deal with each item of a collection separately, it is often convenient to group the collection of objects together into a container.

Usually the container object itself is relatively uninteresting — what is important is its contents, and the fact that users can move an object into or out of the container, sort the contents into different orders, perform operations on all the objects in the container, etc. Familiar containers include directories, folders, lists and catalogs.

Container objects can have their own attributes and actions. For example, in a file system, it is possible to create, delete and rename directory objects as well as performing actions on their contents.

One object containing another is shown in the user object model diagram as a relationship (typically with the name 'contains').

User object action

User object action is something thought of by the user as an action you can perform on a real-world object. For example, create, delete, check validity, sign to authorize, send, attach (to another object), file.

User object actions are used to document the actions the user can perform, and to specify system behavior.

User object subtype

A type of user object may have one or more subtypes, organized into a classification hierarchy. A user object subtype:

- has the same attributes as its parent type, plus (optionally) additional specialized attributes;
- has the same actions as its parent type, plus (optionally) additional specialized

actions (also some of the parent type actions may have a more specialized effect);

- has the same relationships with other objects as its parent type, plus (optionally) additional relationships.

A user object subtype should be perceived by the user as a specialized variant of its parent object type. However, the subtype and its parent should be sufficiently different for the user to distinguish between them easily, and so that the user considers it worthwhile distinguishing the subtype.

Appropriate use of subtypes helps the user to form a clear mental model; and is convenient for specification of object attributes and actions, as complex objects can be specified more concisely and with less redundancy.

Notation — user object model diagram

A user object model diagram is used to visualize the types of object and the relationships between them. The notation is an extension of a widely used entity—relationship modeling notation (from Information Engineering), and uses the symbols shown in Figure 7.3.

The precise diagram notation used for user object modeling does not really matter for GUIDE. Any object modeling notation which includes object types (or classes), subtypes, association relationships and aggregation (or composition) relationships could be used (e.g. Rumbaugh et al., 1991; Coad and Yourdon, 1991).

Note that attributes and actions are part of the user object model but are not usually shown on the diagram.

The annotations at the ends of the relationship line show how many object instances at one end of the relationship are related to how many at the other end. This is known as the 'cardinality' of the relationship.

The annotation nearest to the object shows the maximum number, which may either be one (a line) or many (a crowsfoot). The other annotation shows the minimum number, which may be either zero (shown as O) or one (a line). This is illustrated in Figure 7.4.

Figure 7.4 is interpreted to mean the following:

1. A Department employs zero or many Employees (a minimum of zero and a maximum of many).

2. An Employee is employed by exactly one Department (a minimum of one and maximum of one).

The annotations can be combined in various ways to describe different types of relationship.

7.2.1.3   Aggregation notation

The 'aggregation' relationship (recognizable by a thicker line and a rectangular blob at the aggregate end) is used where one object 'consists of' or 'is composed of' instances of another object.

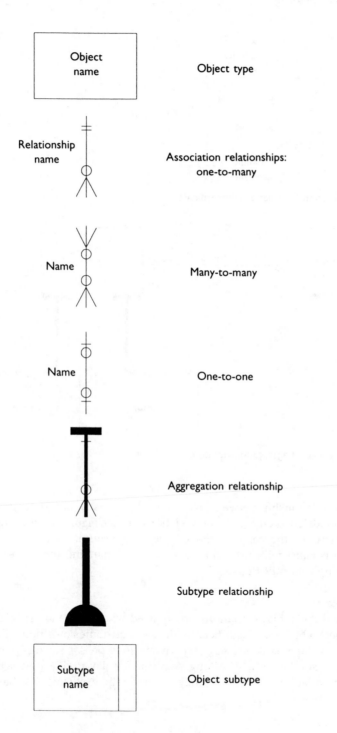

Fig. 7.3 Notation for user object model diagram

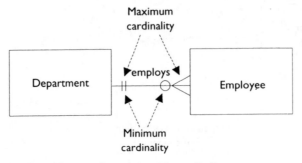

Fig. 7.4   Notation for relationship cardinality

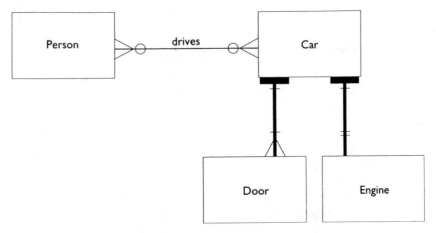

Fig. 7.5   Example of aggregation notation

For example, the relationship between a Car object and its Doors (or Engine, or Wheels) would be modeled as an aggregation relationship (see Figure 7.5). In contrast, the relationship between the car and the people who drive it is an association relationship (a thinner line with no rectangular blob) – changing the Driver does not change the composition of the Car.

Subtype notation

Object subtypes and the subtype relationship are used where there are specialized subtypes of an object which have significantly different attributes or actions. Figure 7.6 shows the example of a Bank Account, where one subtype is a Savings Account paying interest and another is a Checking Account for day-to-day transactions. (Linking these with a blob indicates that they are mutually exclusive, i.e. Savings *or* Checking.)

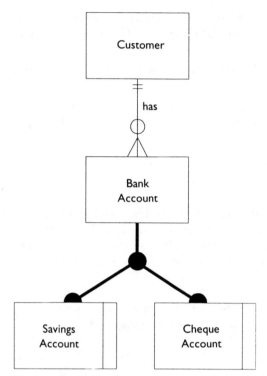

Fig. 7.6 **Example of subtype notation**

Where used

Model User Tasks   Each task scenario is expressed as a sequence of actions on user objects.

Design GUI   Views of user objects are used as the basis for initial window design. User object attributes and actions map into window controls. Relationships between user objects are used to identify and validate navigation between windows.

Quality criteria

- Does the user object model make sense to members of its target user class as a set of objects in the system? (Are the objects familiar, recognizable, intuitive?)
- Does the user object model have the right objects, actions and attributes to support the task models?
- Is each of the objects amenable to visualization?

- Is it possible to simplify the user object model for users who only perform simple tasks? (e.g. can some information or functionality be hidden from novice users?)
- Have existing user concepts and terminology been retained where appropriate?
- Do the user object models provide coverage of all the information content of the data model? (i.e. each element of stored data should be used in at least one user object).

7.2.2   Glossary

The glossary is an alphabetical list of terms which will be used by end-users to describe the state and behavior of objects in the system. Each term has a brief definition.

The glossary includes names of objects, attributes, actions, relationships, values of attributes and any other user terms that are used in the system.

Where used
GUI Design   Words in the glossary are used for window titles, names of menu, items, names of controls, text of error and information messages, help text.

Quality criteria

- Does the glossary contain all user terms needed for the system?
- Does the glossary contain similar terms with different meanings which will confuse users?
- Does the glossary contain avoidable synonyms, where two different terms have the same meaning?
- Does the glossary correspond to users' normal vocabulary for describing business objects and actions?

7.2.3   Action–object matrix

This is a matrix showing how update actions affect objects. The matrix may be considered to be part of the user object model, as it summarizes user object action definitions in a tabular view.

Notation
Each column represents a user object and each row represents a user object action. There are four types of effect:

C Create (create a new occurrence of the object type)

R Read only (information is read from the object to check the validity of the action or to produce its output)

U Update (either the attributes of the object occurrence or its relationship links are updated)

D Delete (an occurrence of the object is deleted)

A cell may show more than one effect, e.g. C/U.
There is an example of the matrix notation in Figure 7.15 (in the case study example).

Where used

The action–object matrix is used to check the consistency and completeness of the user object model.

Quality criteria

- Are all the objects and update actions shown in the matrix?
- Are all effects shown on the matrix?
- If there are any objects which have no create action (or no update action, or no delete action), is this in fact correct?

7.3   PROCESS

7.3.1   Check for multiple models

The first activity in defining the user object model is to assess whether multiple models are required, and to identify the group of users for each user object model. In a large system there may be two or more user classes for whom the 'objects in the system' are almost completely different. In these circumstances, rather than attempting to define a single object model for all users, it is better to define two or more user object models and have these form the basis of two or more subsystems. For example, in a telesales system, operators may be concerned with objects such as prospective customers and individual orders, whereas managers may perceive the system as being about weekly costs, revenues and profits, and statistics on operator performance (number of calls, average length, value of sales).

In this situation the system will require two subsystems, one geared to the tasks and concerns of operators, and the other to managers. In order that the system support a coherent mental model for each group, it is best to develop two user object models, and design each user interface subsystem around a focused user object model.

In general it is not necessary to have a separate user object model for every user class. An object model should be broad enough to cover the requirements of several user classes concerned with the same objects.

As user objects are identified and the models drawn, the initial partitioning into multiple user object models may be revised.

If there are any common objects which occur in two or more models, these should have attributes and behavior which are consistent between the models. This is not normally difficult to achieve, as the data model acts as a system-wide shared model underpinning and integrating any user-specific user object models.

7.3.2   Identify objects

User objects are identified from three sources:

(i) discussions with users;

(ii) task models and scenarios;

(iii) (optionally, if one is available) a data model.

7.3.2.1   Identify objects from users

Ask the users what objects are relevant for their tasks. Interactive workshop sessions or interviews may be used.

- What objects do they perform the tasks on, i.e. what objects are created, deleted, updated, linked to other objects or enquired about?
- What other objects are used in the task, i.e. what objects are used as containers, tools, devices, inputs, reference sources?
- What additional objects would be useful if they were available or feasible?

7.3.2.2   Identify objects from task models

Analyze the task models and task scenarios to identify the objects that are used. The most effective approach is to discuss each subtask with the people who perform it, and ask the following questions:

- What is created or changed by this task?
- What objects are used or referred to in performing the task?

Such objects will usually be mentioned in task or subtask names or goals, or in the detailed descriptive text for a subtask or task scenario. Objects will usually be nouns or noun phrases, such as customer, price list, invoice, accounts statement, spares catalog. Some nouns such as customer name or invoice date are not objects, but attributes of other objects.

Readers who are familiar with data modeling should note that many of these objects are not 'entities' in the entity–relationship modeling sense. Some of them will correspond to a set of entity instances, e.g. a single price list object may be equivalent to a set of product instances, each with a name, a code and a price. Other objects may be documents which contain information from several entities. For example, an account statement may include information from the customer entity, account entity and several instances of the payment entity. Other objects will correspond to devices (e.g. printer, mail out tray) or other people within the organization (e.g. accounts department, sales manager).

Review these task objects to decide which are required as user objects. For each object consider a number of questions:

- Does the user need to see and interact with the object to perform their tasks?

- Does the object group together related information in a way that helps the user to perform a specific task?
- Does the object exist in the business world, and will it continue to exist with the new system?
- Is the object a useful system object, which the user needs to see and interact with (e.g. printer, fax machine) or should it be invisible to the user (e.g. modem)?
- Is the object just an artifact of the old system, which will be made redundant by the new system? (If so it is probably not required in the user object model, unless it is still a helpful illusion for the end-user.)

The user objects should reflect the business world and the requirements of user tasks. At the same time they should avoid merely automating the forms and procedures of the current system, as this would fail to take advantage of the opportunities of GUI technology.

If the object is merely a source or recipient of information in the task and the user does not need to see or manipulate the object, then the object may not be required as a user object. An alternative is to interact with the object via some standard communication mechanism such as an electronic mail mailbox.

Consider whether there are any innovative ideas for introducing new GUI objects to perform the tasks more effectively, e.g. spreadsheet objects.

7.3.2.3   Identify objects from the data model

We do *not* recommend that you produce a data model just to serve as a stepping stone towards identifying objects. (If you do not already have a data model, you might as well start directly with the object model.) However, if a data model for the proposed system is already available, it is often easy for users to identify user objects from the data model. The user object model is usually simpler (i.e. there are fewer user objects than entities).

When examining a data model, how do you know which entities to select as the basis for user objects?

Working with the user, select the entities which:

- the user sees as important objects in their world;
- are useful for performing user tasks;
- the user wants to be able to see and select independently of other objects;
- the user wants to perform actions on;
- have some data.

The entities which normally become user objects are those that represent objects which have an independent real-world existence (sometimes known as 'kernel entities' or 'fundamental entities'). These entities tend to have a simple primary key (i.e. a single attribute whose value uniquely identifies an occurrence of the entity). For example, car is a kernel entity, with primary key vehicle registration number, and would become a user object.

The entities which *sometimes* do not become user objects are the following:

- Entities which are used to describe some characteristic of a more substantial entity. In data modeling these are referred to as 'characteristic entities', in that they are often created by normalization of repeating groups of characteristics.

- Entities which are used to express a many-to-many relationship between two more substantial entities. Such entities typically have a compound key formed from the keys of their masters (in data modeling these are referred to as 'associative entities', as they model associations between entities).

In the case of characteristic and associative entities, a judgment has to be made as to whether the user sees the entity as an object, or merely as providing additional information about another object. Entities which just provide extra information do not usually become user objects. Characteristic and associative entities *perceived by the user as objects* do become user objects, usually part of a larger aggregate object.

This process is illustrated in section 7.4.

7.3.3   Create user object model diagram

Combine the list of potential user objects from the users and the task models with the user objects identified from the data model. Some rationalization of duplicate objects may be needed.

Take care to give each object the name that the user wants to call it in the interface.

Analyze the relationships between the objects. For each user object, consider which other types of user object it is directly related to. For example, a Person object may 'own' a Car object. Define the cardinality of the relationships (one-to-many, many-to-many, etc). For example, one Person may own many Cars, but each Car is owned by one Person.

Use a user object model diagram to show all the user objects and the relationships between them. Where a data model diagram exists, the topology (layout) of the user object model diagram will often be similar.

There will often be 'contains' relationships, showing container objects (such as lists) related to the objects they contain. Many-to-many relationships are common and one-to-one relationships are quite acceptable.

Note the number of occurrences of each user object (e.g. there is only one System object, but there are 1000 Customers and 9000 Orders.)

7.3.4   Define user object attributes

Define the attributes of each object, i.e. the pieces of information the user knows about the object. For example, a Person object might have a Name, an Address, an Employer, a Date of Birth, a Photograph, a Signature and a List of Leisure Activities. Note that

Photograph and (handwritten) Signature are perfectly sensible attributes, even though they are not conventional database fields.

The criteria to use in deciding whether a piece of information should be an attribute of a particular user object are whether it is useful to support a task, and whether it seems sensible to the user. (Avoidance of redundancy, extent of normalization, etc., are not appropriate quality criteria for user object models.)

Some attributes may be added later, as the interface evolves during prototyping.

Where a user object is identified from a data model entity, its attributes often include all the attributes of the entity. However, it may also include repeating groups of attributes which were in related characteristic or associative entities, and attributes of parent entities.

If the system will store data in a database, at some point it will be advisable to define a logical data model. It is useful to relate the user object attributes precisely to this data model, both to cross-check the interface design and later for implementation, when interface elements will need to be connected to database data. For any object which has attributes from more than one entity, associate the user object with the relevant entities and relationships. A good way of doing this is to draw the relevant fragment of the data model.

7.3.5   Define user object actions

Identify the actions the user will need to perform on (or using) the object, such as Print, Calculate, Authorize, Send to, Allocate to, Add.

User object actions are identified from user tasks, and from discussions with users.

Most user objects will have actions to Create or Delete. Establishing (or removing) a relationship between one user object and another is another common action. Some actions relate to the whole user object, while other actions may only relate to part of the object.

Additional user object actions may be identified and added later, while expressing task scenarios as sequences of user object actions, and during prototyping.

Define each action in terms of the following:

- A brief narrative description
- Any input
- The required effect on object attributes and relationships
- Any output

User object actions describe the 'behavior' of objects in the system. They are the main means of specifying required system functionality. The actions on a user object are considered to be part of the object.

7.3.6   Create action−object matrix

Create a matrix to show how update actions affect objects.

The action−object matrix provides a useful way of checking the scope and complexity of actions. Most user object actions only affect one user object. However, where an action does affect more than one object, this is significant for GUI design. When the user performs the action on one object, will they expect the effects on other objects to occur?

Construction and review of the matrix often leads to additional actions being identified, to actions being redefined, or to additional effects being noted.

7.3.7   Check for dynamic behavior

For each object in turn, consider whether there is significant dynamic behavior.
  For the actions of an object, consider the following:

- Can the actions be invalid, depending on the prior state of the object?

- Are there any constraints on the sequence in which the actions can occur?

For example, for a particular person the Divorce action is only possible in the 'married' state, or (equivalently) after a Marry action.

If there is state-dependent behavior (or ordering constraints among the actions), apply the dynamic modeling technique in Chapter 8 to the user object. This will help to clarify the preconditions for each action, and to define the effects more precisely.

7.3.8   Review glossary

The glossary is built up progressively throughout task analysis and user object modeling, adding and defining terms as they are encountered. At this point the glossary is reviewed and refined.

Check whether the glossary is complete – are all the technical terms used in the task model and user object model which might be used in the GUI defined in the glossary?

Check whether there are any synonyms in the glossary, where two different terms are used with the same meaning. Rationalize these, by deciding with users which term will be used consistently throughout the user interface.

Check whether there are any homonyms (where the same term is used to mean two different things), or terms which are so similar that they will cause confusion to users. Where necessary, modify terms to avoid this.

7.3.9   Validate user object model

Check with real end-users that the objects, relationships, attributes and actions are recognizable and correspond to their understanding of the world.

Example   121

■ 7.4 EXAMPLE ▬▬▬▬▬▬▬▬▬▬▬▬▬▬▬▬

This section develops the user object models for the UniSoft Helpline system.

7.4.1   Check for multiple models

In the example, the users have been divided into six user classes. The more technical user classes have a shared understanding of the objects in the system (i.e. a common user object model), but the business users require a simpler view. This gives us two user object models:

UOM1 Helpline – technical staff user object model (advisors, customer support manager, second-line support)

UOM2 Helpline – business staff user object model (salespersons and business managers).

We also consider the mental model formed by customers of 'what is in the Helpline system'. These people are remote indirect users who will not see the screen or receive printout; they only know what they are told on the telephone. Consequently they require a very simple user object model.

UOM3 Helpline – customer contact user object model (customer contacts)

Diagrams for the three models are shown in Figures 7.10, 7.11 and 7.12 later in this section.

7.4.2   Identify objects

We identify objects from users, tasks and from a data model.

7.4.2.1   Objects from users

Talking to helpline advisors identifies several candidate objects:

Customer
A Customer is an organization which has purchased UniSoft products and whose staff may call the Helpline for advice. There is no doubt that Customer is a user object.

Bug/Problem
A Bug is a known error in the software product. This is an important object, and is called 'Bug' in the current system. However, there is a question as to what is the best name. The system needs to hold all kinds of 'known problem', whether this is a software bug, a documentation error, or a common user error or misunderstanding. Calling all these things 'bugs' is very confusing. It is agreed that this user object will be called 'Problem'.

Call

Telephone calls are important objects in the Helpline environment, and each call is recorded separately by the current system. However, this causes various difficulties, as one telephone call may contain many new customer queries (on different topics), but on the other hand a single query may involve subsequent phone calls to and from the customer. Modeling both queries and calls as objects, with a many-to-many relationship, would be complex for the system and confusing for the user. The best way to model calls in terms of user objects is not immediately obvious at this point.

Software Change Request

A Software Change Request (SCR) is an important document in the process of correcting software bugs. These are relevant in the Helpline business system but are outside the scope of the current Helpline computer system. At present advisors have to telephone second-line support and ask about SCRs. It is agreed that SCR should be a user object.

7.4.2.2   *Objects from tasks*

The task models and task scenarios produced in Chapter 6 are discussed with Helpline Advisors and the customer support manager to identify user objects which the system should support.

Resolve customer query

We start with the critical task, Resolve Customer Query (see Figures 6.5, 6.6 and the associated scenario descriptions in section 6.4). Starting with the most important tasks is generally a good idea, as it helps to clarify your ideas about how the main objects should be modeled. (As you will see, this applies to the modelling of Call and Query in the Helpline.)

The central object of this task is a *Query*. During the task a Query is created. The goal of the task is that the Customer is satisfied about the Query. (Another way of expressing this is that the goal of the task is that the Query should end up having status 'ClosedOK'.) Therefore, Query is identified as a user object. 'Query' has been chosen as the name for this object because it is broad and neutral — is a suitable name for requests for information or assistance as well as for reports of suspected software malfunctions.

The customer support manager decides that Query is in fact the central business object of the Helpline group. Rather than giving the customer a 'call reference', the manager wants to be able to give a unique 'query reference' for each distinct Query.

This clarifies the modeling of Calls and Queries. Query will be the main user object, and phone calls are just events that happen in the life of a Query. Another way of phrasing this is that from the user's perspective the 'objects in the system' will be Queries — part of what you know about a particular Query is the phone call in which it was raised, and any other phone calls in which it was discussed.

We consider the subtasks of Resolve Customer Query in turn:

Subtask 1 — Identify Customer

Customer is clearly an important object.

Customer organization is not a separate object, just another way of referring to Customer.

Example   123

A *Contact* is a person working for a Customer organization who calls Helpline. This initially seems like an object, but after discussion it is agreed that the contact is not a separate object but something which is known about a Customer. Consequently it is modeled as an attribute (list of Contacts) of a Customer. The following points indicate that it is not worth modeling as an object:

- A Contact object would have few attributes and no actions except Create.
- Contacts only have unique identities within the scope of Customers. (Joe Schwartz at Downtown Bank is not the same as Joe Schwartz at State Mutual Insurance.)

Maintenance is not an object, but is an attribute of Customer, indicating whether the Customer has paid for a UniSoft maintenance agreement.

Subtask 2 — Identify Problem
Problem is clearly another major 'object in the system', i.e. a user object. The task involves finding (or creating) a Problem which is the cause of the Query. As discussed above, Problem is a more general name than Bug.

'Known Problem' is just another way of referring to Problem.

Advisor is referred to in 'ask other advisor', but is not an 'object in the system' here, so is not considered worth modeling as a user object at this point.

Keyword is referred to in the task scenario ('try keyword "Install — Upgrade"'), and this could be an object. We decide, however, that the user prefers to think of keyword as an attribute of Problem (i.e. one of the things you know about a Problem is that it has some keywords which help you to find it).

Helpline system. The task scenarios refer in various places to 'system' (e.g. resolve using *system*, known problem recorded in *system*, check query reference from *system*). This refers to the Helpline system, which is an important object we had not noted before as a user object.

Subtask 3 — Advise Customer
No further objects here.

Subtask 4 — Log Query
This subtask is concerned with the Query object. Status, Priority, Responsibility and Action Date are not objects, but attributes of Query.

Provide query status
This task is concerned with the Query object, and to a lesser extent with the Customer object. No new objects are identified.

Monitor advisor workload
Advisor. At first glance, this suggests that there might be a new object called 'advisor workload'. Considering it more carefully, we see that the object is an 'Advisor'. Workload is an attribute of Advisor (i.e. something you know about an Advisor).

Another attribute of Advisor is their Queries (the set of Queries they are currently responsible for). Discussion reveals that 'workload' is precisely a summary of the current Queries, indicating how many they have and how urgent they are.

From the task perspective of the customer support manager it is important to be able to see Advisors as 'objects in the system', so they are definitely required as user objects.

7.4.2.3   Objects from the data model

The data model initially proposed for the Helpline system is shown in Figure 7.7.

In order to illustrate the process of creating a user object model, the derivation of objects from entities is discussed in some detail. (In practice, if user objects had been identified in detail from users and tasks, the data model might just be used to check that all data had been accounted for.)

Customer is seen by the user as an object, as discussed above. (Note that it is a kernel entity.)

Contact is not seen by the user as a separate object, but as something known about a Customer. Note that it is a characteristic entity, which may have been formed by normalizing a list of contacts.

Call is seen by the user as an object, but including it leads to a very complex model. As discussed above, it is decided to regard Query as the object.

Query is definitely a user object.

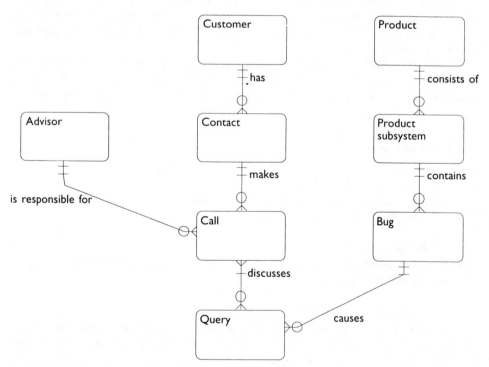

Fig. 7.7   Data model initially proposed

Example   125

Advisor was previously identified as a required user object.

The entities on the right-hand side of the data model (Product, Subsystem) turn out not to be objects in the system, but a framework for classifying and retrieving problems.

7.4.3   Create user object model diagram

The various user objects which have been identified are gathered together in Figure 7.8 and the users' understanding of the relationships between them is analyzed.

A Customer may raise 'zero to many' queries, but each query belongs to exactly one Customer.

An Advisor may be responsible for zero to many queries. A query may have one advisor responsible for it, or none.

The System could be thought of as having 'contains' relationships with all the other objects, but showing these in the diagram is not helpful. Apart from these relationships, it is not related to other objects.

These objects and relationships are shown in Figure 7.9.

Consider the remaining objects and relationships.

A Software Change Request 'defines the solution' to zero or more Problems, but each Problem is only solved by one SCR (or none).

A Problem may 'cause' zero to many Queries, but each Query is caused by a single Problem. (Or a Query might not be linked to any Problem.)

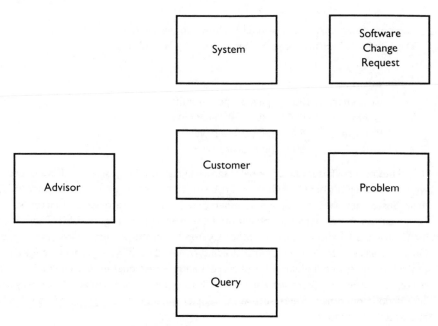

Fig. 7.8   User objects for technical staff

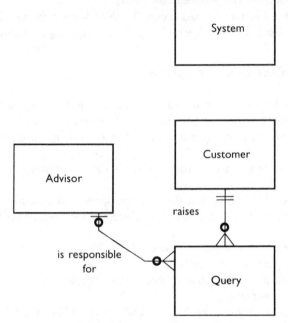

Fig. 7.9   Partial user object model

The completed user object model is shown in Figure 7.10. The number of occurrences of user objects are as follows:

System	1	
Advisor	6	
Customer	1000	(plus 30 per month)
Query	15,000	(plus 500 per week)
Problem	600	(plus 10 per week)
SCR	500	(plus 5 per week)

The business staff user object model is shown in Figure 7.11. Business staff are not concerned with the distinctions between Queries, Problems and SCRs. They want to know what Queries their Customers have raised, and whether they have been resolved satisfactorily.

The customer contact's user object model is even simpler (Figure 7.12). There is no need for Customers to know about the other Customers in the System, or to have any idea that Queries are linked to Problems, which are in turn linked to SCRs. It is adequate for a customer to think of the system holding a set of current and historic queries, each identified by a query reference, and with the attributes date, status, description and responsible advisor. Any necessary information from other objects, such as SCR implementation date, is collapsed down and viewed as an attribute of Query.

Example   127

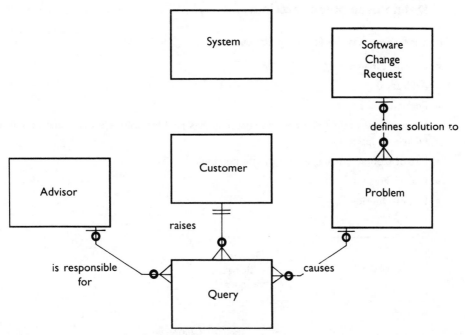

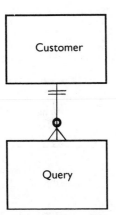

Fig. 7.10   User object model for technical staff

Fig. 7.11   User object model for business staff

Fig. 7.12   User object model for customer contact

7.4.4   Define user object attributes

Customer user object has the following attributes:

- Company name
- Address
- Phone number
- Maintenance status (whether the customer has paid for software maintenance and Helpline support)
- List of Contacts (each with a phone number)
- List of Sites
- List of Queries

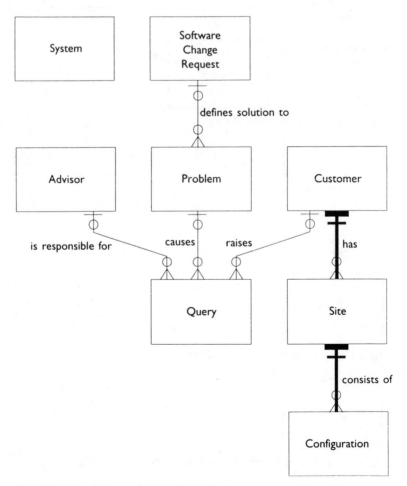

Fig. 7.13   User object model showing Customer as composite object

Example   129

Enquiring further about the list of Sites, we learn that there are other attributes which relate to Site (Site Address, Date Last Visited), and also attributes which relate to configurations of individual computers on a Site (Type of Hardware, Operating System, Clock Speed, etc.). Each Site may have several types of computer with different configurations.

The current user object model presents all this information just as attributes of Customer. It will be clearer for the user if we structure the information by introducing some component objects — Site and Configuration. A Customer has a number of Sites, and a Site consists of several Configurations. These relationships are aggregation relationships — Sites and Configurations are not just loosely associated to a Customer, they are part of a Customer.

We can confirm that these are aggregation (i.e. whole — part) relationships by the kind of reasoning below. If we deleted the Customer from the system, we would delete all their Sites and Configurations. If the Customer changed their organization name, we would change the name of their Sites and Configurations. If we allocated a Customer to be the responsibility of a particular Helpline advisor, that advisor would by default take responsibility for all the Customer's Sites and Configurations.

We extend the user object model to show this (Figure 7.13).

The user-perceived size and format of each attribute is defined, for example, as follows:

Company name   40 characters
Address   4 rows of 32 characters each

The data model entities and relationships which are used to store the Customer object information are shown in Figure 7.14.

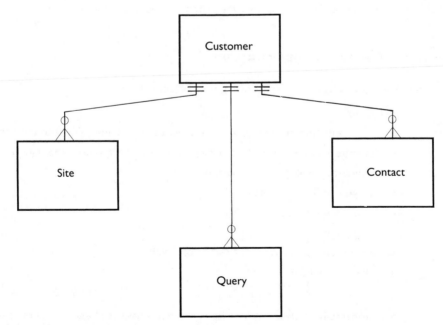

Fig. 7.14   Data model fragment to support Customer user object

This illustrates an important point. The user thinks of the Customer as a single object, and expects to be able to interact with it as a single object, i.e. to be able to select, create, delete, update the Customer as a whole, without having to think about its underlying structure of entities. Note that Query is a user object in its own right, but that the data model fragment for Customer also refers to the Query entity.

Query user object has the following attributes:

- Query ref
- Query name
- Priority
- Status (closedOK, waiting for info, being investigated, etc.)
- Next action
- Action responsibility
- Escalation level (level of management involved)
- Customer name
- Contact
- Problem ref
- Query description
- Technical history (cumulative technical details)
- Event history (list of events, each with date, time, person and event description)

The Event History acts like an audit log — each time a significant event happens, more information is appended to it so that the history of the query can be traced.

7.4.5   Define user object actions

The Query user object has the following user object actions:

- Create
- Merge (with another query, when a duplicate has accidentally been created)
- Associate (link to the Problem which appears to have caused the query)
- Dissociate (unlink from a Problem)
- Change priority (see below)
- Change responsibility
- Change status
- Escalate (change management escalation level)
- Make Problem (see below)
- Subsequent call

There is deliberately no Delete — because once a query has been logged it cannot be deleted. Each action is specified; this is illustrated for the actions 'Change Priority' and 'Make Problem'.

Example   131

1. Change Priority
   - Purpose is to increase or reduce the priority of a query (if its significance changes for the customer).
   - Input — new priority, comment.
   - Effects:
     - update Query Priority attribute to new value;
     - add event to Query Event History, with date, time, advisor, new priority and comment;
     - if linked to a Problem, and new Query Priority is higher than Problem Priority, update Problem Priority to new value of Query Priority.
   - Output — none.

2. Make Problem
   - This creates a new Problem based on the current Query. It is only used when it is not possible to Associate the Query to a known Problem as the cause of the Query.
   - Input — none.
   - Effects:
     - create Problem with unique Problem Ref, set Problem priority to Query Priority;
     - associate Query to the new Problem;
     - add event to Query Event History, with Date, time, advisor, Problem Ref.
   - Output — confirmation of Problem created, and Problem Reference.

7.4.6   Create action–object matrix

The matrix (Figure 7.15) shows which objects are affected by actions (in this case the user object actions on Query).

Most of the effects on other objects are what the user could predict:

	Customer	Advisor	Query	Problem
Query. Create	U		C	
Query. Merge			U	
Query. Associate			U	U
Query. Disassociate			U	U
Query. Change Priority			U	U
Query. Change Responsibility		U	U	
Query. Change Status			U	
Query. Escalate			U	
Query. Make Problem			U	C
Query. Subsequent Call			U	

Fig. 7.15   Action–object matrix

- If you can create a Query for a Customer, you add the Query to that Customer's list of Queries.
- If you associate a Query to a Problem, the Query becomes one the Problem's list of associated Queries.
- Make Problem creates a new Problem, etc.

One hidden effect which could surprise the user is that changing Query priority changes Problem priority. This is necessary to enforce the business rule that a problem has the priority of the highest priority associated Query. Unexpected effects such as this should have warnings in the user interface and allow the user to confirm.

7.4.7   Check for dynamic behavior

Query has some sequences of actions which are not valid. For example,

- Associate, Associate (because you cannot Associate a Query to a second Problem without dissociating from the first)
- Merge, Associate ('Merged' Queries are redundant duplicates that have been merged into a main query to get rid of them without losing trace of them. Several actions are not available on merged Queries.)

We conclude that the Query object has significant dynamic behavior which needs to be analyzed. This is discussed in the example in Chapter 8.

The other user objects in this example do not have dynamic behavior requiring further modeling.

7.4.8   Review glossary

A sample of the glossary entries are reproduced below:

Escalation level   an attribute of Query, indicating the highest level of management to whom the Query has been escalated.

Maintenance   an attribute of Customer, indicating whether they have paid for UniSoft's maintenance and the Helpline service.

Merge   an action on Query and Problem. Used to rationalize duplicates.

Priority   an attribute of Query and Problem, indicating how important it is to resolve it urgently.

Problem   an object consisting of a known problem with a UniSoft product, or familiar type of problem caused by user'error.

Query   an object consisting of a request from a Customer for advice or assistance. This is the main unit of work in customer support.

Showstopper   a value of the Priority attribute of Query and Problem. Indicates that
the query or problem is preventing the Customer doing further work using the product.

No synonyms or name clashes are found. (They are more likely in bigger systems.)

Having completed the user object model for the Helpline case study, you may wish to look
again at section 6.4.6 in the previous chapter, in which the Helpline task scenarios are expressed
as actions on the Helpline objects.

7.5   PRACTICE TIPS

7.5.1   Redundancy in object models

This section discusses some technical issues on the relationship between user object
models and data models, and is addressed particularly to people with a data modeling
background who have to relate the GUI design to the data modeling and database
design parts of a project. It is recommended that you skip over it on a first reading.

In user object models information is sometimes modeled as an attribute of two
different objects at the same time, i.e. it is modeled redundantly. This does not imply
that the data will be stored redundantly, as the object model is mapped back onto
a (relatively) normalized data model.

Redundancy in the user object model is not always an error − it may be required
for the user object model to model accurately the user's understanding of objects.

The following section discusses how typical forms of user object model redundancy
relate to common structures of relationships in data models.

7.5.1.1   *Associative entity redundancy*

An associative entity is frequently treated as 'part of' two different objects. For
example, in a course booking system one might have entities Order, Course Presentation (a particular course being given on a specific date), and delegate booking (one
person booked on one Course Presentation) as shown in Figure 7.16.

An Order user object would include as an attribute the list of delegates booked on
this order (in effect the lines of the order). A Course Presentation user object would
include a list of delegates booked on this Course Presentation (literally the 'delegate
list'). To maintain consistency, any addition or removal of delegates, or change of
delegate names, must be reflected in both user objects.

7.5.1.2   *Type−instance redundancy*

Some entities are effectively 'types' or 'descriptors', which hold information which
applies to other entity types. For example, a data model may include a Customer

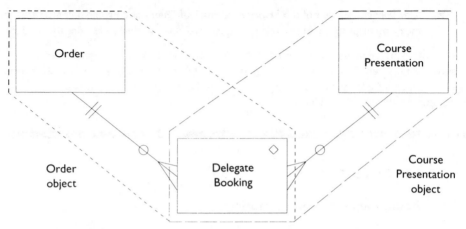

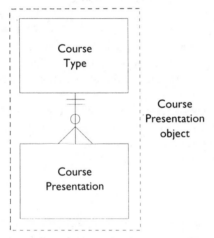

Fig. 7.16   Associative entity redundancy

Fig. 7.17   Type–instance redundancy

Type entity as well as a Customer entity. Information about the Customer Type (e.g. percentage discount) applies to each Customer of that Customer Type. The user is unlikely to conceptualize this distinction (which is concerned with normalization), and is more likely to think of percentage discount as an attribute of each Customer.

For a second example, the course booking system could have an entity Course Type, as shown in Figure 7.17.

Course Type would have a name, description, course syllabus and other attributes related to the course as a whole. Course Presentation has attributes specific to a particular time the course is given – start date, venue, lecturer, etc.

A user would think of the course description and syllabus as attributes of the Course

Presentation, so the user object for Course Presentation will overlap with the user object for Course Type, implying redundancy.

7.5.1.3   Whole—part redundancy

Where one object is part of another, there is often redundancy. Deleting the part, or changing the state of the part, often requires consequential adjustment to the whole object to maintain consistency.

For example, the whole object may maintain a count of the number of parts, or a total which summarizes the total value of the parts. A further example is where the larger object is actually a container object such as a list.

There are also situations where attributes of the whole are perceived (redundantly) by the user as if they were attributes of the part (e.g. location, color, ownership, date of creation).

7.5.1.4   Other redundancy between related entities

Other relationships can also be interpreted in a way that leads to redundancy between user objects. For example, in the familiar case of Customers having many Sales Orders, some of the Customer attributes may also be perceived by the user to be attributes of a Sales Order, e.g. the customer name and address could be part of the user object Sales Order.

For another example, consider the Course Presentation and Venue entities in a course booking system, as shown in Figure 7.18.

In the data model, the address and telephone number of the venue are attributes

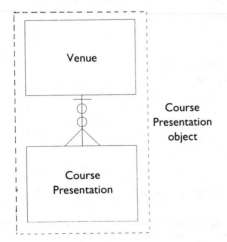

Fig. 7.18   Other redundancy between related entities

of Venue and not of Course Presentation. However, the Course Presentation user object may also have these as attributes.

In contrast with the situations discussed above, note that a Course Presentation is not 'part of' a Venue, nor is Course Presentation an instance of Venue.

7.6   SUMMARY

This chapter describes how to create a user object model. Major points include the following:

- The objective is to enable users to form a coherent mental model of the objects in the system.
- A key benefit is that user object modeling leads the designer towards a flexible and intuitive object-based GUI.
- The technique is based on standard object-oriented analysis techniques, but does not require an object-oriented programming implementation.
- The products of user object modeling are:
  - a user object model diagram;
  - a list of attributes for each user object;
  - a list of actions for each user object;
  - a definition of the effect of each user object action;
  - an action−object matrix (to validate the effects);
  - a glossary of user terms.
- The process of user object modeling consists of:
  - checking for multiple models;
  - identifying objects (from users, tasks and the data model);
  - creating a user object model diagram;
  - defining attributes;
  - defining actions;
  - creating the action−object matrix;
  - checking for dynamic behavior;
  - reviewing the glossary;
  - validating the model.

7.7   FURTHER READING

Rumbaugh, J., Blaha, M., Premerlani, W., Eddy, F. and Lorenson W. (1991) *Object Oriented Modelling and Design*, Prentice Hall.
   The GUIDE user object modeling technique is based on the approach to modeling object types and their interrelationships in this influential text on object-oriented analysis.

IBM (1991) *Systems Application Architecture: Common User Access (SAA CUA) Guide to User Interface Design* (document number SC34-4289-00), IBM Publications.
Discusses the importance of the mental model for achieving usability and the importance of organizing the model around objects meaningful to the user. Discusses the relationship between the user's model and the designer's model.

Johnson, P. (1989) 'Supporting system design by analyzing current task knowledge', in Diaper, D. (ed.), *Task Analysis for Human–Computer Interaction*, Ellis Horwood.
This article proposes an object-oriented model derived from the user's task model as a key component of the 'task knowledge structure' (i.e. the user's mental model).

Walsh, P. (1989) 'Analysis for task object modelling (ATOM): towards a method of integrating task analysis with Jackson System Development for user interface software design', in Diaper, D. (ed.), *Task Analysis for Human–Computer Interaction*, Ellis Horwood.
Proposes a conceptual modeling language consisting of objects, actions and relations. This is used to define a user's conceptual model which influences interface design.

Green, T.R.G. and Benyon, D. (1991) 'Describing information artifacts with cognitive dimensions and structure maps', in Diaper, D. and Hammond, N.V. (eds), *Proceedings of HCI 91: Usability Now*, Cambridge University Press.
Introduces a technique (known as ERMIA: Entity-Relationship Models of Information Artefacts) for representing the structure of information in a display, and relating this to the intended user's conceptual model. The purposes and technique are very similar to user object modeling.

Potosnak, K. (1989) 'Mental models: helping users understand software', *IEEE Software*, September.
Discusses what mental models are, how people build them, how to facilitate the process of building a mental model, and how to gain access to people's mental models.

8

Dynamic modeling

8.1   INTRODUCTION

This chapter describes the (optional) technique of dynamic modeling, which is used to analyze and describe the dynamic behavior of user objects. We recommend that you skip this chapter on a first reading of the book, and come back to it as required.

Dynamic modeling is useful where there is significant state-dependent behavior, i.e. where the behavior of an object changes through time, depending on the state that the object is in. In GUIDE the dynamic modeling technique is used immediately after user object modeling (Figure 8.1), as part of the Model User Objects activity.

Some objects have little or no state-dependent behavior. If all the actions on an object are always valid, and may be performed in any sequence, there is no state-dependent behavior. (Except for the obvious facts that the object must be created before it can be updated, and that the final action is to delete it.) For such objects dynamic modeling is unnecessary.

Other objects have a more interesting lifecycle. The set of actions which you can perform on the object at any point in time depends on its current state, which changes through time. This may imply that actions have to be performed in some fixed sequence. Also the effect of an action on an object may vary, depending on the object's state.

Dynamic behavior may not be immediately obvious, and the dynamic modeling technique helps you to understand it and develop a simple model to represent it.

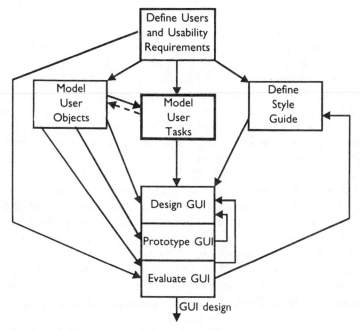

Fig. 8.1   GUIDE context of dynamic modeling

This model guides the designer when constructing the user interface to the object. It is particularly helpful in identifying potential errors, and in designing error prevention and error handling.

Because dynamic behavior is sometimes complex and difficult to understand, it is important to have an appropriate diagrammatic notation to help visualize the behavior. Several notations have been used for this purpose.

GUIDE recommends using Harel's statechart notation. This is an enhanced form of state transition diagram which is increasingly accepted as the most powerful form of dynamic modeling for object-oriented analysis.

The dynamic modeling technique can also be used to analyze and design the behavior of windows, i.e. the window states in which the user is allowed to perform particular window actions. This is illustrated briefly in section 8.5, but is not discussed in detail as it is less often required.

8.1.1   Objective

To define the dynamic behavior of user objects.

8.1.2   Benefits

Dynamic modeling helps the analyst/designer to understand the behavior of the objects in the system. Having a coherent model of behavior is a prerequisite to presenting this behavior in the user interface in a manner which is clear, coherent, intuitive and predictable to the user. (The converse is that if the designer does not understand the dynamic behavior of the underlying objects, the user interface is likely to cope with object dynamics in *ad hoc* ways which are confusing to the user.)

A dynamic model is a useful practical input to GUI design, particularly to the design of error-handling. It shows when actions will be invalid, and the GUI designer can take steps to cope with the user's inappropriate attempts to perform them. This might be either by some preventive action in the user interface such as menu-dimming, or by some recovery action, such as informing the user via a warning that the action they tried to perform was not allowed.

A dynamic model consolidates the user object model, by validating and refining the definitions of user object actions. Dynamic modeling encourages the analyst to ask questions about preconditions for actions, and the effects (postconditions) of actions on object state. This often exposes ambiguities or missing logic, and results in a more precise specification of user object behavior.

The dynamic model can also be used to validate task scenarios, by checking that each scenario consists of a valid sequence of user object actions. In other words one can check that the task scenarios do not specify actions in an invalid sequence, or where the action preconditions are not satisfied.

8.1.3   Inputs/outputs (Figure 8.2)

- *Input* — user object model, comprising objects, attributes, actions and relationships.
- *Output* — dynamic model: for each user object with significant state-dependant behavior, a dynamic model diagram and associated notes on states and the validity of actions.

8.2   PRODUCT — DYNAMIC MODEL

A dynamic model is a model of the dynamic behavior of a user object. It defines the following:

- Significant states of the user object.
- The ways that actions depend on the state and affect the state.

The dynamic model consists of the following:

- A dynamic model diagram (showing states and transitions).
- Supplementary notes specifying states and actions in more detail.

The main concepts are event/action, state and transition.

State
An object may have one or more states. Each state is a stable point in its life, which

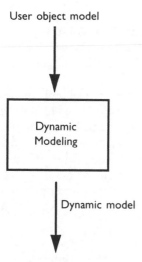

Fig. 8.2 Dynamic modeling inputs and outputs

the object stays in for some period of time. A state can be expressed in terms of the object's attributes and relationships.

Event/action

An event is something that happens to an object. It is atomic in the sense that it happens or does not happen; it cannot have 'half-happened'. In general, an event may cause an action — the event is the trigger, the action is the change in the state of an object as a result of the event.

In GUIDE dynamic modeling, the actions we are interested in are user object actions. The events which trigger these user object actions are almost always users performing some action in the GUI (a window action) which requests the user object action. At this point we are not concerned with these window actions. In these circumstances we can simplify the diagrams and discussion by not showing the events separately. (Each time we show an action in a statechart diagram, you can regard it as meaning the action and the corresponding event which requests it.)

As far as the end-user is concerned each action happens instantaneously, i.e. one moment it has not happened, the next it has.

Actions are specified in terms of their precondition (the state in which the object must be for the action to be valid), and their effect (the way the state of the object is changed by the action).

Transition

A transition is a jump between states; it is labeled with the name of the corresponding action. If an object is in a particular state, then only the actions which label transitions out of the state are valid.

Notation — statechart

A 'statechart' is an extended state transition diagram. It describes the behavior of an object as a set of states, with transitions between states each labeled with the name of the action (event) which caused the transition. The basic notation is shown in Figure 8.3.

Figure 8.4 shows a very simple example of a statechart for a library book object. There are two states, 'In Library' and 'On Loan', and five actions the librarian user can perform on a book: Acquire, Borrow, Renew, Return and Sell. The diagram shows that when a book is in state 'On Loan', only actions Return and Renew are valid. (Actions Borrow and Sell are not valid because they cannot start from state 'On Loan'.)

The problem with the standard state transition diagram notation is that as the number of states increase, the diagrams become very complex and difficult to read. The statechart notation reduces this problem by introducing two concepts for managing complexity: *composite state* and *concurrent state*.

Composite state

Frequently a collection of states can be treated as one state for certain purposes. This reduces diagram complexity by reducing the number of transition lines. The collection is referred to as a composite state, and the states inside as 'substates'.

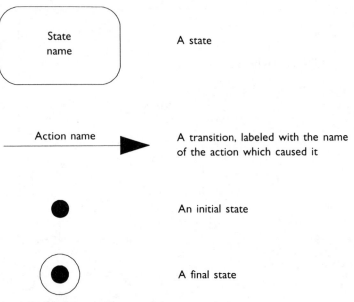

Fig. 8.3   Basic state transition diagram notation

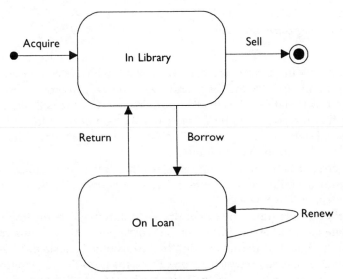

Fig. 8.4   Example of simple statechart diagram

Our previous diagram was oversimplified. In reality only a subset of the books 'In Library' will be on the shelves available for loan. Some newly acquired books will still be 'In Acquisitions', other books may be Withdrawn from circulation for a period of time (e.g. for repair), and later reissued for circulation. These extra states and actions are shown in Figure 8.5.

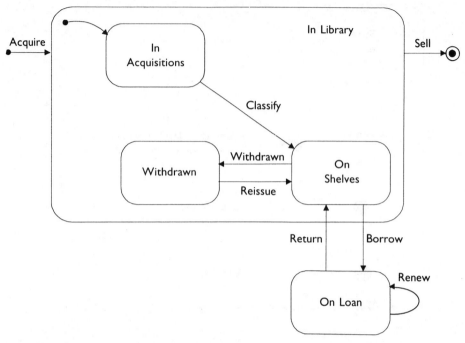

Fig. 8.5 Statechart showing composite state

Figure 8.5 introduces 'In Library' as a composite state, which is composed of the three states 'In Acquisitions', 'Withdrawn' and 'On Shelves'. Any transition which applies to the composite state applies to all of its substates. For the Sell action to be valid we require that the book is in the library, but we do not need to distinguish between the three substates, so the transition is drawn from the composite 'In Library' state. This avoids two extra transition lines.

As well as outward transitions from composite state, there can be outward transitions from specific substates within the composite. In Figure 8.5, the action Borrow is only valid from the substate 'On Shelves'.

Note also that the Acquire transition can be drawn to the outside of the 'In Library' box. The start state icon and arrow in the top left corner show that on entering 'In Library' the default initial transition is to the 'In Acquisitions' substate. In general the initial substate can depend on which action caused the transition, but in this case there is only one and so the transition from the start state into 'In Acquisitions' is not labeled.

These states and state-dependent behavior will need to be presented to the user in the GUI. If someone tries to borrow a book which is in the library but withdrawn, the GUI must prevent the user performing the borrow user action, and explain why the action is not valid. For example, the GUI might dim the menu item for Borrow, and/or display a message such as 'Book not available for borrowing as it is withdrawn for repair'.

Concurrent behavior

Some user objects have dynamic behavior which involves concurrent state, i.e. an object is in two or more states simultaneously. These normally reflect different aspects of the object's life, and the concurrent states may change independently of each other. Statechart diagrams include a notation for describing concurrent behavior, by partitioning the dynamic model into two or more concurrent states.

Consider as an example a film star who may be Hired on a film contract (only after contract approval of course) and may subsequently either finish the film or be fired.

However, he or she also has a life outside the film set; may get married and, who knows, divorced. Being a good Christian, the film star only takes part in monogamous marriages and due to 'exclusive' contracts is only working on one film at any one time.

The statechart diagram in Figure 8.6 shows the film star's life.

To indicate the concurrent behavior a dotted line is drawn separating the two distinct parts of the film star's life. Note that the film star is always in two states at once, and that each behavior has two separate start states. There is no implied sequencing between the Marry and Be Hired actions because the two actions occur on opposite sides of the dotted line.

It is possible for an action to occur in more than one concurrent state, in which case it causes transitions in all the concurrent states in which it occurs. For example, a film star's spouse might always sue for divorce when the film star is fired from a film contract. Figure 8.7 shows the resulting diagram.

If the film star is unmarried, then the Be Fired action merely causes a transition back to the same state; if the film star is married, then the Be Fired action causes

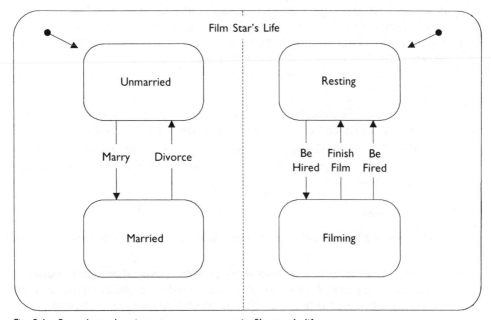

Fig. 8.6   **Statechart showing concurrent states in film star's life**

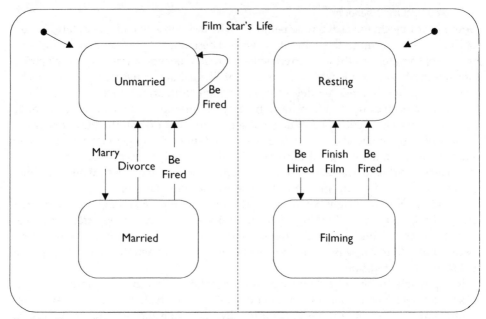

Fig. 8.7   Concurrent state with one action affecting both states

a transition to unmarried as well as to Resting. Note that for an action to occur it must be valid (or irrelevant) in all of the concurrent states, i.e. there must be a transition labeled with the action name from each state that the film star is in.

As with all composite states, a transition drawn from the boundary of the composite state will affect the object whatever the substate; for example, Figure 8.8 indicates that whatever the film star is doing in his/her life, death will stop it.

Where used

Model Tasks   The dynamic model is used to validate the use of objects in task scenarios, to check that the action sequences are permissible.

Design GUI   The dynamic model identifies potential user errors, and is used for designing error prevention and error handling. Object states may influence choice of views.

Quality criteria

- Does the dynamic model show all state-dependent behavior that will be visible to the user?
- Is the dynamic model as simple as possible? (Any dynamic constraints increase complexity for the user and tend to reduce usability, so constraints and state-dependent behavior should be eliminated wherever possible.)

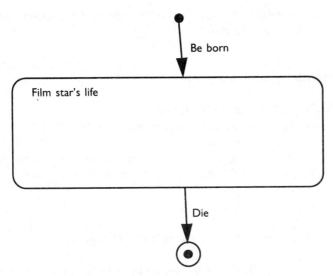

Fig. 8.8   Example of a transition from the outer state

8.3   PROCESS

The process describes activities to produce a dynamic model for a user object. The starting point for this process is a user object, including the list of actions which affect it.

8.3.1   Analyze applicability of actions

For each action on the object, ask the users: 'Is it always valid to do this?' For some actions, such as Change Address, the answer will be 'Yes'. For other actions, such as Marry or Make Payment, the answer will be 'No'. There are some situations (i.e. states of the object) in which the action is valid, and others in which it is not valid. These are 'state-dependent' actions.

Note that most user objects exist for a relatively long period of time, much longer than one editing session. A common situation is that the action the current user wants to perform on an object may not be valid, because of the state the object is already in (from an earlier session).

8.3.2   Identify object states

For each action which is sometimes valid, give a name to the state of the object in which the actions is valid, and a name to the state in which it is invalid. Where possible, use standard user terminology for these states.

For example, the state in which the Marry action is valid is 'Unmarried', and the state in which it is not valid is 'Married'.

8.3.3   Draw dynamic model diagram

Draw a diagram showing all the states identified.

Attempt to rationalize the states, by grouping related states into composite states. Where appropriate show concurrent states.

Add all state-dependent actions to the diagram as transitions from one state to another. If appropriate, rationalize the states and transitions by introducing further composite states.

8.3.4   Express each state in terms of object attributes

Relate the states in the diagram to the attributes and/or relationships of the object.

For example, the states may correspond to the values of a 'status' or 'state' attribute of the object:

> State 'Draft' means 'document status = draft'
>
> State 'Approved' means 'document status = approved'
>
> State 'Cancelled' means 'document status = cancelled'

Alternatively the states may be expressed by some equation involving the object's attributes, e.g.

> State 'Overdrawn' means 'account balance < 0'
>
> State 'In Credit' means 'account balance > 0'

Sometimes the states may be expressed in terms of the presence (or absence) of a relationship to another object, e.g.

> State 'Married' means the object participates in an 'is-married-to' relationship.

8.3.5   Validate dynamic model

For each state, check the set of actions which start from this state with users. Confirm that each of these actions is valid in this state, and that these are the only valid actions (apart from the actions which are not state dependent).

For each action, confirm that the transition to another state shown by the diagram is always true.

For the diagram as a whole, check that it is possible to reach each state from the start point; and that it is possible to leave each state (except any final state(s)).

Example   149

■ 8.4 EXAMPLE

In the Helpline case study, the Query object has significant dynamic behavior.

8.4.1   Analyze applicability of actions

The actions on the Query object are analyzed as follows to identify state-dependent actions.

Create	no prior state
Change Priority	not if merged
Change Status	not if merged
Merge	not if merged
Associate	not if already associated, or if merged
Dissociate	only if associated, not if merged

Note that all actions except Create are state-dependent, i.e. for each action there is at least one state of the Query object in which the action is not valid.

8.4.2   Identify object states

Start with the Change Priority action.

The state in which it is not valid could be called Merged.

The state in which it is valid could be called Not Merged, but Live is chosen as a more positive name for the state. (The name Active was considered, but rejected because many of these not-merged queries will have status 'closed' and will actually be inactive, so to call them Active would be confusing.)

So we have two states: Live and Merged.

The Change Status action leads us to the same two states.

The Merge action also leads us to Live and Merged. Merge is valid if the current state is Live, and invalid if the current state is Merged.

Associate — this refers to states Live and Merged, but also leads us to identify new states Associated and Not Associated. Associate is valid if the current object state is Live and Not Associated, otherwise invalid.

Dissociate leads to the same states as Associate.

8.4.3   Draw dynamic model diagram

Our first attempt at a diagram is shown in Figure 8.9. We have drawn the four states, and some of the transitions which seem immediately obvious.

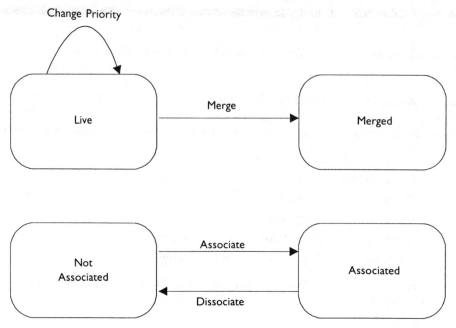

Fig. 8.9 First draft of dynamic model for Query

We investigate the relationship between the states by asking the users questions.

'Is it possible to be Live and Associated?'   'Yes'

'Is it possible to be Live and Not Associated?'   'Yes'

'Is it possible to be Merged and Associated?'   'No'

'Is it possible to be Merged and Not Associated?'   'No'

'So all Associated and Not Associated objects are Live?'   'Yes'

This establishes that Live is a composite state, with substates Associated and Not Associated. We redraw the dynamic model diagram to show this in Figure 8.10.

The diagram prompts two further questions:

'Are all Live queries either Associated or Not Associated,
or are there any other possibilities?'   'There are no others'

So our composite state Live is precisely the composition of these two substates.

'When a new Query is created, is it initially Associated
or not?'   'Initially not associated'

Figure 8.11 shows this information added to the statechart.

Example   151

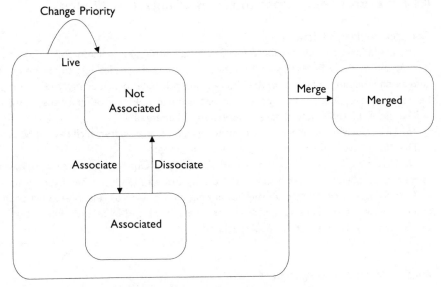

Fig. 8.10   Rationalized dynamic model with composite state

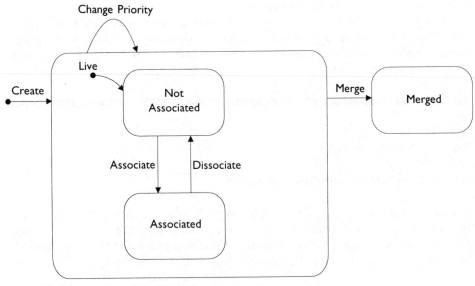

Fig. 8.11   Final dynamic model for Query object

8.4.4   Express each state in terms of object attributes

Consider the Merged state.

We could invent a new attribute for Query called Merged Indicator, with values No and Yes. An alternative which will give the user less to think about (and less to see on the screen) is to extend the range of values of the Query Status attribute to include Merged. This is possible because when a Query is merged we do not need to hold any other status information.

Therefore, Merged state means 'query status = merged'.

The Live state is now defined to be everything else, i.e. any Query which has not been merged. Therefore, Live state means 'query status ≠ merged'.

The Associated state refers to the situation where a Query object is currently associated to a Problem object which is believed to be the cause of the Query (see user object model).

Therefore, Associated state means 'Query has an is-caused-by relationship with a Problem' and Not Associated means 'Query does not have an is-caused-by relationship with a Problem' or alternatively 'is Live but is not Associated'.

8.4.5   Validate dynamic model

We check Figure 8.11. For each state, the set of actions starting from this state is valid. However, they are not the only valid actions — we have omitted Change Status. This is added to the diagram — like Change Priority, it is a transition from Live to Live.

The state transitions are correct, in that each action has the same effect as the definition of user object actions in the user object model.

The diagram as a whole looks sensible. It is possible to reach every state from the start point. The only state it is not possible to leave is Merged. We confirm with the customer support manager that this is what is intended — Merged is supposed to be a final state, and Merge an irreversible action.

8.5   PRACTICE TIPS

8.5.1   Example of window dynamics

The dynamic modeling technique can be applied to GUI objects such as forms and controls. Dynamic models are useful when programming the behavior of an existing control or when designing a new control. This is best illustrated by an example. In this section we will describe the dynamic behavior of a ComboBox.

8.5.1.1   The ComboBox control

A ComboBox is combination of a drop-down list and a text edit control (hence the name). Its appearance in Windows is shown in Figure 8.12. Users can either select

Fig. 8.12   A ComboBox

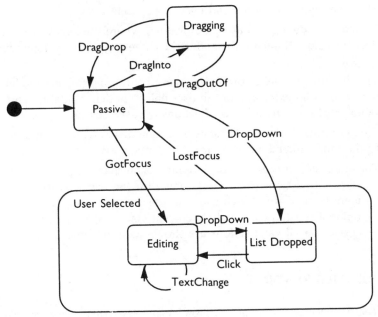

Fig. 8.13   Dynamic model for a ComboBox

the contents of the box from a drop-down list, or they can edit the text directly. The window actions which the user can perform on a ComboBox are as follows:

Event	Description
GetFocus	The user has clicked on the ComboBox
TextChange	The user has typed text into the ComboBox
DropDown	The user has clicked on the drop-down arrow
Click	The user has clicked on an item in the drop-down list
LoseFocus	The user has clicked outside the ComboBox
DragDrop	The user has dropped another object onto the ComboBox
DragInto	The user has dragged another object into the ComboBox
DragOutOf	The user has dragged the object out of the ComboBox

8.5.1.2   The dynamic model

Figure 8.13 shows a Harel statechart which describes the behaviour of a ComboBox.

8.6   SUMMARY

This chapter describes the dynamic modeling technique, which is used to investigate and document the state-dependent behavior of objects in the system. Major points include the following:

- The technique is optional and used highly selectively.
- Dynamic modeling is only recommended where the behavior of an object (i.e. the valid actions and their effects) changes significantly depending what state it is in.
- The dynamic model is produced just after the user object model, and is regarded as an extension of the user object model, validating and making more precise the definitions of actions on user objects.
- We recommend an extended state transition diagram known as a 'statechart' as the most suitable notation for a dynamic model.
- The suggested process for developing a statechart is:
  − start with actions (which are known for the user object);
  − identify states for which some actions are not valid;
  − rationalize composite and concurrent states;
  − check that all valid actions are shown as transitions.

8.7   FURTHER READING

Harel, D. (1987) 'Statecharts: a visual formalism for complex systems', in *Science of Computer Programming*, vol. 8, pp. 237–274.
The original article in which Harel defined the statechart notation and illustrated how it could be used. Well worth reading if you want to use statecharts to produce large dynamic models. Includes some additional notations not described in this chapter.

Rumbaugh, J. et al. (1992) *Object-Oriented Modelling and Design*, Prentice Hall.
The most influential text on object-oriented analysis, defining OMT (object modeling technique). This includes the Harel statechart technique as the dynamic modeling notation, and gives clear examples of states, events and actions specified in terms of effects on the state of attributes and relationships in the corresponding object model.

Browne, D. (1994) *Structured User-interface Design for Interaction Optimisation (STUDIO)*, Prentice Hall.
Recommends the use of statecharts for dynamic modeling, and discusses their use (with some interesting examples) for representing the dynamic behavior of complex windows.

9

Style guide definition

9.1   INTRODUCTION

This chapter considers the following topics:

- Why it is important to produce an application style guide.
- What a style guide consists of.
- The process of developing a style guide.

An application style guide defines the style standards for a single application system. Many organizations have style standards which apply across multiple applications, to achieve consistency between systems. This higher-level document is referred to as a corporate style guide (sometimes known as an installation style guide).

If the organization has already agreed a corporate style guide, this forms the basis for defining the application style guide. The application style guide extends and specializes the corporate style guide with application-specific details (Figure 9.2).

Style guide definition is an activity in which GUI design experience and human factors expertise are extremely important. It is one of the areas of GUI design where practitioners are most likely to require expert advice and assistance from outside the project team, e.g. from a consultancy organization. However, even if an external consultant or a human factors expert from another part of the organization is involved, it is crucial that the GUI designers and the GUI programmers in the project team are actively involved in drafting and agreeing the style guide. A multidisciplinary team is ideal, with a human factors person, one (or more) GUI designers, and one (or more) GUI programmers or technical environment experts. A senior GUI designer in the project team should take on the role of promoting the application of the style guide, and extending and maintaining it throughout the project.

The application style guide needs to be used by anyone in the project performing GUI design or GUI programming. The content and style of the guide need to be tailored to the people who will use it.

Recalling the 'usability iceberg' discussed in Chapter 1, style is only 'skin deep', it is concerned with the surface of the interface rather than what is 'in the system'. The style guide is therefore a set of standards for this interface surface, while in GUIDE it is the user object model which provides the standards for the deeper level of the system. Although appropriate and consistent style is important for usability, it is not sufficient on its own. The user wants to achieve their task goal, which means being

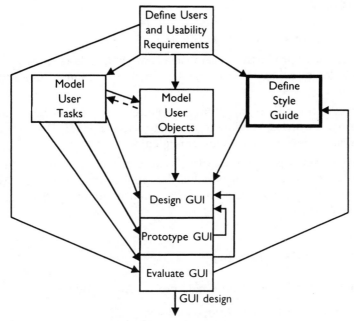

Fig. 9.1   Context for defining application style guide

enabled to perform certain actions on objects in the system. Style is concerned with the interface mechanisms, which for the users are merely a means to this end. Good style is often nearly transparent, like a glass window — the user hardly notices the interface, all their attention is on the objects they see through it (e.g. an experienced Windows user hardly notices the windows).

There is a large amount of literature on user interface style. In a book of this size it is only possible to mention some key practical issues, and to refer the reader to the sources in the Further Reading section for further information. Of particular interest are some of the books of 'guidelines'. These summarize research findings and the judgments of user interface experts on a wide range of design topics, menus, use of color, layout, typefaces, etc.

9.1.1   Objectives

- To define a standard style for the user interface in an application style guide, so that users perceive a uniform 'look and feel'. ('Look' refers to appearance, 'feel' refers to interactive behavior.)
- To select a style which enhances usability by being appropriate to the users and their tasks.

9.1.2   Benefits

- A more consistent user interface style.
- Increased user productivity, because a consistent style reduces what users need to learn and remember, resulting in shorter training time and fewer user errors.
- Reduction in the huge range of choices offered to GUI designers in color, font sizes and styles, window controls, etc. (See Appendix D for an example of a system developed without a style guide.)
- Increased developer productivity, because developers are applying and specializing standard formats rather than re-inventing new ones. Also it is more effective to start with standards, than to attempt retrospectively to achieve consistency.

9.1.3   Inputs/outputs (Figure 9.2)

The main inputs to the Define Style Guide process are as follows:

- The corporate style guide (if one exists).
- Commercially available environment style guides, such as the style guide for

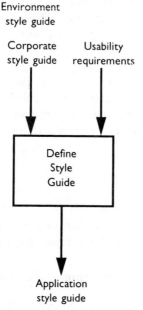

Fig. 9.2   Define Style Guide inputs and outputs

Microsoft Windows, OSF/Motif or the Apple Macintosh (see Figures 9.4—9.6 for examples of these environment styles).

- The usability requirements for the users of this application.

Other inputs include the following:

- External standards or regulations such as ISO 9241.
- Relevant literature such as user interface design guidelines or books.
- Known constraints of the target development environment and tools.

9.2   PRODUCT — APPLICATION STYLE GUIDE

An application style guide is a document defining the consistency standards which have been agreed for an application's user interface.

It often includes the following:

- References to any environment style guide or corporate style guide on which it may be based.
- Design principles (e.g. the system should offer informative feedback) (see section 9.2.1 below).
- Standards for window interaction — opening, closing, navigation between windows, etc.
- Standard window layouts, showing examples.
- A window hierarchy diagram, showing how standard windows are related to each other (see section 9.2.2 below).
- Standards for the naming, appearance, sequence and behavior of menus and push buttons.
- Standards for the use of keyboard keys.
- Standards for the use of graphics, tables and diagrams on screen.
- Standards for the use of window controls, and the mapping of data types to window controls.
- Standard names, symbols and formats.
- Standards for the use of color, type, fonts, etc.
- Standards for how common user object actions are supported.
- Standards for integration of applications or objects (e.g. standardize on Cut and Paste via the clipboard, or on drag and drop conventions such as those in Windows 95).
- A conformance checklist for critical areas of the standard.

(Some style guides include a glossary of user terms, but in GUIDE we recommend that the glossary is part of the user object model, as this is where the user's objects and actions are defined.)

Because the purpose of the application style guide is to maximize usability by facilitating an appropriate style of interaction, the style guide should be primarily user oriented rather than technically oriented. Obviously all the standards in the guide must be technically feasible on the target hardware and software platform, but the central thrust of the application style guide should be a 'human factors' objective of defining the most usable human–computer interaction standards.

For each topic distinguish between *mandatory* standards which you are committed to enforcing consistently, and *recommended* standards which are for guidance (but where the decision is left to the GUI designer's discretion).

9.2.1   Design principles

There are a number of well-established design principles which, if followed, increase the usability of a user interface. A style guide should remind designers of the design principles which are the agreed 'ground rules' for good style. Most of the environment style guides have a section on design principles, but there are also some useful ones from other sources.

The 'eight golden rules' recommended by Shneiderman (1992) are a good example of these fundamental user interface design principles, and apply both in the Define Style Guide and Design GUI activities.

EIGHT GOLDEN RULES OF DIALOG DESIGN (Shneiderman)

1. *Strive for consistency* This principle is the most frequently violated one, and yet is the easiest one to repair and avoid. Consistent sequences of actions should be required in similar situations; identical terminology should be used in prompts, menus, and help screens; and consistent commands should be employed throughout. Exceptions, such as no echoing of passwords or confirmation of the DELETE command, should be comprehensible and limited in number.

2. *Enable frequent users to use shortcuts* As the frequency of use increases, so do the user's desires to reduce the number of interactions and to increase the pace of interaction. Abbreviations, special keys, hidden commands, and macro facilities are appreciated by frequent knowledgeable users. Shorter response times and faster display rates are other attractions for frequent users.

3. *Offer informative feedback* For every operator action, there should be some system feedback. For frequent and minor actions, the response can be modest, whereas for infrequent and major actions, the response should be more substantial. Visual presentation of the objects of interest provides a convenient environment for showing changes explicitly.

4. *Design dialogs to yield closure* Sequences of actions should be organized into groups with a beginning, middle, and end. The informative feedback at the completion of a group of actions gives the operators the satisfaction of accomplishment, a sense of relief, the signal

to drop contingency plans and options from their minds, and an indication that the way is clear to prepare for the next group of actions.

5. *Offer simple error handling*   As much as possible, design the system so the user cannot make a serious error. If an error is made, the system should detect the error and offer simple, comprehensible mechanisms for handling the error. The user should not have to retype the entire command, but rather should need to repair only the faulty part. Erroneous commands should leave the system state unchanged, or the system should give instructions about restoring the state.

6. *Permit easy reversal of actions*   As much as possible, actions should be reversible. This feature relieves anxiety, since the user knows that errors can be undone; it thus encourages exploration of unfamiliar options. The units of reversibility may be a single action, a data entry, or a complete group of actions.

7. *Support internal locus of control*   Experienced operators strongly desire the sense that they are in charge of the system and that the system responds to their actions. Surprising system actions, tedious sequences of data entries, incapacity or difficulty in obtaining necessary information, and the inability to produce the action desired all build anxiety and dissatisfaction. Gaines (1981) captured part of this principle with this rule *avoid acausality* and his encouragement to make users the *initiators* of actions rather than the *responders*.

8. *Reduce short-term memory load*   The limitation of human information processing in short-term memory (the rule of thumb is that humans can remember 'seven plus or minus two chunks' of information) requires that displays be kept simple, multiple page displays be consolidated, window-motion frequency be reduced, and sufficient training time be allotted for codes, mnemonics, and sequences of actions. Where appropriate, on-line access to command-syntax forms, abbreviations, codes, and other information should be provided.

These underlying principles must be interpreted, refined, and extended for each environment.

In general, GUI designers should attempt to conform to these principles at all times. In practice there are certain circumstances where this may not be possible or desirable, notably the following:

- Where the principles conflict, and one has to be traded off against another.
- Where a principle has to be compromised in order to meet some higher priority usability requirement (e.g. access by the public with no training).
- Where it is not technically or economically feasible (e.g. Undo on every action may be very expensive, or technically impossible).

Part of the GUI Evaluation process involves using these design principles as a checklist to identify usability problems.

Many usability problems arise from violating basic design principles. So as well as bearing these principles in mind when performing GUI design, we can use them as a review criterion during usability evaluation. This is precisely the approach recommended by Nielsen in *Usability Inspection Methods* (Nielsen and Mack, 1994). Nielsen studied common usability problems, and built up a checklist of short, 'easily-checkable' review points which are in a convenient format for usability evaluation.

Not surprisingly, they emphasize many of the same points as Shneiderman's list of principles.

Nielsen's checklist of ten principles is as follows:

Visibility of system status: The system should always keep users informed about what is going on, through appropriate feedback within reasonable time.

Match between system and the real world: The system should speak the users' language, with words, phrases and concepts familiar to the user, rather than system-oriented terms. Follow real-world conventions, making information appear in a natural and logical order.

User control and freedom: Users often choose system functions by mistake and will need a clearly marked 'emergency exit' to leave the unwanted state without having to go through an extended dialogue. Support undo and redo.

Consistency and standards: Users should not have to wonder whether different words, situations, or actions mean the same thing. Follow platform conventions.

Error prevention: Even better than good error messages is a careful design which prevents a problem from occurring in the first place.

Recognition rather than recall: Make objects, actions, and options visible. The user should not have to remember information from one part of the dialogue to another. Instructions for use of the system should be visible or easily retrievable whenever appropriate.

Flexibility and efficiency of use: Accelerators — unseen by the novice user — may often speed up the interaction for the expert user such that the system can cater to both inexperienced and experienced users. Allow users to tailor frequent actions.

Aesthetic and minimalist design: Dialogues should not contain information which is irrelevant or rarely needed. Every extra unit of information in a dialogue competes with the relevant units of information and diminishes their relative visibility.

Help users recognize, diagnose, and recover from errors: Error messages should be expressed in plain language (no codes), precisely indicate the problem, and constructively suggest a solution.

Help and documentation: Even though it is better if the system can be used without documentation, it may be necessary to provide help and documentation. Any such information should be easy to search, focused on the user's task, list concrete steps to be carried out, and not be too large.

9.2.2   Window hierarchy diagram

The window hierarchy is a diagram showing window classes (i.e. the standard types of window in a system), and how they are related to each other by specialization or 'subtyping' relationships. We suggest the diagram forms part of the style guide.

The most generalized window class is at the top of the hierarchy, with window classes becoming more specialized down the hierarchy. Each window class is a more specialized version of the one above. It 'inherits' all the controls (e.g. edit fields, scroll

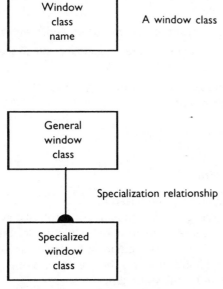

Fig. 9.3   Window hierarchy notation

bars, option buttons) and window actions (menu commands, etc.) of the more general window class, and adds some more for its own special purpose.

Notation
The window hierarchy is a simple hierarchy using the notation shown in Figure 9.3. A larger example is shown in section 9.4.

Where used

GUI Design   The application style guide is used in choosing how to represent information and functionality in the user interface.

Prototype GUI   Standard windows from the application style guide may be implemented as window templates, which are used to assist in the rapid prototyping of windows which conform to the standard.

Evaluate Usability   One of the evaluation criteria is conformance to the style standards in the application style guide.

Quality criteria

- Is the application style guide usable by developers in the sense of:
  - being well-structured;
  - being unambiguous;

-    being small enough to work with;
-    containing concrete examples?
- Is the application style guide appropriate for the users and their tasks?
- Is the application style guide relevant to and technically feasible in the target environment?
- Has the application style guide been formally agreed with users and developers as a mandatory standard?

9.3   PROCESS

9.3.1   Identify basis for style guide

Establish what the application style guide will be based on.

If the organization has a corporate style guide which is relevant for GUI systems, this is usually adopted as the basis. If there is no corporate style guide, the most sensible choice is usually to base the application style guide on the environment style guide for the target GUI environment. Figures 9.4–9.6 show examples of windows with Microsoft Windows, Macintosh and OSF/Motif styles.

Most environment style guides include the following:

- Design principles (such as those quoted above).

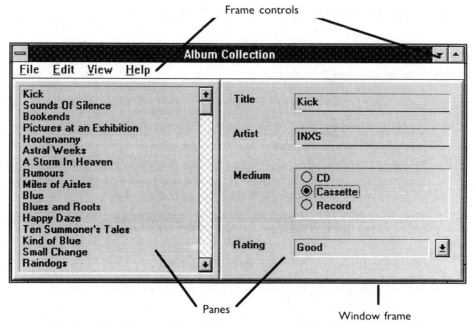

Fig. 9.4   Window with Microsoft Windows style

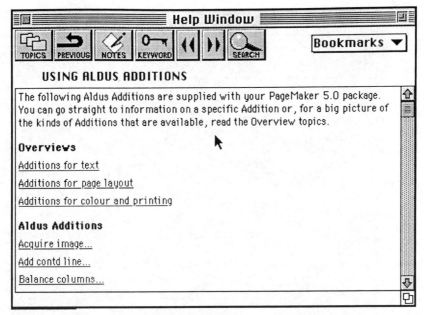

Fig. 9.5 Window with Apple Macintosh style

- Standard controls available in the environment (e.g. drop-down list, scroll bar).
- Standard menu headings (e.g. File, Edit, View, Help).
- Standard window actions (e.g. Copy, Save, Delete), showing how the dialog is managed.
- Standard highlighting and selection rules.

Identify whether there are any other national or international regulations or standards to which the user interface must conform.

(If the organization does not have a corporate style guide it may be advisable to develop one at this time, in parallel with the application style guide. This will require significant additional effort, because the corporate style guide must be sufficiently general to apply to several systems and groups of users. It may need to include different versions of the standards for different hardware or software platforms.)

9.3.2   Consider style implications of users and usability requirements

The most suitable style depends upon characteristics of users, their tasks and their usability requirements.

For example, one of the general principles of GUI design is that the user should feel he/she is in control. However, in public access systems (e.g. touchscreen airport

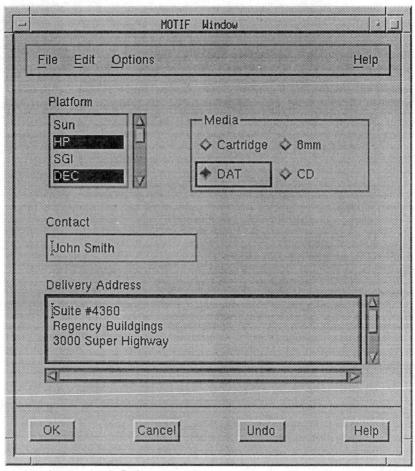

Fig. 9.6   Window with OSF/Motif style

car rental systems) where most users only use a system once and receive no training, it may be best to have a style where the system is more in control, and leads the user through the interaction.

If the users are already familiar with a particular application style, the amount of time and effort they spend learning a new application style will depend on how similar the new style is to the existing; the more similar it is, the less time and effort will be spent learning it. As a style guide developer, you should consider how much users' current knowledge of an existing system can be *transferred* to a new system. Such harmonization of styles is particularly important when people will use the new application system in parallel with other systems (such as wordprocessing).

Record any design decisions in the application style guide.

9.3.3   Review style of similar applications

In GUI design, as in various other areas of human activity, one of the most effective ways for a relatively inexperienced practitioner to achieve a good style is to study the style of an expert.

Many commercially available software packages have had a considerable investment in achieving a uniform and effective style, and the style may have evolved over time in response to customer feedback. When a new application system is being designed it is often possible to identify high-quality, commercially available systems which have similar users, tasks or functionality.

Provided that you are not going to compete with these products, it is neither a crime nor an admission of failure to adopt a style which has already proved to be successful in another system, or is familiar to your users.

For example, if you were designing the user interface to allow people to input and view fax messages on their PC, you might review several electronic mail packages to examine their style, as there are similarities in the user population and functionality.

If there are comparable systems with quite different styles, it would be useful to perform a brief comparative usability evaluation to investigate which style is more usable (see Appendix E).

9.3.4   Define window hierarchy

Define the standard window layouts for the system, including the style of controls to be used on each type of window (e.g. pull-down menus, push buttons or a mixture).

Organize these standard types of window into a window hierarchy. For each window class, define the standard behaviors which will be available (e.g. Open, Save, Minimize, OK, Cancel, Help).

Check that the window hierarchy is a true specialization hierarchy — lower windows should be more specialized, providing all the behaviors of their parents.

9.3.5   Define other detailed standards

Define all the other style issues listed in section 9.2. Working from the basic environment style guide or corporate style guide, consider how the application style guide should be more specific, by ruling out certain controls or options, including additional specialized controls or terms, or providing more detailed guidance.

Restrict controls to be used
Restrict the set of window controls to use by selecting some and excluding others. Some developers are attracted to controls because they are clever or ingenious or look 'sexy' in some way (e.g. temperature or pressure gauges). From the user's point of

view, each additional type of control in a system is an overhead, something else they have to learn and a potential source of confusion and distraction. Therefore, usability is often promoted by agreeing in advance a standard subset of controls which will be used.

Define new or specialized controls

It is sometimes appropriate to design or use special controls in addition to the standard controls defined in the environment style guide. Each such control should be defined in detail in the application style guide, including the following:

- Its appearance.
- Its window actions.
- Its selection rules.
- The states it can be in, and the valid transitions between states. The dynamic modeling technique and notation described in Chapter 8 is recommended as a practical approach to defining the state-dependent behavior of a control. Note that in this context the states are states of the interface object (e.g. selected, dropped-down) and the actions are window actions (e.g. mouse click on button). See section 8.5.1 for an example.

Color and font

Do set specific standards early for detailed choices like color and type font. Even where there is no 'best' solution, select one of the range of sensible acceptable solutions and make this the standard. This pre-empts unacceptable choices and promotes consistency. It is better to be overconstrained and subsequently to agree some exceptions than to lack guidance and have each designer make a different choice.

Map data types to controls

Consider the data types which occur in the type of application for which the style guide is intended. Decide how each data type should be mapped onto a type of window control, e.g.

- Boolean (yes/no) to a check box, e.g. ☒ **No Smoking Room**:
- Integer less than 10 to a spin button, e.g. 4

9.3.6   Validate style guide

The application style guide should be validated in various ways:

- To ensure that it is acceptable to end-users, and will result in windows which will satisfy usability requirements. This usually involves user reviews, discussion of examples, and prototyping some of the standard layouts and interaction sequences.

- To ensure that it conforms to external regulations, standards and environment style guides.
- To ensure that it is acceptable to the designers and developers. It is important to reach agreement among these people.
- To ensure that its recommendations are technically feasible in the target environment.
- It is also common to ask an expert outside the project team to review the application style guide.

This validation will lead to revisions.

9.3.7   Organize support and enforcement

To make an application style guide effective, it needs to be built into the project. There are both technical and organizational aspects to this:

- Making it productive, easy and fun to use by integrating it into the technical development environment.
- Ensuring its use by incorporating it in staff roles and procedures.

The best way of making a style guide productive to use is to integrate it into the design and development environment. This can be achieved by developing window templates that already have the standard layout, standard controls and standard functionality. To design a new window the designer starts with the appropriate template and adds specialized features. Another good idea is to configure development toolkits or libraries so that they contain all the agreed controls readily to hand (and no 'excluded' controls). Some GUI environments enable parts of the style guide to be given automated support, either by setting standard defaults, by generation of windows in standard styles, or by automatic validation that a design conforms to style rules.

Choose a form of delivery for the style guide which will maximize its use. Designers and programmers may prefer an electronic document available on their workstations to a paper one – certainly a shared electronic document on a network is easier to update regularly. Also consider including demonstration programs – GUIs are inherently visual and interactive, and an example you can 'play with' on the screen is far more informative and compelling as a standard than a paper printout with a long textual description.

Build the application style guide into your project roles and procedures. Agree who in the team will have the lead responsibility for coordinating style and for maintaining and enforcing the style guide. Ensure that the style guide has a simple checklist for its mandatory rules that is simple to use in reviews. Decide at what point(s) in your design process you will check conformance to the style guide. For example, you might make this part of a peer design review as soon as each initial window has been designed, and you might also check style guide conformance as part of one of the early usability evaluations.

9.3.8   Extend and evolve style guide

As the overall GUI design process progresses, the style guide slowly evolves. This mainly involves adding further elements, but sometimes prototyping or evaluation demonstrates that the style is not suitable, and earlier style decisions are reversed. Three common forms of extension are as follows:

- Recognition of common controls or patterns of interaction. If the same thing is done in a number of places, then incorporate it into the style guide. This is similar to identifying opportunities for reuse in object-oriented programming, though here the primary emphasis is on consistency for the user rather than productivity for the programmer.

- Documentation of major GUI design decisions. When the application style guide is first drafted (early in the project), many GUI design decisions will not yet have been made. (Some may not even have been identified as issues to be decided.) The style guide should be extended to document any subsequent decision which will affect several windows.

- Resolution of inconsistencies. During initial GUI design, prototyping and evaluation, designers and users will notice inconsistencies between different parts of the emerging design. Some of these will be tolerated, but in any cases where it is agreed to resolve the inconsistency by standardizing on one of the styles, the agreed version should be added into the style guide.

(See also section 9.5.3.)

▓ 9.4 EXAMPLE ▓▓▓▓▓▓▓▓▓▓▓▓▓▓▓▓▓▓▓▓▓▓▓▓▓▓▓▓▓▓▓▓▓▓▓

9.4.1   Identify basis for style guide

In the Helpline system example, Microsoft Windows 3.1 is identified as the target GUI environment. This is dictated by corporate standards — the organization has a large network of PCs running under Microsoft Windows, and has a corporate strategy that all new internal application systems will be Windows-based.

Consequently, Microsoft's manual *The Windows Interface: An Application Design Guide* is identified as the relevant environment style guide which the Helpline system should conform to. Conformance to this style guide should ensure that the 'look and feel' of the new system will be similar to other Windows applications, reducing the learning time.

UniSoft does not have a corporate style guide for internal systems. The project's external advisor recommends that a corporate style guide should be produced before the application

Example   171

style guide to ensure consistency across systems, but the project manager decides that this would cause an unacceptable delay to the project. In the absence of a corporate style guide, the Microsoft guide is taken as the basis for the application style guide.

9.4.2   Consider style implications of users and usability requirements

All the classes of user are experienced users of Microsoft Windows, so Windows style is familiar.

In documenting users and usability requirements, users were asked what application software they use most frequently. The answer was:

- UniSoft's own software products
- Wordprocessing (Microsoft Word for Windows)
- Electronic mail

The user interface style of the electronic mail system is not highly regarded, and the system is due to be replaced, so it is decided this should not influence the style guide. It is decided to harmonize the style as closely as possible with UniSoft's software products, and with Microsoft Word.

One of the usability requirements is that sales staff and other infrequent users must be able to use the system with only five minutes training. This will only be achievable if the system seems 'obvious' because users are able to transfer their skills from other systems.

9.4.3   Review style of similar applications

The software Helpline is a specialized type of customer support helpdesk function. Various commercially available helpdesk packages are examined, to investigate their interface style.

The most widely used style, even in the Windows systems, consists essentially of forms with views of the main objects (Customers, Queries, etc.). This is useful information. It indicates that at present the leading software houses have not discovered (or at least not yet implemented) a graphical presentation or visual metaphor that is significantly more effective than this for helpdesk work.

One of the packages has some elegant features, including an overview window which allows the manager to see everyone's workload at a glance, and to allocate work by dragging and dropping queries between advisors. We make a note of this, to consider during design whether we can use something similar.

9.4.4   Define window hierarchy

Based on the environment style guide and the standard types of window in Microsoft Word and UniSoft's software products, the window hierarchy is defined as shown in Figure 9.7.

We decide that there will be a standard type of object maintenance window (Primary Object Window), which will be similar in behavior no matter which user object is being maintained.

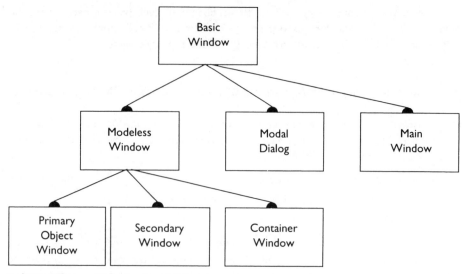

Fig. 9.7 Window hierarchy for Helpline system

The definition of each window is as follows:

- Basic Window has a size, a title bar and a system icon.

- Modeless Window has a menu bar with drop-down menus for File, Edit and Help. Having a modeless window open does not prevent the user interacting with other modeless windows.

- Primary Object Window is a modeless window used to display the main view of an object. It has a standard menu bar with File (New, Open, Save, Delete, Print, etc.), Edit (Cut, Copy, Paste, Undo), View (with a list of the available views of the object) and Help. Its layout always has the identifier (name or reference) of the object instance in the top left corner, and various controls to represent the attributes of the object (e.g. edit controls, list controls, combo controls).

- Secondary Window is used to display and edit more detailed information about an object, or a component object. It adds an Edit menu option (Cut, Copy, Paste, Undo). It is dependent on a primary window. If the primary window opens a different instance of its object, the content of the secondary window changes to display this instance. If the primary window closes, the secondary window closes.

- Container Window is a window used where the viewed object is just a container. The user has little interest in the container, but is interested in viewing and manipulating the contents, moving objects in and out of the container, etc. There is a View menu with an Include option (to set filters for which objects to display). Familiar examples of containers include file directories and product catalogues.

- Modal Dialog is used to capture additional input to perform a window action (such as number of copies to be printed, or confirmation of a deletion.) It has no menu

Example   173

bar options, but uses push button controls for <Action Name> (or 'OK') to complete the input and confirm the action, and 'CANCEL' to abort. When a modal dialog is open other windows in this application are disabled.

- Main Window has a login dialog and a set of icons, each of which represents a dependent Primary Object Window.

At this point in the design process, each window shown in the window hierarchy is a type of window, which defines the common layout and behavior which several windows may follow. One can think of it as an abstract template — in fact it is useful to draw the template, and even to implement it in the prototyping environment. Templates for Primary Object Window, Modal Dialog and Main Window are shown in Figures 9.8–9.10.

In GUI design, the window hierarchy will be extended to show the actual windows in the system, which will be further specialized versions of these general types.

9.4.5   Define other detailed standards

Use of view menu

Where there is too much information to display in one window, selection of which attributes to display will be controlled using the View menu to choose among alternative panes.

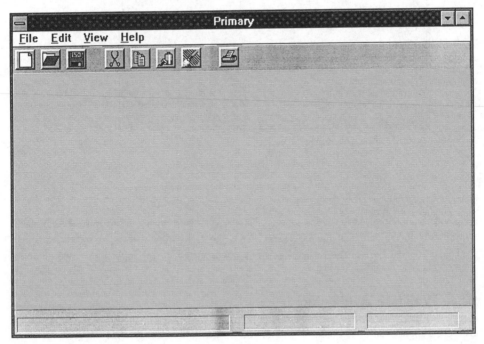

Fig. 9.8   Template for Primary Object Window

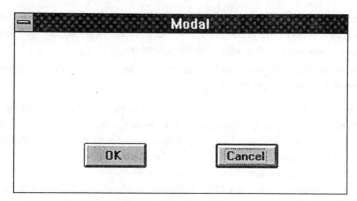

Fig. 9.9   Template for Modal Dialog

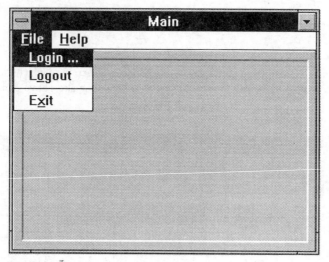

Fig. 9.10   Template for Main Window

Help style

Help will be implemented for every window. The Help subsystem will conform to the standard Windows Help 'look and feel' (i.e. black text on a white background with green hypertext links).
   (These are just two of the design decisions documented in the application style guide.)

9.4.6   Validate style guide

Our draft application style guide was reviewed by our whole design team, several Helpline advisors, and the customer support manager. Various revisions were made as a result.

9.4.7   Organize support and enforcement

As shown above, for each window class we built a standard template using our GUI prototyping tool, Microsoft Visual Basic. This integrated the style guide into the prototyping environment. We also set up libraries of the standard controls we had selected for use.

The senior designer took on the role of style coordinator. On the review procedure, we decided that reviews during initial GUI design would be informal, but that we would use Nielsen's checklist (see section 9.2.1) and check for style guide conformance as part of the usability evaluation (i.e. at the end of each design/prototype/evaluate cycle). Chapter 12 describes this.

9.4.8   Extend and evolve style guide

The style guide evolved in various ways.

One example was the icons on the tool bar. We started out with about ten icons on the standard Primary Object Window, and were pleased because we had made a productivity gain by building lots of functionality into the template which we received for free on each window built from it (e.g. New, Save, Print, Next, Prior). We later discovered that for some objects some of these controls were of no use to the user — for Queries and Problems which have a meaningless numeric reference, Next and Prior are of no interest, and are just a distraction. So we removed these from the standard template for Primary Object Window.

9.5   PRACTICE TIPS

9.5.1   Pitfalls

There are a number of pitfalls which frequently undermine the effectiveness of application style guides. Common problems include the following:

- A style guide is drafted and circulated but not properly agreed. Developers do not feel committed to it and ignore it. The best way to achieve developer commitment is to involve GUI designers and programmers in the creation and maintenance of the style guide, so that they feel identified with it and have a sense of ownership, i.e. of it being 'our style guide'.

- The style guide is not usable by developers, because the material is not well organized, or contradicts itself, or does not include examples, or is too big.

- The style guide is produced too late for the initial GUI design. It is very difficult (sometimes impossible) to change a designer or programmer's mind once they have committed to doing a design in a particular way.

- The style guide does not clearly distinguish between mandatory rules, and material which is merely guidance on good practice.

- The style guide is not enforced, either because it is too vague or ambiguous to be enforced, or because the project manager does not insist on compliance.

9.5.2   Interaction with GUI design

In some projects you do not know what the standard windows in the style guide should look like until you start the GUI design. In this situation you define what you can in the style guide, and then start the GUI design and sketch some initial windows. You identify the commonalities between these windows, and go back and define the window classes in the application style guide.

9.5.3   Dealing with exceptions

When you define a standard style and try to enforce conformance to it, there will inevitably be situations where people argue for exceptions to the standard. Sometimes there is no real basis for making an exception, it is just a designer or programmer wanting to put a stamp of individuality on a window design. In this case the senior GUI designer (and the project manager) must insist on following the style guide, or it will lose credibility.

However, it is common to encounter real exceptions. These are situations in which, although the standard style is best in most cases, some other style is better in this special case. In these situations the design team have to make a choice between the local advantage of the non-standard style, and the general advantage of maintaining consistency. It is important to be able to discuss such situations openly, and (where appropriate) to agree (and record) exceptions to the style guide. Sometimes the exception is so common that it is worth incorporating it into the style guide (i.e. use control A, unless condition C, in which case use control B).

9.5.4   Influence of previous experience

A designer's previous experience tends to influence their style. Prolonged exposure to environments like the Apple Macintosh tends to encourage a flexible, object-based style where the user is in control. In contrast, people who have become accustomed to designing screen-at-a-time mainframe transaction processing often have difficulties in adjusting to the radically different mindset required for good GUI design. We have seen one GUI system designed by ex-mainframe staff which forced the user through a twenty-screen sequence of full-screen windows, and failed to take advantage of the GUI environment at all (except for the large, brightly colored logo on every screen!).

9.5.5   Programming of window templates

Consider using a GUI development tool to specify the windows in the window hierarchy, especially if you have already chosen the development tool for your project. This will increase productivity because developers will start with a partially implemented window. Consistency will also be enforced more easily because developers are provided with predefined windows which exhibit some of the required look and feel.

The amount of effort to be invested should be related to the return you get through the use of the window hierarchy. The usefulness of the window hierarchy depends upon the tool you buy. Tools fall into two categories:

- *Copy based*   With these tools, the template window in the style guide is copied to form the basis of the new window, but thereafter the window is evolved by the developer. Most tools fall into this category, because the developer can manually copy the template. Visual Basic is a good example of this type of tool.

- *Inheritance based*   With these tools, the template window is specialized by the addition of new controls and additional behavior, but it is still linked to the original template and if that template is changed, then the windows derived from it are kept in step. This is very useful if the style guide changes after a significant amount of development has taken place. The tools based upon a full object-oriented paradigm (such as SmallTalk) are inheritance based, as well as some of the more specialized GUI development tools such as PowerBuilder.

There are variants of both these types which, when constructing a new window from the template, can be parameterized by a data source, say a database table, and specific controls added to the new window to maintain the data in the data source. These provide a very efficient mechanism for building initial working prototypes.

It is almost always worth defining standard window layouts, containing controls such as icon bars and menus. It is also worthwhile adding to the windows examples of the various controls which the developer will be using, indicating the look (color, shading) required for that type of control. Both categories of tools will repay investment in this type of preparation.

Defining standard behavior (or feel), such as the effect when a user selects a control, may also be worthwhile. The behavior of a control can be very dependent upon the use to which the control is put, and frequently the developer has to program much of the behavior on a case-by-case basis. Inheritance-based tools provide more reuse in the area of control behavior, so will better repay any investment.

Style guides built in this way can also be used to capture much of the intended system architecture, by embedding code in the window templates. Thus much of the code to implement, say, a mail-enabled application, or an ODBC connection to a server

DBMS, will already be present when a developer creates a window based on such a template. Tools are emerging which support this 'application template' approach to building systems, such as Enterprise Developer and SQL Windows Quick Objects.

9.6   SUMMARY

This chapter describes the creation of an application style guide. Major points include the following:

- The objective of a style guide is to achieve consistency of user interface style (i.e. look and feel).

- There is no single 'best' style. Choices of style are made in an attempt to satisfy the already-agreed usability requirements and user classes of the application.

- An application style guide is almost always based on the environment style guide for the GUI environment you are designing for.

- An application style guide consists of a set of standards, some of which are mandatory and some merely recommended. It should restrict the choice of window controls, colors, fonts, etc., to promote consistency.

- The process for creating an application style guide includes:
  - identifying a basis for the style guide;
  - considering usability requirements;
  - reviewing the style of related applications;
  - defining a window hierarchy;
  - defining various detailed standards;
  - validating the style guide and obtaining agreement to it;
  - organizing support and enforcement;
  - extending and evolving the style guide throughout the project.

- To be effective, the application style guide needs to be a living document, which represents the shared beliefs of the team about how the user interface should look, and which is integrated into the development environment.

9.7   FURTHER READING

Microsoft (1992) *The Windows Interface: An application design guide*, Microsoft Press.
   The Microsoft Windows 3.1 environment style guide.

Apple (1987) *Human Interface Guidelines: The Apple desktop interface*, Addison-Wesley.

IBM (1991) *Systems Application Architecture Common User Access: SAA CUA guide to user interface design* (document number SC34-4289-00), IBM Technical Publications.
   Gives overview of CUA and describes the process of interface design for CUA91.

IBM (1991) *Systems Application Architecture Common User Access: SAA CUA guide to advanced interface*

design reference (document number SC34-4290-00), IBM Technical Publications.
An alphabetic reference guide to each of the interface components in CUA 91. This is the IBM CUA environment style guide.

OSF (1991) *OSF/Motif Style Guide*, revision 1.1, Prentice Hall.

Nielsen, J. (ed.) (1989) *Coordinating User Interfaces for Consistency*, Academic Press.
Describes general approaches to achieving user interface consistency.

Nielsen, J. (1993) *Usability Engineering*, Academic Press.
An authoritative book on usability engineering, including substantial discussion of evaluation.

Nielsen, J. and Mack, R.L. (1994) *Usability Inspection Methods*, John Wiley.
An authoritative book with a chapter describing each of the main inspection and evaluation methods. The inspection principles are in Chapter 2, 'Heuristic Evaluation'.

Smith, S.L. and Mosier, J.N. (1986) 'Guidelines for designing user interface software', Report MTR − 10090, Esd-Tr-86-278, Mitre Corporation, Bedford, Mass.
An extensive and authoritative set of guidelines, mostly formulated in relation to character-based interfaces but many of which are applicable to GUIs.

GUI Guidelines (1993) Corporate Computing Inc., Sausalito, Calif.
An example of guidelines available in both book and hypertext format. Gives detailed guidance on a range of specific style and design issues.

Shneiderman, B. (1992, 2nd edn) *Designing the User Interface: Strategies for effective human−computer interaction*, Addison-Wesley.
Describes and discusses all the main interaction styles, and gives useful practical guidance.

10

GUI design

10.1   INTRODUCTION

This chapter describes how to design the graphical user interface.
  The GUI design is developed from three main products:

- The user object model
- The task model
- The application style guide

  The content of the user interface is derived from the user object model. What the user will see in windows is views of user objects, and the system will enable the user to perform actions on these objects.
  The organization of the user interface is partly object-based, and partly derived from the task model. For each task we identify which views of which objects are required to support the task, and what navigation is needed from one window to another.
  The 'look and feel' of the user interface is derived from the application style guide (Figure 10.1).
  Even though the GUI design is based on these earlier products, designing the GUI is a highly creative act which can add to (or detract from) the usability of the system. Experience of GUI design, design skills, familiarity with style guidelines, and understanding of human–computer interaction are all helpful.

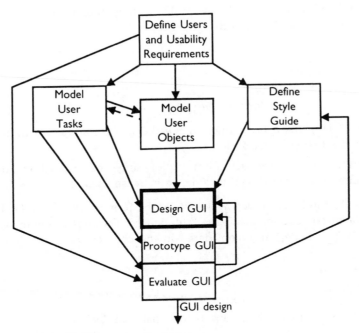

Fig. 10.1   GUIDE context for GUI design

The initial GUI design is unlikely to be acceptable, but should be reasonably well-structured and provide a sound basis for prototyping. Prototyping and usability evaluation are then used to drive a process of iterative redesign, with the GUI design being progressively improved until it satisfies all relevant usability requirements.

This chapter addresses the central question of the book: 'How do you design the GUI?'

To answer this question, the chapter introduces a number of concepts, and has more technical detail than other chapters. If you find any of the material difficult on a first reading, skip over it, and continue through to the Helpline case study in section 10.4 which shows a concrete example of the way the GUI design evolves.

10.1.1 Objective

To design the appearance and user-visible behavior of the graphical user interface.

10.1.2 Benefits

- Quickly produces a well-structured initial GUI design.
- Provides a systematic approach to design which assists inexperienced designers to achieve acceptable initial GUI designs.
- Avoids various kinds of design problem, (e.g. highly modal interfaces, fragmentation of objects in the interface).

10.1.3 Inputs/outputs

There are two main contexts for GUI design:

- Initial design, where the products from earlier analysis and modeling are used to build a first-cut GUI design.
- Redesign, where feedback from prototyping and evaluation suggests modifications to the design in order to increase usability.

If all goes well, the initial design will provide the framework for the GUI, with successive iterations of redesign making tactical changes. The emphasis in this chapter is on initial design. Redesign is considered in the chapters on prototyping and evaluation.

10.1.3.1 Initial design

Figure 10.2 shows the inputs and outputs to initial GUI design.

- *Tasks and scenarios* Tasks to be supported define the scope and context of

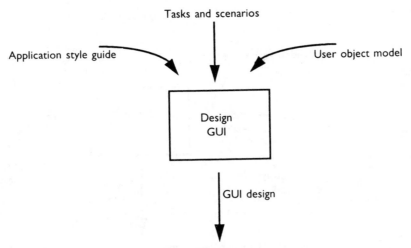

Tasks and scenarios

Application style guide

User object model

Design
GUI

GUI design

Fig. 10.2 Initial GUI Design inputs and outputs

GUI design. Task scenarios are used when defining the detailed user interaction.

- *User object model*   The objects which the user manipulates in order to achieve the tasks. If any of the user objects have dynamic models, these are also an input to GUI design.

- *Application style guide*   This defines the look and feel of the GUI. It defines standard windows which can be used as the basis for specific window designs, and a set of controls which can be used in the design.

10.1.3.2 *Redesign*

Figure 10.3 shows the inputs and outputs associated with iterative redesign of the GUI. Note that the inputs to initial design may still be valuable, but are not the major driving force behind redesign.

- *Prototype feedback*   The feedback from constructing a prototype of this GUI design. This feedback will suggest revisions to the design as a result of exploring the initially designed interface with the user.

- *Evaluation results*   Evaluation of the interface will reveal usability problems which need to be addressed. The results may be accompanied by suggested modifications in order to achieve the desired usability.

10.2   PRODUCT – GUI DESIGN

A GUI design consists of a set of windows, which comprise the interface. Each window contains a set of controls, through which the user communicates with the system,

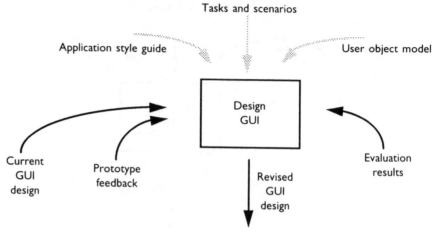

Fig. 10.3 Iterative redesign inputs and outputs

and a set of window actions. A window action is an action the user can perform on a control (e.g. click a push button) in order to achieve some effect (e.g. displaying information in the window, moving to another window).

The relationships between windows are shown by two diagrams:

- A window hierarchy diagram, which shows how windows inherit their layout and behavior from standard windows.

- A window navigation diagram, which shows how users can move from one window to another.

The design may be documented in various ways:

- in paper sketches;
- in a GUI prototyping tool;
- in textual description of window actions (e.g. in a wordprocessor document);
- in a CASE tool (e.g. to associate window controls with the entity attributes in the underlying data model).

Typically the design starts to take shape as paper (or whiteboard) sketches, and is progressively incorporated either into a (paper) design specification (which may include screen layouts captured from the prototype); or into a GUI prototype which becomes the embodiment of the evolving design.

The balance between these forms of design documentation will depend on the type of system being designed and the type of prototyping tools being used. Note, though, that because a prototype is always a partial implementation, it is important to have some design documents which record design features that have been agreed but not yet implemented.

10.2.1 Window

A window is effectively a communication channel through which the user looks to see and interact with the objects in the system (user objects). The exact nature of the windows in a GUI varies widely, depending upon the contents of the application style guide. Typically, a window has a frame, which defines its boundary, and one or more panes through which the user can view objects. The frame contains various controls (such as a menu bar), and performs various functions (such as resizing, minimizing to an iconic form, and maximizing to fill the current screen). Each pane in the window contains a number of controls through which the user interacts with the object.

Figure 10.4 shows a simple window with typical components.

10.2.2 Control

A control is a user interface object through which the user communicates with the system. Controls have three basic functions:

- To allow the user to perform actions.
- To allow the user to see the state of the objects in the system.

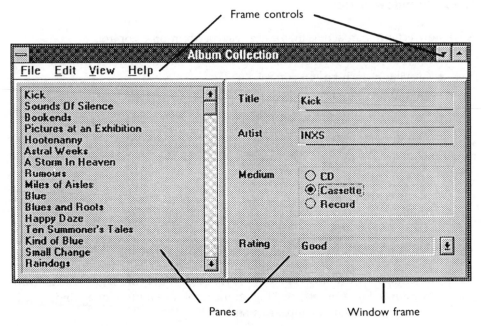

Fig. 10.4 Example of simple window with typical components

- To allow the user to enter data.

Simple controls may be limited to just one of the above functions; more complex controls allow the user to perform two or all three functions. Each GUI environment has its own set of standard controls. Some controls are available in most environments, e.g. menu, label, text edit, push button, option button, check box and scrollable list. A text edit control is an example of a control used to display and enter data. A push button control is an example of a control used by the user to perform an action.

The application style guide will provide a starting set of controls, which will probably be implemented by the GUI tools being used. There are some differences in appearance and behavior of these controls between environments; the controls for the relevant target environment should be used during specification and design. This is part of the general philosophy of conforming to the architecture and design conventions of the target GUI environment.

Increasingly, third parties are creating complex controls which allow the user far more sophisticated interaction. Some examples are graph controls, which display data as graphs rather than numbers, and grid controls, which display sets of related information. During the project, specific controls may be developed, or purchased, to meet a specific need. The new control should be incorporated into the application style guide.

10.2.3 Window action

A window action is an action that a user can perform on a control.
    Window actions include the following:

- Clicking a push-button control.
- Editing text in a text edit control.
- Dragging and dropping an icon.

Each window action will have an effect, as understood by the user, which must be documented in the design. There are three places where that documentation may appear:

- In the central definition of a control in the application style guide. Certain window actions on a control will have a standard effect, e.g. editing text in a text edit control will have the effect of changing the text it maintains.
- In the standard window types in the window hierarchy. Where a window is derived from a standard window type, the effect of performing the action is defined once (in the application style guide) but is the same in all derived windows. For example, clicking on the minimize button for a window will cause the window to appear as an icon.
- In the definition of the current window, where the effect is specific to this window. (Often the control on which the user performs the window action

does not appear in the parent window.) An example of this is clicking a push button control, where its effect may be specific to this particular control on this particular window.

The effect should be expressed in terms of user object actions (i.e. changes to the underlying objects in the user object model); and/or changes to the appearance of the windows visible in the interface.

A window may have many window actions which have the same effect. For example, a wordprocessor may have menu commands Format Paragraph Center to center a paragraph. The same effect may be obtained by a combination of keyboard keys, e.g. Alt-F, P, C; or by pressing an icon on a 'button bar'. In the case of a multiline edit control, there will be a scroll bar with which to scroll down, but simply pressing the down-arrow key may have the same effect.

When documenting these cases it is sufficient to state that the window action has the same effect as one already documented.

10.2.4 Window navigation diagram

Window navigation is concerned with how the user opens new windows and transfers focus from one window to another. These transitions are referred to as 'navigation'. The designer needs an overview of window navigation to plan how the user will be able to perform tasks requiring more than one window. A window navigation diagram shows a number of windows and the navigation paths between them.

Note that the window navigation diagram does not show every possible way that the user can move from one window to another. GUI environments allow multiple windows to be open at one time, and provide the user with mechanisms for choosing which window will be 'active' (e.g. click the mouse on a window and it becomes active). Moving between windows in this way does not have to be described using a navigation diagram.

Notation
Figure 10.5 shows the notation used in a window navigation diagram. Changes of view within a single window (i.e. changes in the panes or controls which are visible in a window) are not shown on the window navigation diagram.

Example
A simple example of window navigation is the transition from a primary window which presents a view of an object, to the modal dialog which prompts the user to select a specific object instance to open. This is shown in Figure 10.6. On completing the selection, the user is returned to the primary window (this is shown by the lower arrow).

See Figures 10.19 and 10.20, and Figure 11.6 for larger examples of window navigation diagrams.

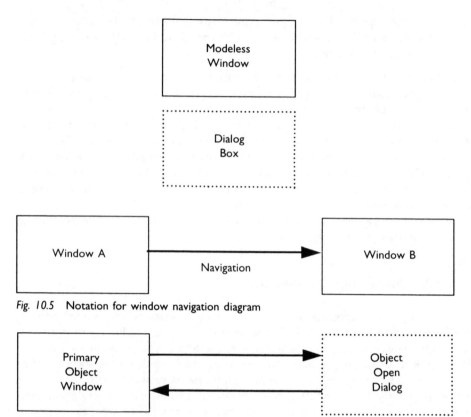

Fig. 10.5   Notation for window navigation diagram

Fig. 10.6   Simple example of window navigation

10.2.5 Window hierarchy diagram

The window hierarchy diagram defined in the application style guide forms part of the GUI design (see Chapter 9, Figure 9.7).

During GUI design the window hierarchy may be modified, or extended as new styles of window are designed.

10.2.6 Window dependencies

In the simplest case, a window is completely independent of all others and is unaffected by actions taken in any other window. Typically, however, certain windows have special relationships with each other, which can limit their independence. Most GUI environments support some kind of dependency between windows, e.g. IBM CUA defines a 'primary' window having 'secondary' windows; and a 'window group' consisting of a number of windows.

These dependencies define how the windows behave in response to certain actions. For example, when a primary window is closed (or iconized), all its secondary windows are automatically closed (or iconized). When a secondary window is closed, the primary is not affected. In contrast, the dependencies in a window group are symmetrical. Closing any window in the group closes them all.

Microsoft Windows has a related concept of 'parent' and 'child' windows.

Where used

The GUI design is used in GUI Prototyping, GUI Evaluation and eventually in the construction and testing of the production system.

Quality criteria

- Is the GUI design sufficiently complete to build a prototype and exercise it using task scenarios?
- Does the GUI design provide adequate support for user tasks, as documented in task scenarios?
- Does the GUI design assist the user to form an appropriate mental model of the system based on the user object model?
- Does the GUI design conform to the application style guide?
- Is the GUI design likely to satisfy the agreed usability requirements?

10.3   PROCESS

This section describes the process used in initial GUI design, where the products of earlier stages are used in order to design initial windows and navigation. The redesign process is rather different, in that the designer is reacting to specific problems or suggestions for change, with the emphasis on updating the design in line with those suggestions. (Chapter 11 includes discussion of redesign.)

The suggested process for initial GUI design is as follows:

1. Define views of user objects.
2. Define windows in terms of their panes, controls, layout and window actions.
3. Express task scenarios as sequences of window actions, defining navigation and revising the windows to provide usable ways of performing tasks.

10.3.1 Define views of user objects

A view of an object presents the information and functionality that a user needs to perform a particular task (or tasks) using that object. Each view should consist of a coherent group of attributes and actions. An initial view of a user object can be defined using a sketch or a GUI painting tool. During prototyping, these initial views will be revised and new views added as required.

Consider using multiple views of a user object if the following conditions apply:

- There is too much information to display in a single view.
- Some information is used frequently in tasks, while other information is not. In this case it may be best for usability to have an uncluttered main view and a supplementary view.
- A user object is used in different contexts or for different tasks. In this case a different view may usefully present the relevant information for the task. For example, the salesperson and the accountant may need different views of the Customer, and would have different user object models with Customer as a common object.
- There are graphical visualizations which will assist the user to interpret or manipulate the object more quickly or effectively. These views are sometimes referred to as metaphors, and their feasibility will depend on the facilities and constraints of the target environment. (For example, the environment may support gauges, hierarchy charts, etc., as custom controls)
- Different tasks involve different types of use. Some views are better for the user inputting new information, while other views are more effective for examining information already in the system.
- Some information relating to a user object is restricted to particular users (e.g. sensitive personal or financial data).

10.3.2 Define windows

Make a first attempt to define the appearance and behavior of the major windows. The following five activities are suggested:

1. Allocate views to windows.
2. Select controls to represent attributes.
3. Define window actions.
4. Define dependencies between windows.
5. Define window instances.

These major windows deal with objects. Windows for object actions are defined later.

10.3.2.1 Allocate views to windows

Allocate each object view to a pane in a window. In doing this, consider which views may need to be seen together, and which are never required by the user at the same time. The objective is to identify the main windows required.

As a starting point, each user object will normally have its own modeless window.

Having a modeless window open does not prevent the user interacting with other modeless windows.

The window may contain the following:

- A single view of the object.
- Alternative views of the object (the user chooses which view to display).
- Two or more views of the object visible simultaneously in different panes.

Decide which type of window from the window hierarchy to use as a basis for the window.

In general a user interface is most flexible if each window consists of one or more views of a single object. Windows showing views of multiple user objects are therefore only introduced where they are needed to make the interface more convenient for multi-object tasks.

Note whether the user object is part of a larger object (as shown by an aggregation relationship in the user object model). An object which is part of another object may have its own window, but another option is to view it in the window for its parent object (e.g. as a pane or list).

Make a first attempt at identifying windows which show multiple objects, justifying them by reference to the tasks they are required for. These windows will be refined, and further multi-object windows may be identified, when expressing task scenarios as window actions (see section 10.5.3).

10.3.2.2 Select controls to represent object attributes

For each attribute of the underlying object consider how it should be presented to the user via a control. The default mapping rules of data type to control type are defined once in the application style guide. This activity applies and refines the general rules.

A key principle is to prevent the user from entering erroneous values. This implies the following:

- Where there is a discrete set of valid values for an attribute, then the control should present only the valid values, via a drop-down list, a set of option buttons or similar multichoice control.
- If a specific format is required for attribute data, then either that format should be enforced by using a control which restricts input, or the entered data should be validated when the user attempts to save the data.
- If the user can see an attribute value but is not permitted to change it, it should be displayed in a control that is recognizably noneditable.
- When a particular attribute is not valid, the control which represents it should be disabled. Care must be taken when doing this that the user understands why the control has been disabled. (One way of achieving this is to allow the user to click on the disabled control for an explanation.)

Select the control that is appropriate for the type of attribute and for the action(s) the user will perform on the attribute in this window. Avoid using controls just because they are novel, colorful or 'sexy'.

Sketch how the controls will be laid out in the window (or use a GUI prototyping tool). Try to keep related information together.

10.3.2.3 Define window actions

Each window already has a number of window actions defined, consisting of the standard window actions for the controls which are used in the window, plus the set of window actions inherited from the parent window in the window hierarchy. In addition, window actions may be added at this point to allow the user to perform user object actions on the objects viewed. The objective is to ensure that there are sufficient window actions to enable the user to perform all the activities they need to in this window.

These additional window actions usually require extra controls, in the form of push buttons, menu options and/or a button bar (a special pane which contains a number of push button controls, whose effect is similar to choosing a menu option).

If a window action is only appropriate for a particular view, then it is best to place the control which supports the window action in the same pane as that view. Alternatively, if the control is attached to the window frame, or in a button bar, then if its window actions are not valid it should be disabled (this is sometimes called greying or dimming). As with disabling controls for invalid attributes, care should be taken that the user understands why the window action is not available.

10.3.2.4 Define dependencies between windows

Review initial windows to identify window dependencies. There are two objectives here:

- To ensure that the behavior of the proposed design is well-defined.
- To make conscious choices over dependencies which will improve usability, for example by eliminating nonessential dependencies, or ensuring that dependencies reduce user effort by 'tidying up' the interface.

Window dependencies are normally used where one window is used to view an object which is part of (or contained in) an object in another window. Window dependencies can often be identified by asking the following questions:

'If this window is closed, should any other windows be affected?'

and

'Must some other window be open before I can open this window?'

and

'If I select a different object instance in this window, are any other windows affected?'

Window dependencies should be defined using the terminology of the specific GUI environment (e.g. Microsoft Windows, IBM Presentation Manager) and implemented using environment-specific mechanisms. Careful use of window dependencies can ensure consistency of interface behavior while reducing effort on both window action specification and implementation.

10.3.2.5 Define window instances

For each window decide whether the user should be able to have more than one instance open at one time. This largely depends on whether the user needs to interact with several instances of the underlying user objects at one time, and whether you can see more than one object instance in a single window.

There are three main possibilities:

- Only one instance of the user object exists, viewed in one window (e.g. the system object, and the system window).
- Multiple instances of the user object exist, viewed one at a time in a single window instance. In this case the window is used to view one user object instance, then the same window is reused to view another object instance. It is never possible to open a second instance of the window.
- Multiple instances of the user object exist, viewed in multiple window instances. In this case each object instance has its own window. When the user needs to see another object instance in the interface, an additional window is opened, without affecting the contents of windows already open. (It is useful to make a note of the number of instances of the window which are expected to be open on the screen at once.)

If the user needs to see more than one instance of a user object at the same time for some task, then consider the third option. (Another alternative is to use a window which has the objects in a list format.)

Otherwise, choose the second option because (i) it will be less confusing for the user, as there will be fewer windows open at once; (ii) the user has less clutter to clear; and (iii) the interface is less complex to develop.

Window multiplicity is a property of the relationship between a window and a user object, and should be specified for each modeless window.

An option which is not discussed above, and which is not recommended, is to have two separate window instances viewing a single object instance.

10.3.3 Express task scenarios as window actions

This step is performed interactively with the user. Task scenarios are walked through the initial windows, in order to enrich and validate the initial GUI design before the software prototype is built. The objective is to shape the evolving GUI design so that it supports user tasks. If tasks are not well supported, the GUI design is extended or restructured as required.

In this step, scenario scripts (i.e. sequences of user object actions representing task scenarios) are expressed as sequences of window actions. Windows and window actions are revised as necessary so that each scenario is a natural and convenient window action sequence.

Note that we are *not* recommending that these sequences of window actions are formally documented. The product is improvement to the GUI design, not a mass of detailed documentation which would not be cost-effective to produce or maintain.

10.3.3.1 Define window navigation

Users often need to move between windows to perform tasks. Users' navigation requirements are identified from the sequences of user object actions, which reflect particular task scenarios.

Where a task scenario includes two or more objects, the user object action sequence shows when the user needs to move from one object to another. Window navigation design is concerned with defining convenient and natural ways of moving from one window to another in the interface. Generally navigation takes place as a side effect of performing specific user object actions such as dragging a control from one window to another to associate two user objects, or opening an object in a list box for more detail. There is usually a mechanism supplied by the GUI environment to allow the user to force navigation, such as clicking with the mouse button on a window frame.

For each task scenario involving two or more objects, review the relevant windows and navigation paths between them on the window navigation diagram. Using the diagram, explore and evaluate alternative navigation paths with the user. If navigation is clumsy and the task is high-volume and/or time-critical, redesign the windows. Allocating views of two or more objects to one window can often reduce navigation. However, there is a trade-off here. A multi-object window designed for a specific task is often less suitable for use in other tasks than a single-object window.

Navigation of object relationships

Related objects for each user object are shown in the user object model. For each related object consider its usage in tasks to assess whether the user:

- needs to navigate from the related object to the current object;
- needs to navigate from the current object to the related object;
- needs to navigate explicitly in both directions;
- does not require direct navigation.

Define window actions to perform all navigation, and show the planned navigation facilities in the window navigation diagram.

Moving between views of a single object

Where there are multiple alternative views of an object, the object window will normally have View menu options allowing the user to change from one view to another. This is not really navigation, but is similar for the user.

The number of views of an object required for a single task should be minimized. Each change of view is a window action which makes the sequence of window actions longer and more complex.

10.3.3.2 Object action to window action

It must be possible to achieve each user object action using window actions, such as pressing a button, editing a control, selecting a menu, double-clicking, dragging, etc.

There are two possibilities:

- A user object action requires several window actions. For example, in a wordprocessor, 'Save Document with new name' (one user object action) becomes:
  - click on 'File' menu option;
  - click on 'Save As ...' menu option (opens dialog box);
  - select required directory in list (with perhaps some scrolling);
  - type required file name;
  - press OK.

  (i.e. five window actions).

- The effect of a single window action is to perform a user object action. For example:
  - the effect of the window action 'Edit Customer Address' in a multiline text edit control is to perform the user object action 'Update Customer Address'.

Each window action is allocated to one or more views, paying attention to the validity of the window action, if it is not applicable to all views.

As soon as the user object actions in a task scenario have been mapped into window actions, the scenario can be prototyped.

This step identifies additional window actions, and may revise the required behavior of window actions.

10.3.3.3 Define modal dialogs

We have already defined the 'object' windows. At this point we identify and define the 'action' windows, for which we use the Microsoft Windows term 'modal dialogs'. When the current window is a modal dialog, no other windows in the application are accessible. When the modal dialog is closed, the user is returned to the window from which the modal dialog was invoked.

Some user object actions are best implemented as a window action sequence using a modal dialog. Three common situations are as follows:

- Additional information is required to perform the user object action (e.g. input of parameters, selection of a target object from a list).
- The user object action involves two or more steps, which must all be performed together (or all cancelled) before other work can be done.
- An explicit confirmation or authorization step is required for an action (e.g. to confirm a delete action).

Overuse of modality reduces user control, so modal dialogs are only used where necessary. In particular, sequences of modal dialogs should be avoided.

The following needs to be done for each modal dialog:

1. Identify a suitable window class from the window hierarchy to use as a basis for this one. (There is often an environment standard.)
2. Define the full information content and controls for editing or display.
3. Define the window actions.
4. Consider how the dialog fits into the window navigation diagram.

The extent of use of modal dialogs is an important aspect of application style. The general approach should be agreed in advance and documented in the application style guide. This activity applies and interprets the general approach.

Whether or not confirmation dialogs are required depends on usability requirements concerning error prevention. There is a trade-off here − confirmation dialogs reduce error rates, but increase keystrokes and time to perform a task.

■10.4 EXAMPLE

This section develops the GUI design for the Helpline case study.

The windows are shown sketched by hand, both to be realistic (this is what we actually did) and because it is what we recommend. During the GUI design process, sketching is often the most effective initial medium. It is very quick, it is recognizably only an unfinished draft, and there is little resistance to making changes and even redrawing completely.

You can use a GUI prototyping tool for the first draft design, but our experience is that when someone has invested time and effort (even an hour or two) in preparing something that looks like a finished window design, there is a danger that they will start to defend it, rather than encouraging criticisms and suggestions that lead to worthwhile change.

10.4.1 Define views of objects

The user object model for the Helpline system was developed in Chapter 7 and the diagram is reproduced in Figure 10.7.

We examine each user object to identify what views are required.

Example   197

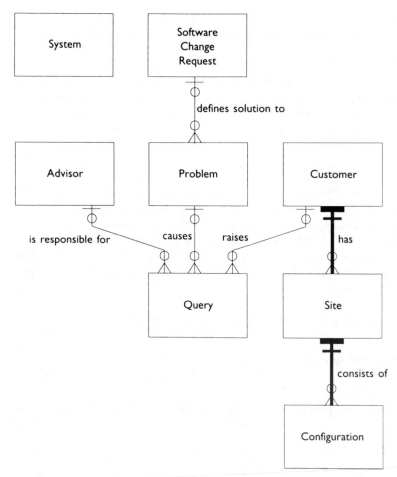

Fig. 10.7 Helpline user object model

Customer
There is too much information to show conveniently in one window, so we have to divide it into alternative views.

Customer information is important at the beginning of a customer query — from the task model (Chapter 6, Figure 6.5) we can see that the required information is Customer Name, Site, whether 'On-Maintenance' and Previous Queries. As this task is high volume and time critical we group the required information into a view, which we think of as a 'Query' view.

Looking at the attributes of the Customer object, we identify that Address, Phone Number, FAX Number, etc., can be grouped into a second view — a 'Contact Information' view.

Site
This just requires a single view showing all the information. There is not much information, and the task contexts do not require any special views.

Configuration
This requires a single view showing all the information (for the same reasons as Site).

Query
Most of the information on a Query can be displayed in a single view. The only problem is that there are two large pieces of textual information, the Event History (history of phone calls, management actions, etc.) and the Technical History. It is acceptable to put these in alternative views because usually a user is either concerned with solving the technical problem or reviewing the managerial history of a query.

Problem
All the information about a Problem can be displayed in a single view. This is adequate for creating new Problems and for examining the stored information on a single Problem.

However, there is another important task context which requires a different view. We know that the Resolve Customer Query task involves attempting to identify the Problem that is causing the symptoms the Customer is reporting. This task is critical so we note that we will require a Problem Identification view of Problem, which provides a summary of several problems.

Advisor
All the information about advisor can be displayed in a single view.

10.4.2 Define initial windows

Window hierarchy
The standard window types in the window hierarchy (in the application style guide) are used

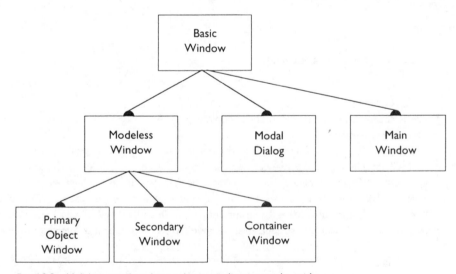

Fig. 10.8   Helpline window hierarchy in application style guide

Example   199

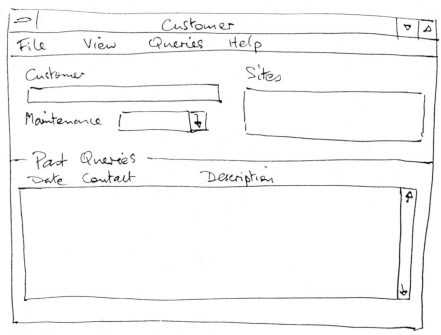

Fig. 10.9   Initial Customer window — query view

to guide the initial window design, so the window hierarchy from Chapter 9 is reproduced in Figure 10.8.

Customer

The Primary Object Window was defined with the intention of being the standard type of window for maintaining user objects.

There is no reason why Customer is exceptional, so we use a Primary Object Window for Customer, and allocate the two views we discussed in section 10.4.1 as alternative views. This is shown in Figures 10.9 and 10.10.

Note how the user object attributes are mapped to controls:

- Customer is represented as a text edit control.
- Address is represented as a multiline text edit control.
- Maintenance is represented as a pull-down list control (Figure 10.11), which assists the user in selecting a valid value (and prevents the input of invalid values).

Sites is represented as a scrollable list control, and Previous Queries and Contacts are also scrollable lists.

The initial Customer window already has some initial window actions. Some of these come from the window hierarchy (in the application style guide), e.g. Open, Save, Next, Prior, Print, and Cut, Copy, Paste. Others are implied by the standard behavior of controls, e.g. scroll list of sites, and set Maintenance value using pull-down list control.

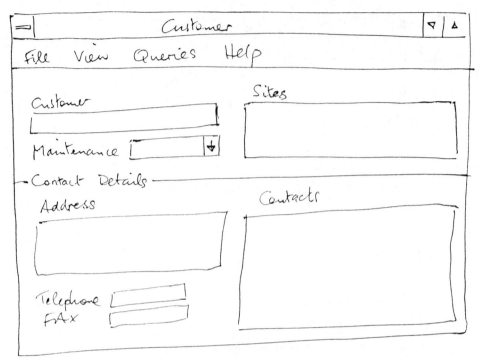

Fig. 10.10   Initial Customer window — contacts view

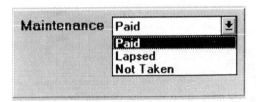

Fig. 10.11   Example of pull-down list control

See section 10.4.3.2 for a more complete example of window actions.

We consider how Customer window instances will be related to Customer object instances. It is not necessary to have two Customer windows open at once, so we will only ever have one Customer window instance, and will reuse this window when we open a new Customer instance.

The Customer window is dependent upon the Helpline system window — in other words if we iconize the Helpline window, we iconize the Customer window. If we close the Helpline window, we close the Customer window.

We proceed in similar fashion through all the user objects to define initial windows. All the initial windows are shown below to give an overall impression of the system, but only interesting features are discussed.

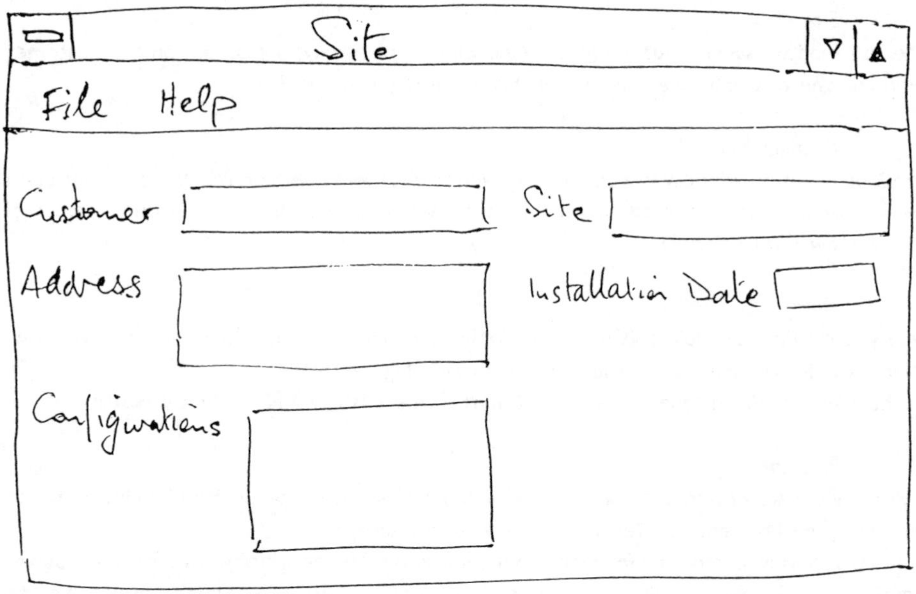

Example   201

Fig. 10.12   Initial Site window

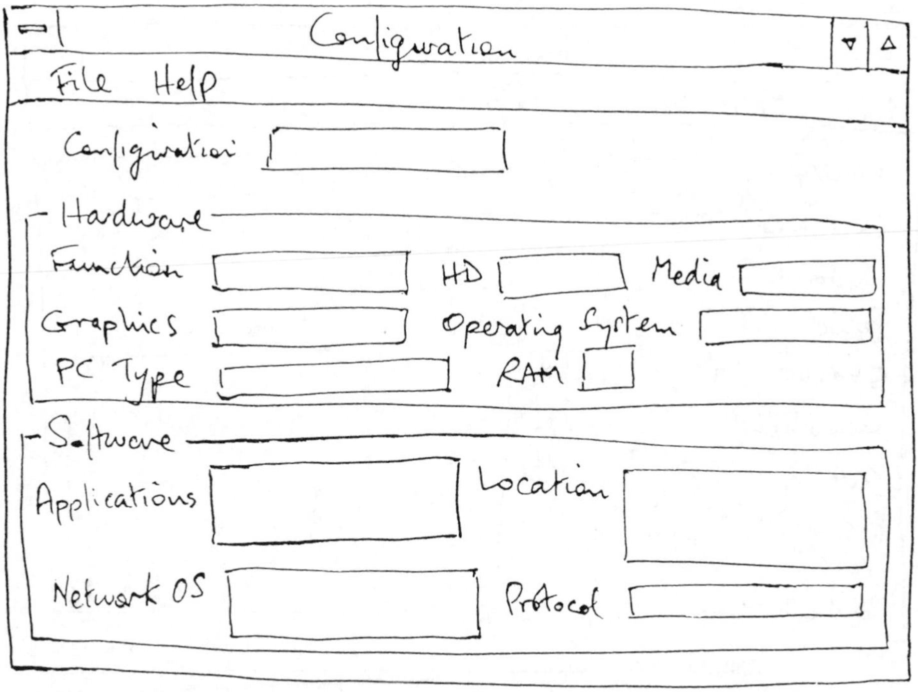

Fig. 10.13   Initial Configuration window

Site

The Site window is a secondary window (see window hierarchy) dependent on the Customer window. There is only one instance of this window (Figure 10.12).

Configuration

The Configuration window is a secondary window (see window hierarchy), dependent upon the Site window (and indirectly upon the Customer window). There is only one instance of this window (Figure 10.13).

Query

Query uses a Primary Object Window. It is only dependent upon the Helpline system window. There is only one instance of the Query window (Figure 10.14).

The View menu on Query has two options: Event History and Technical History.

Problem

A Primary Object Window similar to the Query window is used for the Problem maintenance window. (The Problem maintenance window is not shown.)

A separate view is required for Problem Identification. The design objective for the Problem Identification window is to allow advisers to identify one or more known problems which might cause the symptoms the Customer is reporting. There could be hundreds of Problems in the

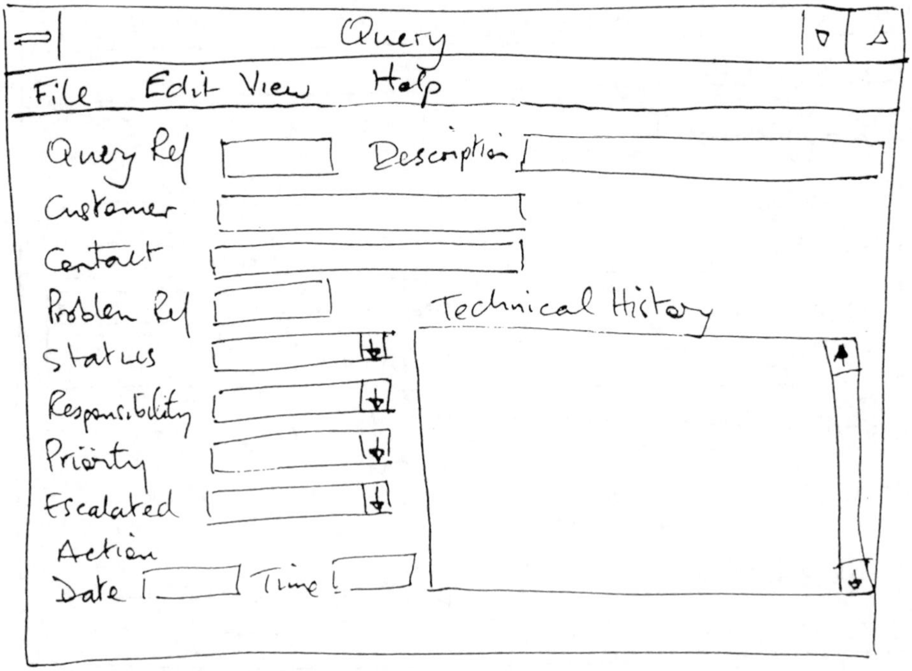

Fig. 10.14   Initial Query window

Example   203

system, and the search for the relevant one may have to be performed in stages — identifying candidate Problems and then checking each one in turn.

We want to have a very flexible mechanism for this Problem Identification task, but at the same time we want to have a familiar (and if possible standard) mechanism, to maximize usability.

Reflecting on standard Microsoft products, we recognize that this Problem Identification task of 'looking for a needle in a haystack' has a direct parallel in the Microsoft Windows help system. A help system often has a large amount of information, and the task is to find the portion that is relevant to a particular situation. The standard solution provided for this is a Search dialog. The user types the initial character(s) of a keyword, selects a keyword (or phrase) from a list, and is shown a summary list of the topics related to the keyword. Selecting one of these topics gives further information on the topic.

We decide that this Search approach will be effective for the Problem Identification subtask, and familiar to Windows users. The initial Problem Identification window is shown in Figure 10.15.

Advisor

A Primary Object Window is used to view an advisor. The information of interest is the list of queries which the advisor is currently responsible for resolving.

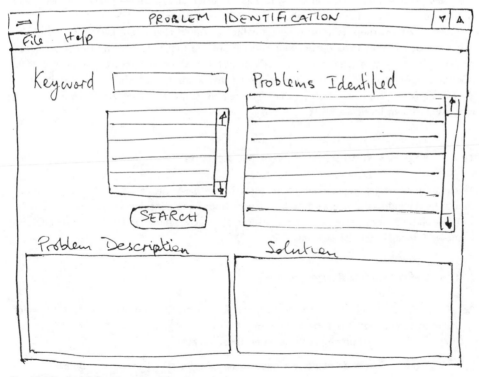

Fig. 10.15   Initial Problem Identification window

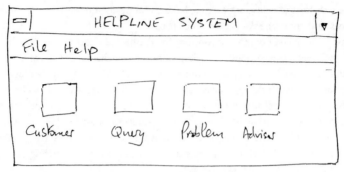

Fig. 10.16   Initial Helpline System window

The Advisor window is only dependent on the System window. It might be important to have two advisor window instances open at the same time. We defer a decision until we consider in detail how the window will support the tasks.

The Advisor window is discussed further and illustrated in Chapter 11.

Helpline system

It is useful to think of the system as a whole as an object, and to think of views of this object and actions on it (e.g. Backup Database, Print Usage Statistics).

In some systems there is a 'root' object, which all other objects are part of or related to (e.g. the Document in a wordprocessing application) and the system shows this root object. In the Helpline system (and in most database systems) there are several top-level objects (Customers, Advisors, Problems, Queries) rather than a single 'root' object, so a sensible top-level view of the system is to indicate that all these objects are 'in the system'. An initial system window is shown in Figure 10.16.

10.4.3   Express scenarios as window actions

The initial window design provides a basic set of object-based modeless windows. Attempting to use these windows to deal with task scenarios leads us to consider window navigation, the way that object actions are achieved by sequences of window actions, and the need for additional windows (especially modal dialogs).

10.4.3.1   Define window navigation

Recall the relationships between the user objects Customer, Query and Problem. (A fragment of the user object model is shown in Figure 10.17.)

Consider the navigation required between these objects:

- From a Customer object we need to navigate to that Customer's Queries.

Example   205

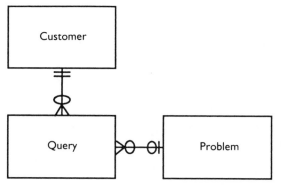

Fig. 10.17   Part of user object model for Helpline system

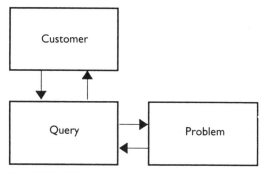

Fig. 10.18   Window navigation diagram

- From a Query we need to navigate to the Customer who raised the Query.
- From a Query object we need to navigate to the Problem which caused the Query.
- From a Problem we need to navigate to all the Queries caused by this Problem.
- In contrast, there is no direct relationship between Customer and Problem, so there is no navigation requirement in either direction.

The resulting window navigation links are shown in the window navigation diagram in Figure 10.18.

Resolve customer query − scenario 1

This high-volume and time-critical scenario script was developed in Chapter 6, section 6.4.6.

Consider the window navigation required for the scenario, as shown in the window navigation diagram in Figure 10.19.

Unfortunately this structure of windows and navigation does not support this critical scenario well.

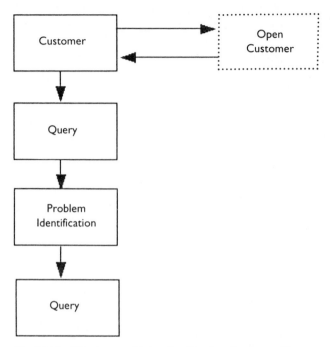

Fig. 10.19 Window navigation for Resolve Customer Query

Open Customer

Examine Customer Details

Create new Query

(*problem point*)

Identify Problem

Complete Query Details

Save Query

At the 'problem point' above, a new Query has been created and the Query window opened, displaying a Reference and the Customer Name. The problem is that this window does not support the user's task goal — the advisor wants to identify the problem as quickly as possible, and this window does not provide the information or functionality to assist with this.

We resolve this by modifying the GUI design, combining a very slim view of the newly created Query into the Problem Identification window, and allowing the advisor to navigate directly from Customer to Problem Identification as shown in Figure 10.20.

The progression through the user interface now corresponds very closely to the progression through the task scenario, with each window providing the information and/or actions to support a particular subtask.

Example   207

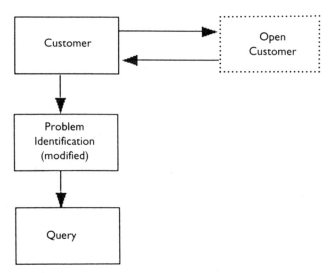

Fig. 10.20   Revised window navigation diagram for Resolve Customer Query

The revised design for the Problem Identification window is shown in Figure 10.21.

10.4.3.2 Object action to window action

The Problem Identification window (Figure 10.21) has four panes:

- A view of the Query.
- A pane to define the search criteria.
- A pane containing a list of Problems which meet the search criteria.
- A pane showing the textual description of the selected Problem.

Some of the window actions for the Problem Identification window are described below.

For the Problem Identification window, many window actions are defined purely by the nature of the controls, and consequently would not need to be described specifically for this window. Two specific examples are shown in Figure 10.22.

Some window actions are defined because this window is specialized from 'Modal Window' in the style guide for this project (Figure 10.23).

Lastly, there are window actions which are specific to this window (see Figure 10.24).

The Resolve Customer Query scenario has object actions which need to be expressed in terms of window actions.

Some object actions are achieved by very simple window actions. For example, Associate (an action on Query to link it to a specified Problem) is expressed simply by pressing the push button control labeled 'Associate' (window action 'Associate'). Note that this button has been positioned in the Query pane because it is an action on Query (Figure 10.21).

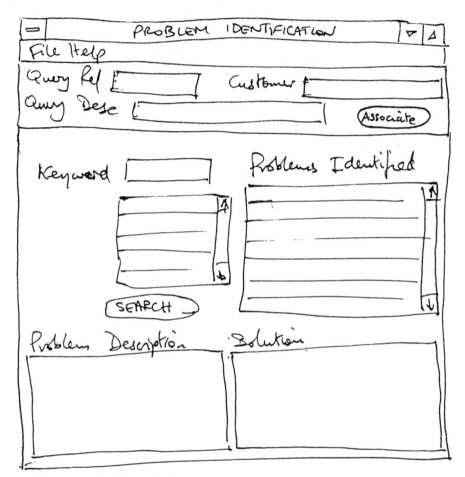

Fig. 10.21   Revised Problem Identification window

Identify Problem is a simple user object action on Problem, but requires several window actions.

The sequence of window actions for the Identify Problem action is (expressed in terms of the window actions in Figure 10.24) as follows:

1. Position in Search window.

2. Select Keyword.

3. Show Problems. -

4. Select Problem.

Example   209

Window action	Effect	How to perform the window action
Edit text	Change the text in the Text Edit Control	Type characters into the control
Select list item	Select an item in the List Box (which becomes highlighted)	Click on the desired item in the list box

Fig. 10.22   Window actions defined by controls

Window action	Effect	How to perform the window action
Move	Move the window on the screen	Click on the frame of the window and drag-and-drop the resulting outline
Move	Move the window on the screen	Click on the minus control to drop the menu and select Move. Drag-and-drop the resulting outline
Close	Close the window	Double-click on the minus sign control on the window frame
Close	Close the window	Click on the minus control to drop the menu and select Close

Fig. 10.23   Window actions defined in the style guide

10.4.3.3 Defining modal dialogs

Some object actions need an additional modal dialog to be introduced.

For example, Merge is an action on Problem which allows one Problem to be merged with another. (This is necessary if a duplicate Problem has accidentally been created.)

The Merge action requires the user to supply some additional information — the Problem to be merged with, and optionally a textual comment. A modal dialog is added to the GUI to enable the user to enter these (Figure 10.25).

In addition, the Merge action is not reversible, so the system needs to warn the user and ask the user to confirm the merge. This requires another modal dialog (Figure 10.26).

This section has shown examples of initial design. Examples of redesign are given in Chapter 11, section 11.4.

Window action	Effect	How to perform the window action
Associate	Associate the selected problem to the current Query	Click the Associate button
Position in search window	Position the user in a chosen part of the keyword list	Type the keyword initial letter(s) into the search keyword control (the list moves to display keywords with this initial letter). Note that this is additional behavior of the Edit Text window action defined above
Select keyword	Select a search keyword	Click on a keyword in the search criteria pane (this action is almost redundant with the basic definition of Select List Item in the first of these tables)
Show problems	Show the set of problems associated with the current keyword (the short descriptions of the identified problems are displayed in the Problem list)	Click the Show Problems button in the search criteria pane
Show problems	Show the set of problems associated with the current keyword	Double-click the current keyword in the search criteria pane
Select problem	Select a problem from its short description (the textual description of the selected problem is then displayed)	Click on a problem in the problem list pane
Cancel	Stop identifying a problem and return to the previous window	Click on the Cancel button
Cancel	Stop identifying a problem and return to the previous window	Click on the minus control to drop the menu and select Close (note that this is additional behavior of the close window action from the previous table)

Fig. 10.24 Window actions defined specifically for this window

10.5   PRACTICE TIPS

10.5.1 Simplicity

In initial window design we recommend starting with simple, standard, single object based windows. These are easy to learn and flexible to use. A common mistake made

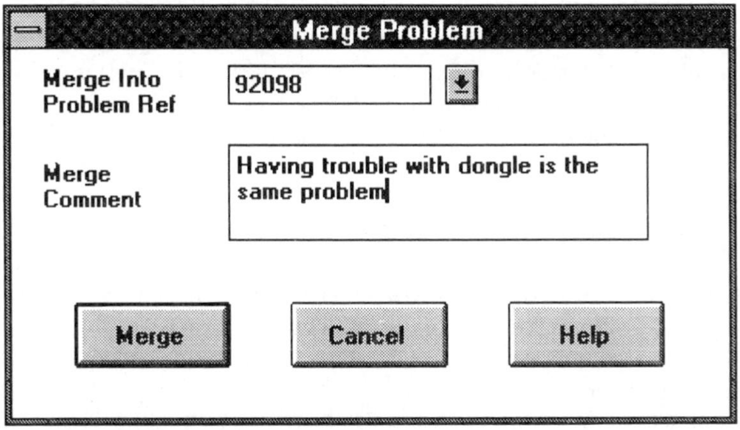

Fig. 10.25   Modal dialog

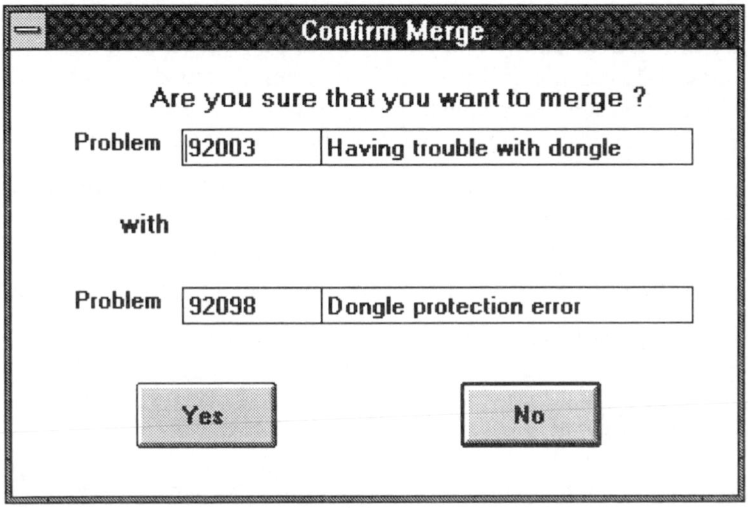

Fig. 10.26   Confirmation modal dialog

by inexperienced designers is to try to make a single window do too much, with the result that it is complex and difficult to use. Start with something very simple and then restructure and add in extra functionality only where it is important to support real tasks.

10.5.2 Multiple window actions

Providing two or more interface mechanisms (i.e. window actions) to achieve a particular effect is an important design approach for achieving high usability. It allows a user to select the mechanism which is most convenient at his or her current level of knowledge or skill and in his/her current task context. Inexperienced users often prefer explicitly labeled actions, even if they take a little longer. Users who perform an action repeatedly prefer a 'shortcut' code because it is faster, even though they have to learn and remember it.

10.5.3 Completeness of GUI design

People often ask us 'How do you know when the GUI design is complete?'

In an iterative design process the early designs are known not to be complete — they are inputs to prototyping and evaluation, so they only need to be complete enough to be useful inputs.

Completeness is an issue with the final GUI design. A GUI design is complete when you have evaluated a realistic prototype with real users, and are confident that any major usability problems have been eliminated and that the main usability requirements will be satisfied by the production version. The second criterion for completeness is that the GUI design documentation (combined with the prototype) must provide sufficiently complete, consistent and unambiguous definition of the design for the production system to be constructed and tested. The amount of formality and detail required depends on various factors, including the following:

- Whether the same team will build the production version. (If there is a handover to another team who have not been personally involved in the design and prototyping, more detailed documentation is required.)
- The skills and experience of the team who will build the production version.
- The complexity of the interface.

10.5.4 Consistency of views

An important consistency issue arises where a user can see more than one view of an object, or where two objects overlap and the user can see the overlapping part in two different windows. It is vital that the two views do not give the user conflicting information about the state of the object.

Suppose, for example, a particular customer's name and address are visible to a user in two windows at once. If the address is edited in the first window, the two views will contradict each other unless the second window is promptly updated, and the user is likely to become confused. Another example is where an object is visible as an element in a list view, and in a single-object view. If the object is deleted in one window, it must disappear in the other, to preserve the coherence of the user's mental model. Such automatic updating of other windows is referred to as notification.

Design of a standard notification scheme is an important part of GUI program design and client—server design, and includes questions of maintaining consistency between several users on different workstations. (Notification is sometimes referred to as 'rippling', because updates appear to 'ripple' from one window to another.)

A related issue is where controls show related information, such as a set of figures and a total. Either use a control which captures all of the information, e.g. a grid control with a total row, or make sure that changes to any of the figures ripple through to the control showing the total.

The need to maintain consistency between multiple views can make both a GUI specification and its implementation significantly more complex, and lead to performance problems.

10.5.5 Use of color

Color can be used to enhance the attractiveness of a GUI, and sometimes other aspects of usability. However, it should be used with caution, as its overuse or abuse may cause usability problems.

Color is not essential to usability — for several years the Apple Macintosh competed effectively with more colorful but less usable GUI systems. If you examine leading GUI office tools today (wordprocessors, spreadsheets, etc.), you will see that most make very little use of color.

Color is a very powerful visual stimulus, and can be used to attract the user's attention to an important piece of information, such as an error or warning message. Note, though, that this makes it harder for the user to focus on other information on the screen.

Color can be used to signal a context, for instance help and error messages (which can be confused by the novice user) may appear in differently colored frames.

Another appropriate use of color is to make distinctions between items. For example, in a list control, color can be used to distinguish the selected item(s) from the other items. Similarly, in an electronic mail in-tray, the 'new' items (to which we wish to draw the user's attention) may be a brighter color than the older items.

Consistency is important in the use of color, and should be managed using the application style guide. Take the standard use of color in your GUI environment as your starting point (e.g. the standard color for a window title bar). Colors tend to be culturally associated with meanings, e.g. red for stop or danger, or (on a map) blue to indicate water, and where relevant you should use colors in harmony with these meanings.

Take care to avoid foreground/background color combinations which are hard to read, bearing in mind that different terminals will give different shades of color, and that nearly 5 percent of the population suffers from some color blindness. Also, some GUI systems need to be used on monochrome PCs. In view of these issues, it is often safest to make color a secondary cue — i.e. the user can obtain adequate information for their task from text, size or shading, and the color information is technically redundant.

10.5.6 Containers and filters

Some user objects are primarily containers, in that the most interesting and important thing about the object is its contents, which is typically a set of objects. Common examples are folders and directories, price lists and catalogs.

There are several standard styles of window which are suitable as views of the contents of a container. Usually the contents are represented either as a list, or as a collection of icons organized in two dimensions. In either case, there is the question as to whether the user needs to be able to apply some kind of filter to the contents, i.e. to view all the objects of a specified type or status and 'hide' all the others. (For example, in an electronic mail system, the user may select a filter to view 'unread' items only.)

If the contents view is presented as a list, the user may require options to present the list sorted into various specific orders. (For example, mail could be sorted by date, or by who sent it.)

10.6   SUMMARY

This chapter is about designing the GUI. Major points include the following:

- The objective is to design an initial GUI which:
  - supports user tasks;
  - presents the user's objects clearly;
  - conforms to the style guide;
  - meets usability requirements.
- GUI design should be iterative, with each design iteration being prototyped and evaluated. Plan for at least three iterations.
- The GUI design product consists of a definition of the appearance and user-visible behavior of the user interface. It includes:
  - window designs;
  - window controls;
  - window actions;
  - window navigation diagram;
  - window hierarchy diagram.
- The process of initial GUI design involves:
  - defining views of user objects;
  - defining initial windows based on these views;
  - expressing task scenarios in terms of these windows, including window

navigation and modal dialogs;
  - revising the windows and window actions to provide users with good task support.

- Redesign is driven by usability problems discovered during prototyping or evaluation, or by failure to achieve usability requirements.

10.7   FURTHER READING

Shneiderman, B. (1992) *Designing the User Interface: Strategies for effective human–computer interaction*, Addison-Wesley.
One of the classic books on user-interface design, recently updated. Very readable, covers a wide range of user interface styles and issues, includes good practical advice.

Hix, D. and Hartson, H.R. (1993) *Developing User Interfaces: Ensuring usability through product and process*, John Wiley.
This book has a summary of GUI design components and guidelines, and an attractive little case study showing how a GUI design evolves, starting as views of objects and being refined to support tasks and satisfy usability requirements. It also contains instructions for a case study exercise which is suitable for a small group of colleagues to work through together.

Browne, D. (1994) *Structured User-interface Design for Interaction Optimisation (STUDIO)*, Prentice Hall.
STUDIO has some useful material in Chapter 3 'Task Synthesis' for designing interaction with complex windows, including examples of how to use Harel statecharts in GUI design.

Laurel, B. (ed.) (1990) *The Art of Human–Computer Interface Design*, Addison-Wesley.
A very readable and interesting collection of short papers on various aspects of interface design, by many of the leading writers on interface design. Includes plenty of practical tips and insights from experience. Includes chapter from Apple with a detailed discussion of the use of color in GUI design.

GUI prototyping

11.1   INTRODUCTION

This chapter describes the GUIDE recommended approach to GUI prototyping. The process consists of building a prototype and informally investigating whether it is usable. This identifies usability problems and suggestions for improvement. The prototype is progressively evolved by incorporating solutions to the usability problems, and other suggested improvements.

The product of the prototyping process is a prototype, which is subsequently evaluated for usability (see Chapter 12). Defects uncovered by the evaluation process are fed back into the next iteration of redesign and prototyping.

We concern ourselves, in this book, with prototyping GUIs for usability, as opposed to the numerous other uses of prototyping in computing, such as technical feasibility or performance estimation. However, some of the measures of effectiveness for a GUI may require a certain level of performance from the GUI prototype in order to allow realistic evaluation (Figure 11.1).

The style of prototyping described in this chapter is sometimes referred to as 'rapid prototyping', because of the rapid succession of versions of the prototype. A rapid prototyping iteration may take a matter of days, and there may be many such iterations during the development of the GUI.

GUIDE draws a conceptual distinction between GUI Design and GUI Prototyping, but in practice the boundary is often very blurred. One activity shades into the other,

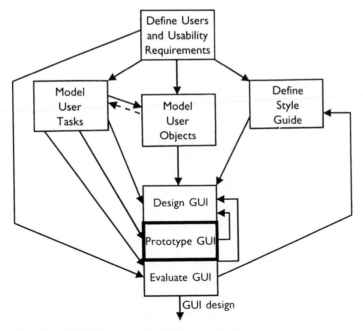

Fig. 11.1   GUIDE context for GUI prototyping

and the same person may be doing both at the same time. It is the same team of people (GUI designers, GUI programmers and users) who do both design and prototyping. Also, there is not a clear dividing line in the design medium: sometimes both the GUI design and the first prototype are paper-based; in other situations, the GUI design is expressed from the outset in a GUI prototyping tool.

The design/prototyping distinction is based on a difference of objective and emphasis. GUI Design is concerned with producing a representation of the required appearance and behavior of the entire user interface. Prototyping is concerned with building a subset of the user interface (and of the underlying functionality), and exploring its properties by interacting with it.

Certainly, amendments will be made during prototyping in order to tune the GUI for usability. On the other hand, during prototyping people may conceive ideas for change to the GUI design, which, although not essential to achieve the goals of this iteration of the prototype, are fed back for subsequent incorporation into the design.

Finally, the dividing line between 'reviewing the GUI design' and 'interacting with the prototype' is often so subtle that it is not worth arguing about.

11.1.1 Objectives

- To investigate, and improve, the usability of the proposed GUI design.
- To provide feedback on the validity of the task model, user object model and style guide.

11.1.2 Benefits

Prototyping allows the developer to deliver successive, executable versions of the GUI rapidly. This provides the following benefits:

- *Better communication with user* The user can obtain early hands-on experience of how the GUI will look, feel and perform. They can assess earlier how it will impact their business. Compared with a more traditional approach where an application is designed, constructed and installed before the user can use it, this provides much more effective communication with the user.
- *Improved design through feedback and iteration* The iterative nature of the approach means that a number of different approaches can be evaluated with the user, and their feedback used to evolve and improve the design.
- *Reduced risk* The risk of producing an unsuitable GUI is greatly reduced.
- *User education* A prototype provides a training/learning medium for the user population. Normally user training is crammed in an at the end of the project, after the system has been delivered. The succession of prototypes allow some training development to be carried out much earlier.

- *Greater user acceptance*   When users feel they have been involved in the design of a product, they are more likely to view it positively and accept it.

11.1.3   Inputs/outputs (Figure 11.2)

The inputs to this process are as follows:

- A proposed GUI design.
- A set of task scenarios which can be used as the basis for investigation.
- Usability requirements.

The outputs from this process are as follows:

- A working GUI prototype.
- Suggested GUI design changes.
- Feedback on the task model, user object model and style guide.

11.2   PRODUCTS

11.2.1   GUI prototype

A GUI prototype is a partial implementation of a GUI design which enables users to interact with the design.

Types of prototype
There are a number of different aspects of a prototype. This section outlines some possible classifications:

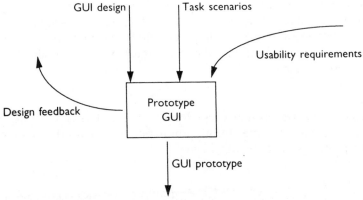

Fig. 11.2   GUI Prototyping inputs and outputs

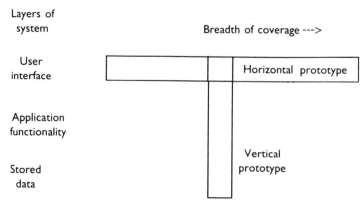

Fig. *11.3*   Horizontal and vertical prototypes

- *Scope*   A prototype may be global or local. A global prototype is one which covers all of the scope of the current increment. A local prototype will concentrate on a specific feature which is particularly vital, contentious or difficult, or where there are several design options.

- *Horizontal/vertical*   A prototype may be horizontal or vertical. A horizontal prototype covers much (or all) of the eventual scope of the GUI, but not very deeply. A vertical prototype covers a few tasks (or software functions) but implements more layers of the eventual GUI and potentially other functionality, such as data management (Figure 11.3). A minimal type of prototype may have very limited breadth and no depth.

- *Evolutionary/throwaway*   A prototype may be intended to evolve into the production system, or it may be intended to be thrown away when it is no longer useful.

- *Fidelity (or realism)*   A prototype may have a variable degree of fidelity (or realism) in relation to the intended GUI system. In the early stages of a prototype it may not be necessary to produce a high-fidelity prototype. As the prototype progresses it is important that the realism increases to ensure that the evaluations conducted on the prototype are applicable to the final production system.

Notation

The GUI prototype is described at a high level by the GUI design, the notation for which was introduced in Chapter 10. All prototyping tools have their own notation in which the prototype must be described.

Where used

The GUI prototype is used in the Evaluate GUI process, where it is formally evaluated for usability.

If an evolutionary prototype is developed, the prototype is (at least partly) used in the construction of the production system.

Quality criteria

The quality criterion is that the GUI prototype satisfies the prototyping objective for this iteration. This typically involves the following:

- Coverage of some defined portion of the GUI design.
- Being 'good enough' to enable user interaction and useful feedback.
- Being sufficiently detailed and complete to support some kind of evaluation.

11.2.2 Feedback to GUI design

A set of problems in the GUI design and suggested solutions, identified during investigation of the prototype. This feedback loop, as opposed to the evaluation report produced by the GUI evaluation process (Chapter 12), is intended to feed back changes which should be made within this iteration.

Notation

Partly a textual description of the problems, but GUI design notation may be used if this expresses a desired change effectively (e.g. a change to the window navigation diagram or window hierarchy).

Where used

In GUI Design, solutions to the problems may be incorporated into the design.

11.2.3 Feedback to models

This is feedback on the validity of the products of earlier steps, specifically the task model, user object model and style guide. As prototyping proceeds, problems may be discovered with the various models from which it was derived. This feedback is a very important benefit of the prototyping approach.

Where used

Model user objects If the user does not recognize the user objects and relationships, or does not find them 'obvious' or natural to use, consider revising the user object model.

Model user tasks Prototyping often identifies additional task scenarios, and may lead to refinement of the task models and scenarios.

11.3   PROCESS

11.3.1   Overview

Figure 11.4 shows the suggested activities for the Prototype GUI process. The activities 'Define prototype objectives' and 'Choose prototyping tool' are usually performed as part of planning the design of an increment and determining the number of iterations (see Chapter 4, section 4.3). These planned prototyping objectives and tools are reconsidered (and if necessary revised) at the beginning of each prototype iteration.

The later activities occur once per iteration.

Figure 11.4 is simplified; in some cases there are several 'builds' happening in parallel, either of vertical prototypes of particular areas, or local prototypes investigating a specific isolated feature. The latter may even require the use of a different prototyping tool. As long as this diversity is controlled it can be a very effective way of working.

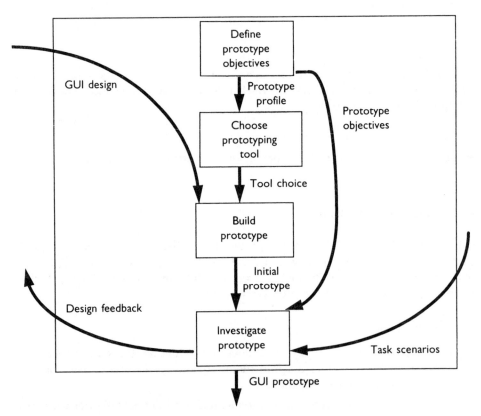

Fig. 11.4   Prototyping activities

The distinction between 'Build' and 'Investigate'

A distinction is drawn between the activities 'Build the prototype' and 'Investigate the prototype'. The boundary between these two is blurred, because the same types of activity are performed in both, namely building the prototype and investigating its usability. There is always some informal evaluation of the prototype as it is being built, and part of the investigation process may involve making changes to the prototype. However, the distinction is worthwhile, because it reflects the practical reality in which developers firstly concentrate on building some significant part of the prototype, and then subsequently investigate its behavior. Users are involved more in investigating than in building.

Comparison with GUI Evaluation

There is some overlap between GUI Prototyping and GUI Evaluation, but they have a different emphasis. Prototyping involves some informal evaluation, but its primary product is a prototype (which has evolved through user and developer feedback). In contrast, GUI Evaluation is about detecting usability problems (using a more formal process involving real end-users and usability experts), and reporting them for later removal.

In practice, you may choose to use some of the evaluation techniques described in Chapter 12 to 'Investigate the prototype'.

11.3.2 Define prototype objectives

Define the objectives of each prototyping iteration. These may be the following:

- To validate the style guide.
- To reach agreement on the GUI support for a particular task.
- To explore the appearance and behavior of a single complex window.
- To satisfy a specific usability requirement, such as making some part of the interface sufficiently simple that it requires no user training.

Consider the type of prototype which is required to meet the prototype objectives. Assessing the acceptability of the style guide might be achieved by constructing a throwaway prototype to demonstrate the interface style of all the major windows in the window hierarchy. Providing a high usability level for a particular requirement may require a vertical prototype covering only a small part of the scope but implementing it fully.

11.3.3 Choose the prototyping tool

Potentially for each iteration, you must choose a prototyping tool. If an evolutionary prototype is being built, then the choice is made early and in later iterations no further choice is required (other than for local, throwaway prototypes).

There are many tools on the market which support GUI prototyping, but your choice will depend upon the type of prototype that you are building. Some examples of current GUI prototyping tools are discussed in section 11.5.4.

A throwaway prototype should be cheap to build and any supporting tool reasonably cheap to purchase. The following are typical choices:

- A flipchart/whiteboard and appropriate pens. Very cheap and can take you far and fast in the early stages. A variation on this theme is to sketch each window on a separate card, and lay them (partially) on top of each other (as they would be seen on the screen).

- A presentation package. This can allow you to present sequences of windows for a particular scenario, perhaps by capturing a series of screen shots from other tools, or the 'look and feel' of the interface (e.g. Microsoft Powerpoint).

- An application-building 4GL. Some systems which require limited flexibility can be prototyped entirely in one of these. They are typically proficient at a specific vertical slice of the overall functionality which can therefore be prototyped with high fidelity (e.g. Microsoft Access).

- A specialized throwaway prototyping package (e.g. HyperCard).

An evolutionary prototype requires a different sort of tool. It is likely to have the following strengths:

- The ability (eventually) to construct production-quality systems.

- The flexibility to allow tuning of the prototype to user requirements.

- Support for fast turn-around of code changes for rapid prototyping.

11.3.3.1 Tool characteristics — development environment

You should choose a prototyping tool with a set of characteristics appropriate for your development environment. Some considerations are the nature of your development team, the complexity of the GUI being developed and the eventual fate of the prototype. Consider the following issues.

Target user
Tools are targeted at a range of users from a computer-literate end-user at one end, to skilled GUI programmers at the other. Tools aimed at end-users are often very useful for constructing early prototypes. Prototypes actually produced by end-users can provide valuable insight into that user's requirements for the production system. Typically, the more skilled the target user, the more powerful and complex the tool.

Target run-time environment
Tools are normally either compiled into a standalone machine code executable, or are interpreted, when at run-time a special program is required to run the GUI.

Compiled code tends to be faster at run-time. There are still major doubts about whether interpreted code is efficient enough to allow the construction of production-quality systems which have high-performance requirements.

Development paradigm

The distinction between compiled and interpreted GUIs also applies in the development environment. Some tools require that the code be compiled before execution, others will interpret the code as written. An interpreted tool will allow a faster turn-around from design to execution because the design can be executed immediately, without compiling first. This saves time as compilation requires that the code for the whole prototype is (at least grammatically) correct.

Representation

Tools differ in how the developer can represent a design. Most tools have a graphical mechanism for describing the window layouts. However, they vary widely in how code is associated with visual controls, from a text-based approach where code is written using a standard text editor and linked via control names, to a graphical approach where references in the code to controls are made graphically.

Some examples of current prototyping tools are discussed in section 11.5.4.

11.3.3.2 Tool characteristics — prototype features

Make sure that the prototyping tool supports the features you require in your prototype. Some potential features to be aware of are listed below.

Type of interface

Make sure that the type of interface which you want to build is buildable using this tool. An obvious question is whether the recommendations in the style guide can be followed using the tool. If it is important that particular media, say video or sound, be included in the prototype, then make sure that the tool supports them.

Integration with other tools

Increasingly, it is expected that the GUI can interact with other applications running on the user's workstation, such as spreadsheets and wordprocessors. Check that the tool you choose provides the necessary degree of integration with the required tools.

Production platforms

If you intend to evolve the prototype into the real system, check that the prototyping tool supports the production platform(s) required. Some tools support multiple production platforms.

Vendor stability

The number of GUI tools in the market place is staggering; not all will survive. Check that the vendor is financially stable and provides good support for the product.

11.3.4 **Build the prototype**

Build the prototype, based upon the GUI design, using the chosen prototyping tool.

It is suggested that the team size for building a prototype be quite small, no more than five developers in all (and often only one to three). Any larger than this and the team tends to fragment, the communication overhead rises, and the prototyping is no longer so rapid. It is important that at least one of the developers is skilled in the use of the chosen prototyping tool. Skilled developers can increase the pace of development both by their own development efforts, and playing a 'technical authority' role in use of the prototyping tool.

At the end of this step you should have a prototype which approximately matches the GUI design. (Some minor design improvements may have been made while building.)

11.3.5 **Investigate the prototype**

Investigate and interact with the prototype, focusing on what is needed to meet the prototyping objective.

The aim of the investigation is usually to identify usability problems which prevent the prototype from achieving the usability levels for the iteration. Defects can either be addressed immediately or deferred. Although there is no 'hard and fast' rule, typically simple problems are addressed immediately and the prototype evolved to remove the defect. More difficult problems may be deferred and swept up in a further build of the prototype. Problems which mean that the objectives of the iteration will not be achieved should (where possible) be dealt with within the iteration. Others should be recorded and addressed in a later iteration, via feedback to the GUI design process.

The most important characteristic of a prototype is that you can interact with it. This does not imply that the prototype has to be built in software, although software obviously offers very rich forms of interaction.

A user can interact with a paper prototype in either of the following two ways:

- By looking at it, discussing it with the designer and mentally 'walking' task scenarios around it.
- By role-playing an interaction. The user takes the role of user, and a designer plays the role of the computer. The 'computer' 'executes' the prototype in response to actions requested by the user. This can be done by pinning the paper prototype to a wall. The developer wields a frame, the size of a prototype window, and in response to user-initiated actions, moves the frame to show the navigation between windows. This is discussed further in Chapter 12.

The development paradigm of the prototype can make a big difference to the effectiveness of the prototyping process. An interpretative tool allows much faster iterations through an investigate/amend cycle, than a tool which requires compilation. Increasingly, machine-executable prototypes are being used from an early stage, as prototyping tools become more and more powerful.

Having at least one user in the prototyping team is essential during investigation. Even the most user-oriented developer is unlikely to perceive the system from the user's point of view. Anyone who is a system developer is, by definition, not a typical end-user of an application system.

The following are some examples of typical usability defects and potential solutions:

- Too many window actions for a user object action. Each task scenario has been defined in terms of a task situation, and the sequence of user object actions that the user performs whilst executing the task. In order to improve the efficiency with which the user performs the scenario, the efficiency of performing the user object actions can often be improved by reducing the number of window actions per user object action, or choosing more efficient ones. Reducing the number of window actions is often achieved by providing more information in a window, thus removing the need for the user to do work in order to access required information. Various forms of acceleration may also be used, such as:
  - short-cut keys for menu options;
  - double-clicking on an object to perform the most popular action;
  - buttons for frequently executed actions;
  - use of 'direct manipulation', as exemplified by 'drag and drop'.

- Poor window navigation. Sometimes performing a sequence of user object actions in a scenario is made difficult by the available navigation between windows. By tuning the flow of control through the windows to a particular scenario, the usability can be significantly improved. A tradeoff to be aware of is that by optimizing the GUI design to make particular tasks or scenarios easy to perform, we may make the GUI less flexible and suitable for other tasks.

- Terminology and labeling. User interaction with prototypes often exposes problems in terminology, e.g. some users may misinterpret a label because they use the same term to mean something different.

- Window layout. Users often respond to a prototype by pointing out ways in which the layout of the controls in a window could be more meaningful or convenient to use.

- Setting of default options. It is often possible to save substantial user effort by careful selection of default options. Prototyping offers the user the opportunity to validate the default settings, and to suggest additional defaults.

■■11.4 EXAMPLE

This section illustrates the prototyping process with some examples from the prototyping of the Helpline system case study.

As discussed in Chapter 4, the project has three increments, and the first increment will have three iterations, each involving GUI design, prototyping and evaluation. Part of the schedule is reproduced in Figure 11.5. In this example, each iteration involves just one prototype.

11.4.1 Define prototyping objectives

We decide on objectives for each of the three iterations.

Iteration 1/prototype 1

- To validate the overall acceptability of the style guide by producing representative windows.
- To validate the main windows required, and their approximate layout.
- To validate the main navigation paths between windows.
- To validate support for various scenarios of the central task (Resolve Customer Query).
- To support evaluation by expert inspection, and user walkthrough of task scenarios.

A very shallow horizontal prototype is adequate for these purposes. The risk of major rework (or even throwing it all away and starting again) is highest at this point, so a very fast, low-cost option is preferred. Also this means that we receive valuable feedback at the earliest possible point in the project.

Iteration 2/prototype 2

- To validate the detailed window content and layout.
- To explore usability by allowing the user to interact with windows in the prototype.

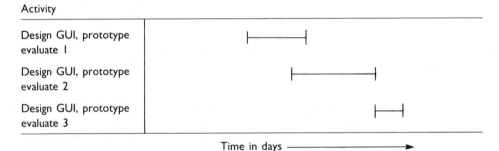

Fig. 11.5 Schedule showing three iterations

Example   229

- To explore support for monitoring and managing Advisor's queries, where the initial GUI design (and thus prototype 1) are believed to be weak.

- To support evaluation by fairly realistic user testing.

A second shallow horizontal prototype is sufficient for these purposes, although it needs to have more interactive behavior, especially the Advisor window. Menu selection and inter-window navigation need to be implemented, but it is not necessary to connect the prototype to a database of sample data.

Iteration 3/prototype 3

- To confirm that modifications have successfully resolved usability problems identified in earlier prototypes.

- To support informal exercising of all task scenarios.

- To support realistic user evaluation.

- To achieve 'planned' levels for some usability requirements, and levels above 'worst acceptable' for all usability requirements.

- In this way, to achieve a sufficient level of confidence in usability to stop prototyping, formally agree the GUI design, and proceed to construction of the production system.

This requires a deeper and more global horizontal prototype, with some vertical slices where there is deeper functionality.

This is the initial plan of the iterations required for the first increment of the Helpline system. Depending on progress and on what is discovered during prototyping, it may be necessary to revise the number of iterations or the objective for a particular iteration. In any case, the objectives for iteration 2 should be reviewed and their appropriateness confirmed after iteration 1 is completed.

11.4.2 Choose the prototyping tools

Prototype 1

We chose pen and wallchart, because of the speed of production and modification, and lack of emotional commitment to a particular design.

A storyboarding or presentation tool like Powerpoint could also have been used for this prototype, but would have taken too long to create and change the screen layouts.

The final version of the paper prototype was carried forward into and superseded by the first software prototype, and the paper prototype thrown away.

Prototype 2

We chose Microsoft Visual Basic 3.0, with no underlying database.

Visual Basic was attractive in this project because: (i) it provided rapid turnaround prototyping facilities; (ii) it could evolve into a production system; (iii) the developers were already familiar with it; (iv) it had been used to build the existing system, which performed well enough to provide reasonable confidence that the new system would have adequate response time.

We decided to begin building prototype 2 (the first software prototype) in parallel with the evaluation of the paper prototype.

Prototype 3

We decided this should be an evolutionary extension of prototype 2 in Visual Basic.

We also decided we needed a small local database to provide sample test data for the Helpline prototype. By increasing the fidelity of the prototype in this way, we expected that the evaluations would be more accurate. We selected Microsoft Access for the database, as an Access database can be defined and populated very quickly, and there is good integration between Visual Basic and Access.

(Note that the Access database was a throwaway prototype. Access cannot support the data volumes or the response times required for the production Helpline database.)

11.4.3 Prototype 1 (paper)

11.4.3.1 Build the paper prototype

Using the GUI design already developed, we 'built' a paper prototype covering all of the user objects in the user object model. The prototype consisted of paper sketches of the windows, 'blue-tacked' onto a large sheet of paper, and connected by window navigation links drawn in pen. As prototyping proceeded, the original window sketches were replaced with updated versions of windows (as they were produced).

Figure 11.6 shows a copy of the paper prototype, much reduced in size. (The original was 3 m by 2 m.) The design for the prototype is discussed in Chapter 10, section 10.4.

11.4.3.2 Investigate the paper prototype

The prototype was pinned to the wall of the customer support office and one of the designers outlined the GUI design to the Helpline advisors. This generated a lot of questions, followed by discussion (and even argument) about how the design should be organized.

After making notes on all the initial criticisms and concerns mentioned, we guided the discussion in the direction of 'walking' task scenarios through the prototype. This generated more comments such as 'I don't do things in that order', and 'You have to remember that the Customer is on the phone, they just want a quick answer, you can't make the advisor look at too many windows.'

During this session, we re-sketched some windows and tacked the revised ones up. We also agreed to go away and think about the more difficult problems, and come back with proposed solutions. The advisors were so energized by the discussion that two of them volunteered to sketch alternative designs for some of the windows.

This is a real benefit of a paper prototype — no one is prevented from volunteering designs because of lack of skill in (or access to) the prototyping tool.

One significant area of discussion and revision concerned Sites and Configurations.

Example   231

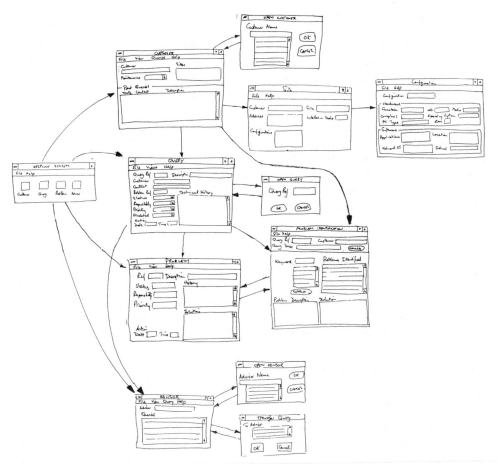

Fig. 11.6 Paper prototype — version 1

Customer Sites and Configurations

Version 1 of the paper prototype (Figure 11.6) shows three separate windows, one for the Customer object, one for the Site subobject, and a third for the Configuration subobject.

One of the main items of information that a skilled advisor uses when investigating a Query is the Configuration being used. In order to obtain this information, the advisor has to perform the following actions:

- Open the appropriate Customer.
- Choose the required Site and open a Site window.
- Identify the Configuration used and open a Configuration window.

This 'drilling-down' through the three layers is too long-winded, especially when the most useful information to the advisor is often in the Configuration (the bottom layer), and is rarely in the Site.

Access to Configuration information needs to be obtained via Customer, but it is suggested that the number of layers of windows be reduced. One window containing all the information (customer details, site details, configuration details) would be too large, so we propose that the Customer and Site windows be retained, but the Configuration window collapsed into the Site window.

The paper prototype was changed to collapse the Configuration window into the Site window. Configuration was put in a lower pane, because it is a view of a different (and subordinate) object.

To minimize the window actions the user must perform before they see configuration data, we agree that when the Site window is opened the Configuration list will default to the top Configuration, and the lower pane will display the data for that configuration. This and a number of other changes were made and a section of the final paper prototype is shown in Figure 11.7.

Accelerators

We identify several situations in which shortcuts will be useful for expert users.

For example, from the Query window a Helpline advisor might want to navigate with minimum effort to the Customer who raised the Query, or to the Problem which caused the Query. While we might support such navigation with (labeled) menu items for novice users, expert users would prefer an icon on the toolbar in the Query window, enabling them to navigate to these related windows with a single mouse click.

11.4.4 Prototype 2 (Visual Basic)

11.4.4.1 Build prototype 2

This prototype was based upon the final paper prototype. The Visual Basic windows were largely copies of those in the paper prototype. Four windows — Customer, Site/Configuration, Query and Problem Identification — are shown in Figures 11.8–11.11 to give an impression of the appearance of the emerging GUI.

An icon bar has been added to help the user execute the most common actions more effectively. This is a common feature in the popular Windows applications.

Advisor allocation

One of the objectives of prototype 2 was to explore how to deal with the manager's tasks, specifically 'Monitor Advisor Workload'. This task can include redistributing queries, in order to cope with sickness, high-priority requests, workload imbalances, etc.

The paper prototype supported this task with an Advisor window showing the list of queries for which a single Advisor was responsible. The window had menu options to choose the advisor to be viewed, and to transfer queries. This was implemented in the initial version of prototype 2, as shown below.

The Advisor window in Figure 11.12 provides the main view. The Open Advisor dialog (Figure 11.13) is invoked by choosing the Open option from the File menu on the Advisor window.

Example   233

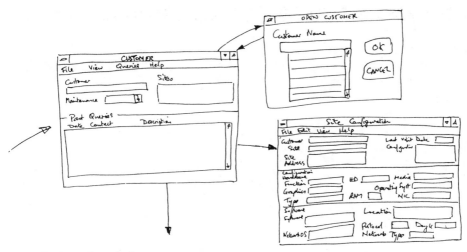

Fig. 11.7 Part of the final paper prototype

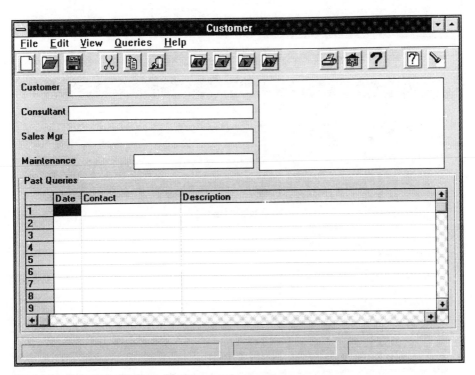

Fig. 11.8 Customer window, showing past queries view

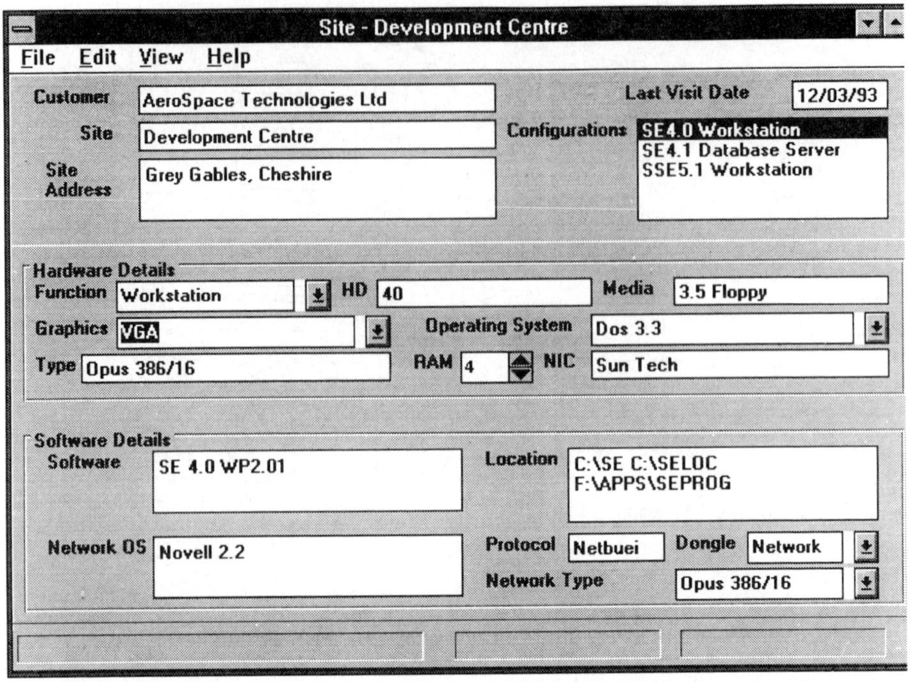

Fig. 11.9   Site/configuration window in Visual Basic

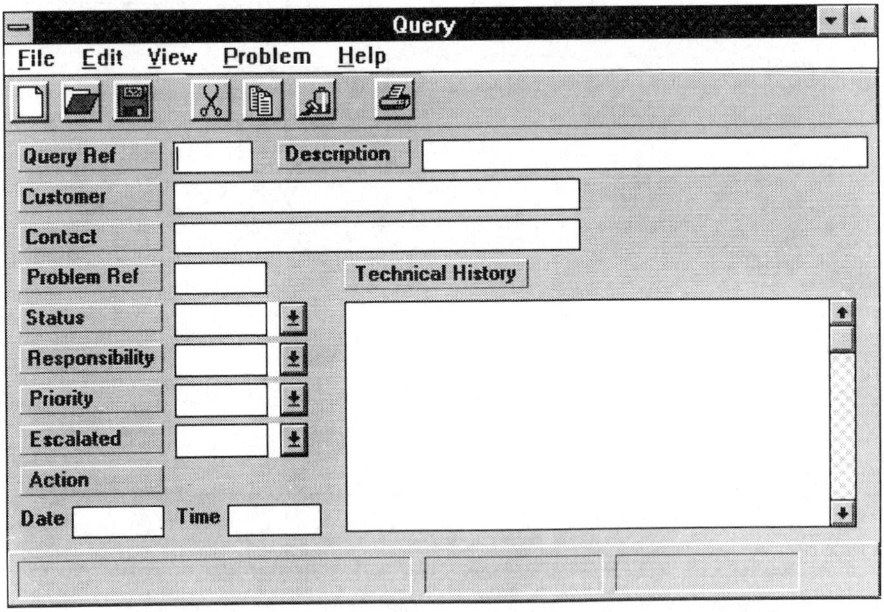

Fig. 11.10   Query window in Visual Basic

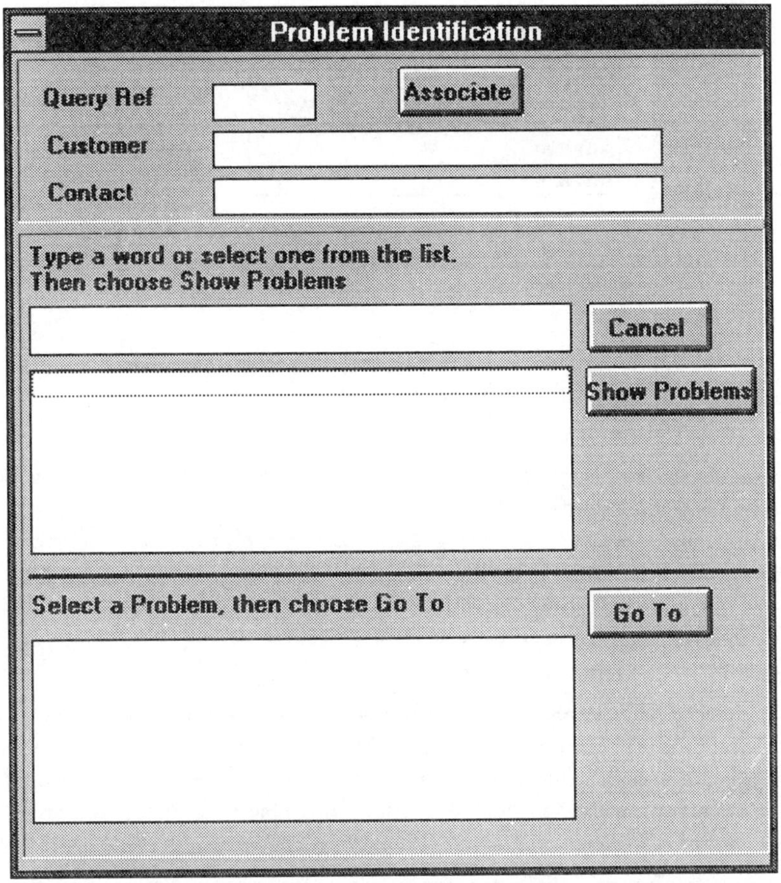

Example   235

Fig. 11.11   Problem identification window in Visual Basic

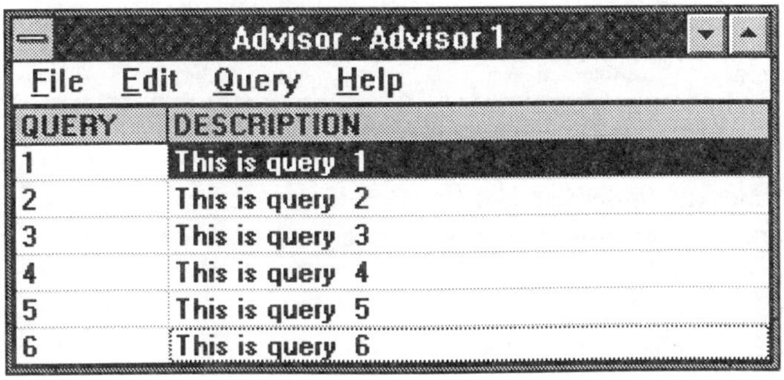

Fig. 11.12   Advisor window at start of prototype 2

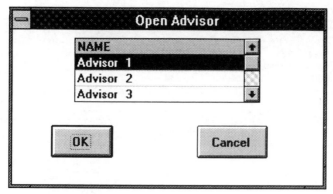

Fig. 11.13   Open Advisor dialog

The Transfer Query dialog (Figure 11.14) is invoked by choosing Change Responsibility from the Query menu on the Advisor window.

The task which was used to investigate this part of the prototype is 'Monitor Advisor Workload', and a task scenario 'Reallocate a Query' (Chapter 6, section 6.4 describes the task and scenario in detail). A usability (performance) target had been established (UR7), which used 'Reallocate a Query' as a task scenario (section 5.4 describes the usability requirements for the system).

> Usability requirement − UR7   The manager must be able to obtain a clear overview of the current situation very quickly. This can be measured by a performance test, which identifies all the information the manager must check to be confident that she 'has a grip on the situation'. The criterion is time to complete the task.

Reqt ref	Usability attribute	Measuring instrument	Value to be measured	Current level	Worst acceptable level	Planned target level	Best possible level
UR7	Expert performance, manager	Monitor Advisor Workload, scenario 1	Time to complete	120 (not auto)	60 sec	40 sec	20 sec

Task − Monitor Advisor Workload

Check how many queries each advisor is currently dealing with and their urgency and reallocate if necessary.

Scenario 1 − reallocate a query

Background: John has two urgent queries, Suzie has several queries but they are all low priority. Mark is on leave.

Example   237

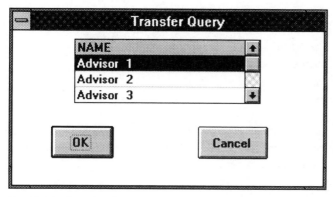

Fig. 11.14   Transfer Query dialog to change responsibility to another advisor

Examine workload   **[All Advisors]**

Note John overloaded

Examine John's current Queries   **[Advisor (Queries)]**

Examine Suzie's current Queries   **[Advisor (Queries)]**

Discuss with advisors.

Manager: 'John, I'm worried that you've got two hot cases there, do you think
it would be a good idea if Suzie dealt with one of them?'

John: 'OK, Suzie, can you take the Saudi Oil query?'

Transfer Saudi Oil query from John to Suzie

[Query.ChangeResponsibility]

11.4.4.2 Investigate prototype 2 (Usability Requirement UR7)

Problems found

Using the scenario 'Reallocate a Query', a number of problems were found:

1. 'Examine workload' was a laborious process; the window actions:
   Select Open from File menu
   Scroll through list of advisors (might be several window actions)
   Select advisor
   Press OK
   Wait for Advisor window (to fill and look at their queries)
   had to be repeated for each advisor.

2. 'Transfer Saudi Oil query from John to Suzie' was too clumsy; the required window
   actions are:
   Select Open from File menu
   Scroll through list of advisors

Select 'John'
Press OK
Select 'Saudi Oil' query
Select 'Change Responsibility' from Query menu
Scroll through advisors
Select 'Suzie'

Press OK

3. 'Examine Current Queries' required that the advisor was currently displayed in the advisor window. In order to examine the queries of a number of advisors, a significant amount of interaction was needed.

Solutions offered

We felt that changes were needed.

Problem 1   The addition of navigation operations (First, Last, Next, Previous) was considered in order to reduce the number of window actions. However, we felt that the key to the problem was that a view of [all advisors] was required. We decided to add a Advisor Overview, containing details about each advisor. The following features were added:

- a vertical gauge for each advisor indicating visually the number of outstanding queries;
- color codes to show the urgency of the most urgent query for an advisor.

Problem 2   We decided to adopt a drag-and-drop mechanism for query transfer. This would operate between the advisor window, containing the list of outstanding queries, and the Advisor Overview. To aid the mechanism, pictures of the advisors were displayed in the Advisor Overview to provide a clear target for the drop.

Problem 3   We decided to display the workload of all advisors all the time.

We incorporate these proposed solutions into prototype 2. Figure 11.15 shows the Advisor Overview window and three Advisor windows.

11.4.4.3 Evaluate prototype 2

During further investigation of Usability Requirement UR7 and the subsequent usability evaluation, the following problems were found:

- There is no indication of an advisor's availability. The manager could use the phone, but this would be time consuming and lose the benefit of computerization.
- The number of windows displayed is too great. Despite the apparent advantage of displaying all advisor workloads constantly, the average complexity of interaction is increased, because the various windows tend to obscure each other. They have to be continually moved and resized to achieve the claimed advantage. Frequently, the Advisor window required has to be made active in order to see all the necessary information. With more advisors, the problem gets steadily worse.

Example   239

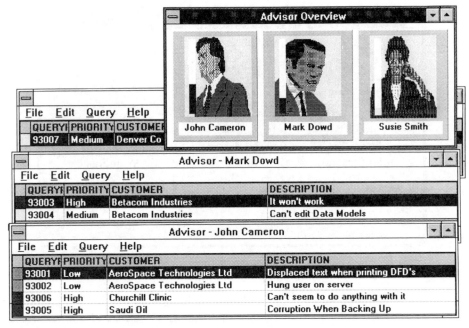

Fig. 11.15   Advisor Overview and set of Advisor windows

■ The vertical gauges indicating Advisor workload are often difficult to read, because of the pictorial backdrop. The color of the bars sometimes clashes with the underlying picture.

We include this example because it illustrates an important point which often occurs on projects. There were serious problems in prototype 2, and we proposed a solution which addressed these problems, seemed plausible and evolved the prototype in a worthwhile direction. However, implementing the agreed solutions introduced new (unanticipated) problems, and so a further iteration was required to restructure some of the improvements.

11.4.5 Prototype 3 (Visual Basic + Access)

Prototype 3 aimed to correct the problems in prototype 2, and to increase the realism of the prototype by using a prototyping database.

11.4.5.1 Build prototype 3

The following changes were made to the Advisor Overview and Advisor window.

Problem 1   Add an indication of the advisor's availability to the Advisor Overview.

Fig. 11.16   Revised Advisor Overview window

Problem 2   Have just a single instance of Advisor window; the current advisor is selected by clicking on the advisor's picture in the Advisor Overview.

Problem 3   Separate out the gauge from the advisor's picture, and show it horizontally.

The final version of the Advisor Overview window is shown in Figure 11.16.

We implemented the suggested solution to problem 2 (only having one advisor window). The layout of the Advisor window did not change, so it is not reproduced again. Reallocating queries is still performed by dragging a query out of one advisor's list and dropping it on another advisor's picture.

In prototype 3 we have an underlying database so we build a realistic implementation of the drag-and-drop interaction, with the Query moving from one advisor to another in the window, and the responsibility attribute of the Query in the underlying database also being updated.

11.4.5.2   Investigate prototype 3

The changes made to the Site window and the Advisor Overview window were found to work acceptably well.

A wide range of task scenarios was attempted by users. This led to requests to improve window navigation by provision of shortcuts. These were implemented immediately by adding extra buttons on the icon bar. Exercising the scenarios also led to a number of small changes in window content and layout.

11.5   PRACTICE TIPS

11.5.1   A typical prototype lifecycle

Although every development is different, there are some 'typical' characteristics of the prototyping lifecycle which are worth noting.

The style guide

The window hierarchy and standard controls and interaction mechanisms defined in the style guide should be validated with the user at an early stage in the project, before much effort has been expended on design. A throwaway, horizontal prototype with limited breadth would be a suitable choice.

The early prototype

Early prototypes are typically global horizontal prototypes, but with low fidelity. Quite often pencil and paper are used because of the speed with which ideas can be conveyed and the resulting suggestions acted upon. The windows will be very closely based on user objects, providing a 'task neutral' prototype, with no particular bias towards user effectiveness at any particular task.

The resulting prototype provides a good basis for further development, because the entire scope of the increment is covered at some level, and to an extent simultaneous development can take place based on a common foundation.

A 'task neutral' GUI can sometimes achieve a reasonable number of the usability requirements without optimization.

The later prototype

As prototyping tools become better, global evolutionary prototypes are becoming increasingly popular, and are started in an early iteration. Vertical extensions to the prototype are developed where a particular task has to be examined in detail. It is often from these that 'task-optimized' sections of the prototype arise.

Local prototypes may be used from time to time to investigate more advanced GUI features such as drag-and-drop window action mechanisms, and embedding spreadsheets and documents. These local prototypes are typically thrown away; the results derived from them are fed back into the main global prototype.

11.5.2   Risks

The two major risks to be addressed when prototyping are controlling the prototyping process, and managing the expectations of the customer (i.e. the person or authority funding the work).

The central issues for control are what to do in an iteration, and when to stop work on an iteration. What to do is defined by selecting a set of task scenarios and usability criteria which should be addressed. This focuses the attention of the developers, ensuring that time is spent in the appropriate areas. Ideally, the work for an iteration is over when the agreed coverage is achieved and the agreed usability levels have been met.

An alternative is to adopt a 'timebox' approach to controlling the iteration. In timeboxing, a fixed duration (e.g. three weeks) is defined for each iteration. The team makes as much progress as possible towards the prototyping objective within this time constraint. It is accepted that progress and problems are unpredictable, the team may not be able to complete the planned work, and that the approach is to do a predefined amount of time (and effort) and then assess it and plan what to do next. The advantages of this approach are the following:

- The difficult question 'Have we done enough yet?' is replaced by a simple question 'Have we run out of time?'
- The project timescales are not jeopardized.
- An 'overengineered' prototype is less likely to be produced.
- It is more possible to plan usability evaluation activities (where one needs to schedule people for user testing, and possibly field visits or the use of usability labs).

The two aspects of managing customer expectations are ensuring that the customer 'buys in' to the prototyping concept, and that they understand the limitations of the prototype. Your customer must understand that the success of prototyping depends upon extensive input from the user community. This typically requires that one or more knowledgeable, full-time users are included in the prototyping team. It also means that typical end-users must be made available to take part in evaluations.

The other common mistake is to assume that a prototype is in some sense a finished product. Clear examples of the prototype's limitations are required in order to dissuade your customer from taking a prototype and attempting to use it in a live situation.

11.5.3 Recording changes

Each time a problem is identified or a change is made to the prototype, make a note of it in the prototyping log. You should record the following points:

- What the asserted problem is.
- What solution or improvement is proposed.
- What decision is made (implement in this prototype iteration, implement in next iteration, wait and decide after evaluation, don't do, etc.).
- The rationale for the decision (why is it thought (un)important, why this solution rather than others?).

In this way you build up a trail of the way the prototype has evolved, and can spot when some enthusiastic user or developer wants to spend time reversing a previously agreed change.

11.5.4 Examples of prototyping tools

There are a large number of tools which can be used for prototyping. The following list offers a brief description of the characteristics of a selection of commonly used tools. These products mostly run under Microsoft Windows or on the Apple Macintosh. (There are also a wide variety of tools available for X-Windows (under Unix).)

Microsoft Office

The products in Microsoft Office (Excel, Word and Powerpoint) have some features which allow the construction of throwaway prototypes. Word templates and macros can be written to produce and populate simple forms. Excel can be used to access and display data in databases, in a fairly inflexible way. Powerpoint can be used to capture screen and other images, to demonstrate general application style guide issues. Microsoft is implementing a common programming language, Visual Basic, throughout all of these tools, which in addition to standardizing the approach to programming these tools will also increase their flexibility.

Target user	end-user
Target run-time environment	the prototypes execute within the Office toolset, so they are essentially interpreted
Development paradigm	interpreted
Representation	almost entirely graphical, with some macros

Hypercard

Hypercard runs on Macintosh computers. It has its own scripting language HyperTalk, which is run interpretively. It also has a built-in library of graphical controls and general functions, and allows grahical placement of controls.

Target user	programmer
Target run-time environment	interpreter
Development paradigm	interpreted
Representation	highly graphical, but with a programming language (HyperTalk), which is required if other than simple interaction behavior is required

Access

Access is both a database and a user interface builder. It supports the construction of forms-based access to database information, including objects such as sound and video.

Target user	end-user
Target run-time environment	interpreter (the Access Engine)
Development paradigm	interpreted
Representation	highly graphical, but with a programming language (Access Basic)

Visual Basic

Visual Basic (from Microsoft) is used to build Windows applications, either as standalone systems or as the client part of a client–server system. Visual Basic is a true GUI prototyping tool, designed to support rapid iteration of prototypes, and increasingly, evolution of a prototype into a production system.

Target user	knowledge of programming, but not necessarily skilled programmer
Target run-time environment	interpreter (Visual Basic compiles into an executable file, but this requires a run-time interpreter)
Development paradigm	interpreted
Representation	graphical window layout, some visual association between controls (filling text and picture controls from a data source via a data control), but complex language (Visual Basic) which has to be used in order to construct any but the simplest application

PowerBuilder

PowerBuilder (from PowerSoft) supports the construction of the client component of client–server systems. It has a powerful GUI prototyping tool, designed to support rapid iteration of designs and evolution of a prototype into a production system. It also has strong support for linking the forms through to a server DBMS, allowing developers to produce SQL in a graphical, 'point and shoot' manner. It also supports inheritance in a window hierarchy, thus directly enabling the construction of style guides.

Target user	knowledge of programming, but not necessarily skilled programmer
Target run-time environment	interpreter
Development paradigm	interpreted
Representation	as with Visual Basic there is graphical window layout. Datawindows (a proprietary facility) can be used to construct quite complex forms which perform database maintenance. A powerful and complex language (PowerScript) has to be used to build more complex applications

Smalltalk

Smalltalk (from Digitalk) is a complete environment, consisting of a development environment, a fully object-oriented programming language, and a large set of prebuilt components which can be used directly or specialized in order to build complete graphical client applications. A competent programmer can build very complex prototypes rapidly. Smalltalk prototypes are frequently evolved into production systems.

Target user	skilled programmer; although the programming language is quite small, detailed understanding of the object-oriented paradigm and detailed knowledge of the prebuilt components is required in order to use Smalltalk effectively
Target run-time environment	interpreter
Development paradigm	interpreted
Representation	if used on its own has little support for the graphical representation of controls, but is often accompanied by a GUI builder which does offer those facilities. A closely related product 'Parts' employs an entirely visual programming interface for building applications

Visual C++

Visual C++ (from Microsoft) is primarily a compiler for the C++ language but also contains tools which help in the creation of production-quality GUIs.

Target user	skilled programmer
Target run-time environment	Windows (native code)
Development paradigm	compiled
Representation	has some support for graphical placement of controls, via one of the support tools, but detailed definition of appearance and all design of interaction has to be coded in C++, a very complex programming language

11.6   SUMMARY

This chapter describes how to build and exercise a prototype of a GUI design. Major points include the following:

- A prototype is a partial implementation of some part of the GUI design, which enables users and designers to validate (and extend) the design by interacting with it.
- Each GUI design iteration will have one (or more) prototypes, enabling user interaction and usability evaluation.
- The products of prototyping are:
  - the working GUI prototype;
  - feedback on the GUI design and proposed enhancements;
  - feedback on the validity of the task and object models and style guide.
- The prototyping process consists of:
  - defining the prototype objective(s);
  - choosing the prototype tool;
  - building the prototype (from the GUI design);
  - investigating the prototype using task scenarios.

11.7   FURTHER READING

Rettig, M. (1994) 'Prototyping for tiny fingers', *Communications of the ACM*, vol. 37, no. 4.
An excellent article on the value of 'low-fidelity' prototyping using paper, cards, etc., for communicating design ideas and achieving multiple early iterations without wasted effort. Contains various useful tips.

Wagner, A. (1992) 'Prototyping: A day in the life of an interface designer', in Laurel, B. (ed.), *The Art of Human–Computer Interaction*, Addison-Wesley.
A short chapter on how an interface designer interacts with a multidisciplinary team to prototype and user-test an interface. Realistic discussion of what you can and cannot do, and what tools to use to produce the prototype.

Hix, D. and Hartson, H.R. (1993) *Developing User Interfaces: Ensuring usability through product and process*, John Wiley.
A good discussion of the principles of prototyping GUIs to achieve usable designs.

Andriole, S.J. (1991) *Rapid Application Prototyping: The storyboard approach to user requirements analysis*, McGraw-Hill.
A useful book on the use of prototyping to design and develop software systems.

Usability evaluation

12.1   INTRODUCTION

This chapter describes how to evaluate a GUI design and prototype to assess their usability (Figure 12.1).

Analysts and designers often have the impression that usability evaluation is something very expensive and complex, which is only feasible if you work on a high-profile system for a major software vendor with a sophisticated usability laboratory and teams of 'human factors' experts. It is important to recognize that even though some evaluations may match this up-market stereotype, it is feasible to perform worthwhile usability evaluations on ordinary application software with limited project budgets and staff expertise.

Usability evaluation is a field in which the 80/20 rule applies. You can often derive 80 percent of the benefit of evaluation for only 20 percent of the cost, with further improvements becoming progressively more expensive. The feasibility and value of low-cost evaluation have been established recently by Jakob Nielsen, who has popularized it under the heading 'discount usability engineering'.

The type of evaluation recommended in this chapter is 'formative evaluation', which is where evaluation feeds back into the design process. Evaluation of this type is crucial to iterative redesign. Evaluation should start as early as possible in the GUI design process, and each major prototyping cycle should end with evaluation. In the prototyping chapter we suggest that you should plan for (at least) three prototyping cycles, so plan also for at least three evaluation cycles. If the prototypes are of the

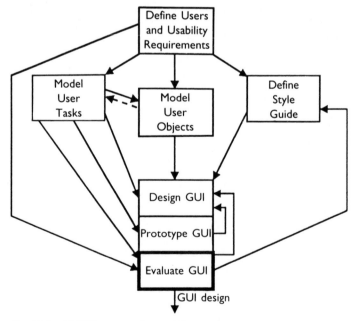

Fig. 12.1   GUIDE context for usability evaluation

same depth, the first evaluation usually produces more useful information and leads to more design changes than the second or third.

This chapter emphasizes evaluation as a process. Evaluation has a product (usability problems and proposed changes, documented in an evaluation report), but the most interesting aspect is the process through which the problems are brought to light.

12.1.1   Objectives

- To identify usability problems.
- To assess whether the GUI design satisfies specified usability requirements.
- To evaluate whether the GUI design will be usable in practice by its intended users.

12.1.2   Benefits

Evaluation frequently uncovers usability problems which are not noticed during informal interactive prototyping.

Evaluation exposes designers to real users in a situation which helps designers to understand the user point of view.

Evaluation provides the information base for deciding whether GUI design and prototyping is complete. If usability targets are met, and there are no serious usability problems discovered, development can move on to the next phase. Alternatively the evaluation results indicate where redesign is required.

Evaluation measures task performance. This gives managers or customers a direct measure of the benefits they receive from the usability of the GUI.

A positive side-effect is that involving users in evaluation frequently increases user interest and acceptance of the proposed system.

12.1.3   Inputs/outputs (Figure 12.2)

The main inputs are as follows:

- The agreed usability requirements (including ways of measuring these, such as task scenarios).
- The GUI prototype, and supporting GUI design documentation.

Other inputs include the following:

- Application style guide.
- User object model.
- Task models and scenarios.
- User class descriptions.

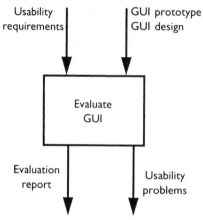

Fig. 12.2   Evaluation inputs and outputs

The output is an evaluation report containing usability problems.

The usability requirements may be modified as a result of experience gained during evaluation. The task model, user object model and application style guide may also be modified as a result of problems identified during evaluation.

12.2   PRODUCT – EVALUATION REPORT

The evaluation report is a report summarizing how the design was evaluated and the conclusions reached. This includes the following:

- An assessment of the extent to which each usability requirement was satisfied. Failure to meet the worst acceptable level of a usability requirement constitutes a serious usability problem.

- A table of other specific usability problems discovered during evaluation (e.g. problems in interaction sequences, layouts, labeling).

- An assessment of the impact of each usability problem on business costs and benefits. This is used to prioritize proposed changes to the design.

- Recommendations for change to the GUI design and (possibly) the application style guide.

Notation
Basically a textual report.

The report should include the usability requirements specification table, updated to show the actual values recorded for the measures of usability.

Quality criteria

- Does the evaluation report reach a clear conclusion on whether the GUI design is acceptable in terms of usability as perceived by the end-user?
- Does the evaluation report assess whether previously agreed usability requirements are satisfied?
- Are the usability problems specified sufficiently clearly to enable redesign?
- Was the evaluation process sufficiently realistic to be valid? (The more similar the users, task scenarios and software are to real-world use, the more valid the assessments of usability will be.)

Where used

The evaluation report is used by the project manager in deciding how much more iterative redesign to do, or whether to stop.

Usability problems and proposed revisions lead to changes in the application style guide, the GUI design and the GUI prototype.

12.3   PROCESS

The evaluation process described here is based on a combination of work by Hix and Hartson (1993), Monk *et al.* (1993) and Nielsen (1993). It consists of five main activities:

- Design the evaluation.
- Conduct evaluation sessions.
- Collect data.
- Analyze data.
- Agree required redesign.

12.3.1   Design the evaluation

12.3.1.1   Select evaluation approach

There are several quite different approaches to evaluating usability, and the first part of the process is to decide what is feasible and most appropriate in the project circumstances.

The emphasis in evaluation may be to identify as many usability problems as possible, which involves rich qualitative data; or it may be to assess whether or not the GUI design satisfies the specified usability requirements, which requires much narrower quantitative data on user performance or error rate.

In practice, the evaluation approach is often selected early in the design process. When specifying usability requirements, it is good practice to plan how they will be evaluated. Also, in planning the GUI design process, evaluations are major project milestones which need to be planned in advance to ensure that suitable users or experts are available at the right time.

The main types of evaluation are as follows:

- Review by human–computer interaction (HCI) expert (or heuristic evaluation).
- User testing (or observation of users).
- Survey of user attitudes or perceptions.

It is common to use two or even all three types in a single evaluation cycle, for example, for each evaluation session to consist of observation followed by some kind of survey, or to combine user testing with heuristic evaluation.

Review by HCI expert or heuristic evaluation

A very quick way of evaluating a GUI is to ask an external HCI expert to review it. An expert is likely to identify a large number of usability problems and to suggest improvements to the GUI design, based on their knowledge of relevant guidelines and familiarity with a large number of user interfaces. A limitation is that an expert will not have some of the problems that a real user performing real tasks will encounter. Expert evaluation is therefore complementary to end-user evaluation.

A less expensive alternative than an HCI expert is to use 'heuristic evaluation', a form of inspection researched and recommended by Nielsen. Since the majority of usability problems are caused by violating a few key principles of interface design, you can identify many problems in a GUI by giving reviewers a checklist of these principles. You ask the reviewers to examine each part of the interface, actively looking for places where any of the principles have been broken. Working from a checklist, it is not essential to have an external HCI expert, the reviewer role can be performed by a GUI designer from a different team. This greatly reduces the cost, making heuristic evaluation feasible in low-budget projects. Nielsen's checklist of ten principles is reproduced in Chapter 9, section 9.2.

User testing/observation of users

Typical end-users are given task scenarios and observed to see how they perform the tasks using the GUI, what errors they make, how long the tasks take, etc. Observation produces rich qualitative data, and can produce quantitative data. Observation of a few users can quickly highlight difficulties.

A form of user testing that is particularly suitable for use by designers who are *not* human factors specialists is 'cooperative evaluation', as described by Monk (1993). Users are encouraged to think aloud about what they are trying to do, and about their reactions to the system's responses. (This is sometimes referred to in the literature as 'verbal protocol analysis'.)

Another aspect of designing the evaluation is to choose the setting. 'Field testing' is when the evaluation is performed in the user's normal work environment. This is most realistic, but it is often difficult for the evaluator to control the environment (e.g. interruptions from other people and tasks). 'Laboratory testing' is when the user participants come out of their work environment and perform the evaluation in a 'usability laboratory' (i.e. a room in the software development area). In laboratory testing, the evaluator has more control and more equipment but the setting is less realistic. It is sometimes feasible to use both, in which case it is usual to perform early evaluation in the laboratory, and use field evaluation later.

Survey of users

Users are surveyed either using a questionnaire, or with a structured interview. In either case the users will be asked to answer a number of questions. Questionnaires can be used on a large group of users, and produce quantitative results. The questions need to be phrased very carefully to avoid biasing the responses. Interviews are possible, but are usually less effective at identifying usability problems than the cooperative evaluation technique, where the evaluator's interaction with the user is structured around the user's reactions to using the software. Alternatively, a questionnaire can be administered first and used to identify specific people to interview and specific usability problems to ask them about.

12.3.1.2 Identify evaluation participants

For both observations and surveys, it is important to select participants who are representative of the user classes for the system (described in Chapter 5). It is best to select users who have *not* been involved in the design and prototyping process. We know that the design team (including its user members) understand and like the interface; the evaluation is trying to establish how other users will cope with using it. If possible select three members of each user class to evaluate. (After three there are diminishing returns from testing with additional participants.) Evaluation is still worthwhile, even if you only have a single user.

The evaluation should specify how much experience of the interface the users will have had. For example, in a survey of the usability of an existing system by experienced users, we might require three months use of the system. In evaluating a prototype, we might specify that users should have fifteen minutes instruction before being observed.

12.3.1.3 Decide session protocol

Plan how the evaluation session will be organized. The 'protocol' (i.e. the format and schedule) depends on the purpose of the evaluation.

An early evaluation intended to increase understanding of how the user interprets the GUI prototype might use a cooperative evaluation style to elicit qualitative information about usability problems. For example:

- Put participant at ease, establish cooperative atmosphere.

- Task scenarios 1–6, participant thinking aloud and evaluator prompting, interspersed with discussion, no time pressure.
- Concluding comments and discussion.

A later session which is more geared to testing whether usability requirements are met might have a more formal format and produce more quantitative information. For example:

- Instructions to participant.
- Initial training.
- Task scenarios 1–3 (timed).
- Free use of system (10 minutes).
- Task scenarios 4 and 5 (timed).
- Usability questionnaire.
- Concluding questions, comments and discussion.

In both cases, the task scenarios are selected from the scenarios described in Chapter 6, and are used to lead the user through the prototype, and/or to test whether the prototype meets usability requirements.

To ensure that participants understand what is expected of them, and are all given the same instructions, it is worth typing out a sheet of instructions. This should include the purpose of the evaluation (what is being measured and why), and make clear that the software is being evaluated, *not* the participants. It is good practice to inform participants of what is involved (e.g. length of time) and of their rights (e.g. to walk out at any time), and to check that they want to participate. Some evaluators ask participants to sign an 'informed consent' form to indicate that they understand and agree to the conditions.

An example set of instructions for cooperative evaluation suggested by Monk is reproduced below. The tone of the instructions gives a flavor of the relationship the evaluator is trying to establish with the participant.

Thank you for agreeing to help with this study. Today we are going to evaluate the usability of a particular computer system called Mind Bender.

Mind Bender stores large numbers of references to academic works rather like the catalogues in a library. It can be used to search for things written on a particular subject, or by a particular author and so on.

The aim of the study is to find out how easy Mind Bender is to use by people like yourself. We want you to use it to help us find out what problems Mind Bender poses and how it could be improved.

We will give you some standard tasks to do using Mind Bender. The aim of this is to allow us to get some information about how Mind Bender supports this activity. We're particularly interested in situations in which Mind Bender encourages you to make errors in selecting commands and misleads you about what it will do. We are also interested in extra commands that would make the system easier to use.

To get this information we shall use a question-and-answer technique. This involves three things.

1. We want you to think-out-loud as you do each task telling us how you are trying to solve each task, which commands you think might be appropriate and why, and what you think the machine has done in response to your commands and why. Think of this as you giving us a running commentary on what you are doing and thinking.

2. Whenever you find yourself in a situation where you are unsure about what to do or what effect commands might have, ask us for advice. If you ask us what you need to know we will suggest things for you to try but if you get really stuck we'll explain exactly what you have to do.

3. In addition we will ask you questions about what you are trying to do and what effect you expect the commands you type will have. This is simply to find out what problems there are with the system. During our conversations, we want you to voice any thoughts you have about parts of the system which you feel are difficult to use or poorly designed.

While you're doing this we'll be noting down the problems you mention but in case we miss any we are going to audio tape our conversation. This recording will be anonymous and treated in confidence.

Remember it's not you we're testing, it's Mind Bender. We are interested in what you think so don't treat this as an examination. Treat it as a structured discussion about Mind Bender. Please feel free to say whatever you think about the system and the tasks you're given to solve.

If a survey is to be used, decide what questions to include and how to score the user responses. Most surveys are only feasible when there is (at least) a reasonably substantial software prototype to evaluate. (Asking people to rate a paper prototype for response time does not produce sensible results!)

As devising valid questionnaires is a time-consuming specialist activity, the most effective approach is often to use a standard usability questionnaire such as SUMI (the Software Usability Measurement Inventory, see Appendix E).

If heuristic evaluation is to be performed, agree the checklist of heuristics to be used. We suggest you start with the Nielsen list in Chapter 9, possibly supplementing it with points from other experts such as Shneiderman, or from your environment style guide (e.g. IBM CUA).

12.3.1.4 Pilot the evaluation

Once the session structure is defined and the materials prepared, run a pilot session to validate the evaluation protocol. You will usually find some problems which need to be ironed out. The pilot need not use a real user.

12.3.2 Conduct evaluation session

Each session is coordinated by an 'evaluator', who is often a member of the design team. Although it might seem better to have an external expert, there are several reasons why it is usually most cost-effective for a member of the design team to play the role of evaluator:

- The evaluator understands the GUI prototype and underlying design intentions better than an external evaluator would.
- The communication flow of feedback from the evaluation session to the design team is faster and richer than if an evaluator had to go away and type up a report. And it is less expensive.

It is the evaluator's responsibility to guide the participant through the evaluation session and to ensure that all relevant observations are recorded. Usually the evaluator stays in the same room as the participant, either in the background, or sitting next to the participant, depending on how much interaction is planned.

If collecting 'thinking aloud' data, the evaluator may need to prompt the participant with questions about what they are thinking or attempting.

Monk (1993) suggests the following questions as being useful in cooperative evaluation sessions. (Note the style of language, which indicates the way the evaluator is relating to the user.)

The following questions will generally give the information you require:

- How do we do that?
- What do you want to do?
- What will happen if ...?
- What has the system done now?
- What is the system trying to tell you with this message?
- Why has the system done that?
- What were you expecting to happen then?

For example:

1. After the users read each task (get them to read it out aloud) ask them: 'How do we do that?' This will yield information about their intentions.
2. As the users consider a menu item ask them: 'What will happen if you choose that item?'
3. When users have entered a command and the system has responded ask them: 'What has the system done?' or 'What is the information on that part of the screen telling you?' This can be followed up by asking the users 'Why has the system done that?', or if they appear confused or surprised ask them, 'What were you expecting to happen?' Finding out about things that did not happen that the users expected is very informative.

Sometimes the participant may get stuck and ask for assistance. If the evaluation includes timing the completion of the task, or counting the number of user errors, the evaluator clearly has to be cautious in the amount of advice given, as assistance will distort the data collected. A compromise is to give hints without telling the participant exactly what to do. For example, to point and say 'Watch this part of the screen carefully.'

12.3.3 Collect data

Observational data is usually based on asking participants to perform predefined task scenarios.

There are various techniques for collecting the observational data:

- *Real-time note-taking* — this is the simplest form. The observer has a stopwatch, and makes notes of what the user does, any errors the user makes, how long each task takes, and any other significant events (such as a long pause while the user thinks about what to do next). It helps to have a structured worksheet prepared in advance (see Figure 12.3).
- *Video-recording* — a video camera is used to record the user's activities, usually focused on their hands and the screen. As well as allowing subsequent analysis, brief excerpts from video-recordings are very compelling evidence to any designers or managers who are skeptical about usability problems.
- *Thinking aloud* — the user is encouraged to 'think aloud' while they are performing the task, and this is captured on audio or video recorder (and/or by the evaluator making notes). The evaluator is likely to have to prompt the user with questions such as 'What are you doing now?' or 'What are you looking for?' It is extremely valuable to have the user describing in their own words what they are attempting to do or what they are confused about. This is very direct evidence of the mental model which the user has developed of the system. An observed user error indicates *that* there is a problem, but it is often the user's own words that clarify *why* there is a problem.

These three techniques are often combined together — the user is asked to 'think aloud', the interaction is video-recorded, and the observer makes a note of timings and any 'critical incidents' such as user errors. Cooperative evaluation combines thinking aloud with video-recording and note-taking, though usually *not* with a stop watch. (Timing someone's performance is likely to inhibit richer forms of cooperation.)

It is worth stressing that it is *not* necessary to have a usability laboratory to perform an observational evaluation successfully. All that is required is a room to run the

Participant Id:		Session date: Session start time: Session end time:				
Task description	Tape counter	No. of errors	Elapsed time	Participant's actions and comments	Evaluator's observations
1. Scenario A 2. Scenario B						

Fig. 12.3 Evaluation worksheet for note-taking

evaluation in, a computer to run the prototype GUI, and optionally an audio or video-recorder.

After the observation session it is worth asking the user if they have any comments on the tasks or their experience of the interface.

As an evaluator, summarize your observations on paper immediately after a session, while the interactions are still fresh in your memory and you can still recall what you meant by brief scribbled notes made during the session. You will have two main types of information:

- Unexpected user behavior.

- User comments (both during their interaction with the GUI and afterwards).

Heuristic evaluation/review by HCI expert

Brief the reviewers on the purpose of the system and the type of users and tasks.

The reviewers work through the interface, noting all the places in which it fails to conform to the checklist of good design principles, or is not consistent with the application style guide.

12.3.4 Analyze data

User testing

Analyze the observational data. Usually the information extracted is quite simple:

- Time to complete the tasks.

- Number and nature of any user errors.

- Any significant pauses, or points where the user got stuck.

- Any user comments which suggest inappropriate conceptualization of the interface.

Most of the important information should already be in the observer's notes – the videotape is used as a backup to allow reanalysis of important incidents. More detailed analysis is possible, but subject to diminishing returns – the most important usability problems are usually found quickly.

In the analysis of user errors, it is important to distinguish between 'catastrophic errors' and more minor errors. A catastrophic error is when a user is unable to complete a task. This may be because they cannot find the appropriate command, or they repeatedly make the same mistake, or because they make a mistake and get into a mess which they cannot undo, or they get stuck in a mode or a part of the interface they cannot escape from. Whatever the precise problem, they reach the point of thinking (or saying) 'I can't get this to work, I give up!' A subtly different kind of catastrophic error is when the user believes they have completed the task success-fully, but actually has not achieved the task goal, or has had some different unintended effect (e.g. transferred money to the wrong account).

In contrast, minor errors are where the user performs an action which does not contribute to the task goal. For example, a user may pull down the wrong menu list to look for a command, and find that it is not there. Or they may attempt an invalid command to which the system responds with an error dialog box. In either case, the user has to back out of their error (wasting further time and effort) and continue with their task.

On timings, note that we are measuring user performance rather than system performance. Much of the time taken to perform a task will be pauses where the user works out what to do next, or errors where time is spent taking a wrong path through the software.

The quantitative results are related back to the specified usability requirements by adding them to the usability specification table (see Figure 12.6). The actual results are compared with the planned, and the worst acceptable.

In analyzing both the observational data and the questionnaires, it is not usually appropriate to use sophisticated statistical techniques. The aim is to identify usability problems, and to assess how important these are to the user. A simple but effective way of doing this is to maintain a list of usability problems, as illustrated in Figure 12.5 below. The 'importance' of each problem is rated as high, medium or low. The strongest evidence of a problem being important is that several users got stuck or made an error and therefore wasted time on it. In many situations the assessment of importance will inevitably be subjective.

Survey data

The survey data is processed through some kind of statistical analysis to convert it into a usable form such as a usability score. A cost-effective way of achieving valid results is to use an evaluation package which comes complete with appropriate statistical analysis (see Appendix E).

12.3.5 Agree required redesign

Review the usability problems in the context of the specified usability requirements. Our objective is that by the end of the last iteration we can measurably achieve all our planned usability levels. (In practice, we sometimes discover that the targets were set so high that it is too difficult or expensive to achieve them, and we have to negotiate lower targets.)

For each usability problem consider the possible solutions. Most solutions consist of redesigning part of the GUI to improve usability, and there is often more than one solution to a problem. Estimate the cost (in time or money) of each potential solution, and how the changes may affect the usability of other parts of the user interface.

A decision has to be made as to which parts of the GUI to redesign in the next prototyping cycle. The project plan for prototyping and evaluation will have allocated a number of days of effort for redesign in the next cycle. The aim is to use this limited resource to obtain the greatest possible improvement in usability, and that this usability will generate benefits for the business.

Start with the 'high-importance, low-cost' problems. It is easy to agree to do these.

Review the 'high-importance, high-cost' problems. If the solutions are feasible with the planned effort, agree to do them. If not, consider whether there are any other lower-cost solutions which would be acceptable (though less than ideal). If it is impossible to find acceptable solutions with available effort, then either the plan must be revised to allow more effort or lower usability requirements must be accepted.

Having resolved the 'high-importance' problems, allocate any remaining effort to solving as many of the medium-importance problems as possible. Their relative value can be assessed by asking 'How much does each hour working on the problem contribute to usability?'

At the end of this process each problem will have a decision noted alongside it, either:

- implement solution in next cycle;
- implement solution in next cycle if time permits; or
- no action.

■12.4 EXAMPLE

This section discusses the evaluation of the Helpline case study developed in earlier chapters.

The project used three iterations of prototyping and evaluation. The first prototype was a paper prototype, the second and third were software prototypes in Visual Basic.

12.4.1 Evaluation I

The first iteration consisted of a paper wallchart prototype shown in Chapter 11. We decided to perform two types of evaluation on this:

- Heuristic evaluation.
- User testing with role play and thinking aloud.

We also performed a brief review of our usability requirements specification. It was not possible yet to measure whether or not the system met the requirements, but we assessed whether at this point it looked likely that we would meet the requirements, or whether we would obviously have difficulties.

Heuristic evaluation
We asked two GUI designers from another project to be our evaluators. We gave them Nielsen's ten principles as a checklist, plus the mandatory sections of the application style guide. They

Example   261

reviewed the paper prototype separately and made their own notes, and then discussed jointly with us the problems they had identified.

User testing

We asked two Helpline advisors each to attempt to perform three scenarios for the 'Resolve Customer Query' task.

This was 'role played' — the advisor played the role of user, and a designer played the role of computer, by moving a large cardboard frame around. The frame concealed most of the paper prototype, but had a hole cut out the size of a window, so the user could see the 'currently active' window. (An alternative way of achieving the same effect is to have each window on a card. As the user points to a control on the card which transfers focus to another window, the evaluator places the next window card on top.)

We asked the advisor to think aloud about what they were trying to do, and to point at the controls they wanted to use. As far as possible the developer remained silent and just moved the frame. We audiotaped the user comments, using a cuff microphone close to the user's face.

12.4.2 Evaluation 2

The second prototype consisted of a set of Visual Basic windows, illustrated in Chapter 11. We decided to perform two types of evaluation on this:

- Heuristic evaluation.
- User testing with scenarios.

Heuristic evaluation

The same two designers assisted us again, using the same checklist. On this evaluation it was possible to apply the checklist to the interactive behavior of the prototype, such as whether it gave adequate feedback on system state. (This clearly could not be judged on a paper prototype.)

User testing

We gave three (different) Helpline advisors scenarios from 'Resolve Customer Query' and 'Monitor Advisor Workload', and asked them to work through them, thinking aloud. A short form of each scenario was used as an evaluation script. (The format of a scenario to give to a user as an evaluation script is slightly different from the scenario format for GUI design: see Figure 12.4 in comparison with the same scenario in Chapter 6, section 6.4.6.)

These sessions were audiotaped, so that we did not have to worry about how complete our notes were of their comments. Our focus was on understanding the user's view of the interaction, and identifying any problems and misunderstandings that they had. We did not time task performance, because of the emphasis on cooperative evaluation. (Cooperative evaluation means a partnership to explore the software together. Measuring someone with

---

Resolve Customer Query — Scenario I

Initial message from customer: 'I'm trying to upgrade from version 4 to version 5 of your DesignAid tool and the installation program is crashing. It's giving a message ERROR SSDB8 FILE MISSING, and then INSTALLATION FAILED.'

1. Find the Customer 'John Smith from NickelCo in Ontario'.
2. Create a new Query in the Helpline system to record the query.
3. Search in the Helpline system for the Problem causing this difficulty. Search using keyword 'Install — Upgrade'.
4. Read out description of Problem and solution.
5. Log the Query by associating Query to Problem, setting Query status to closed and saving the Query.

Fig. 12.4   An example of a task scenario in the format used for evaluation

Problem	Effect on user performance	Importance	Solution(s)	Cost	Resolution
1. Monitor Advisor Workload requires too many windows	35 of 60 sec	High	Only have one Advisor window open	5 hours	Fix
2. Need to identify Problem when no current Customer or Query	NA	Medium	Open Problem Identification window direct from Main window	2 hours	Fix
3. A few Problems are hard to identify using the keyword or free text search strategies	NA	Medium	Implement a third search strategy using a multikeyword strategy	15 hours	Leave

Fig. 12.5   Usability problem list

a stopwatch implies (and induces) a different kind of relationship.) In any case, with no data in the windows, the prototype was not sufficiently realistic.

We also asked the customer support manager to work through all our scenarios for 'Monitor Advisor Workload', thinking aloud. We recorded problems in a usability problem list (Figure 12.5).

12.4.3 Evaluation 3

The third prototype consisted of the Visual Basic windows for the whole interface, with sample data in a prototyping database. We decided to perform three types of evaluation on this:

- Review by an external HCI expert.

Example   263

- User testing of all usability requirements.
- A survey of user-perceived usability using a package called SUMI (see Appendix E).

Expert review

By this point we felt we had eliminated the most obvious usability problems, and could benefit from the advice of an external expert. With the GUI system being small, a half-day consultancy was sufficient for the expert to review all the windows and interaction in detail.

User testing

With this version of the prototype we recruited three Helpline advisors we had not worked with before, and asked them to perform the scenarios we selected as benchmarks for the usability requirements. For the timed tasks and number of errors, we calculated the average result for our three users. The results are shown in Figure 12.6. We also performed timed tests with the customer support manager.

SUMI survey

For this evaluation we decided to use the three advisors and the manager who performed the user tests, and another two advisors. Having at least six responses makes the results more reliable, and you obtain benefit from more of the SUMI analysis facilities.

We asked these users to complete a SUMI questionnaire. For questions which they could not answer because the prototype was so incomplete (e.g. over Help messages), we asked them to mark 'undecided'.

The questionnaire yielded an overall usability score of 50.

In addition to the global usability scale, SUMI produces five subscales which factor out user perceptions of different aspects of usability, as follows:

- *Efficiency:* Whether the user can perform tasks quickly, effectively and economically. Includes software performance and economy of keystrokes.
- *Affect:* The emotional dimension. Whether the user 'feels good, warm, happy or the opposite as a result of interacting with the software'.
- *Helpfulness:* Whether the software communicates in a helpful way and assists in problem resolution. Relates particularly to messages and help.
- *Control:* Whether the software responds in a normal, consistent and predictable way to input and commands, so that the user feels in control.
- *Learnability:* How quick and easy it is to learn how to use, and whether manuals are readable and instructive.

The subscale scores were as follows:

Efficiency	42
Affect	59
Helpfulness	50
Control	56
Learnability	62

Reqt ref.	Usability attribute	Measuring instrument	Value to be measured	Current level	Worst acceptable level	Planned target level	Best possible level	Observed results
URI	Expert performance	Resolve Query scenario I	Time to complete	40 sec	45 sec	40 sec	30 sec	**42 sec**
UR2	Support various problem-solving strategies	Assessment by Helpline manager	Number of strategies	2	2	4	10?	**2**
UR3	User satisfaction — helpline staff	Questionnaire (SUMI)	Total score	18	40	50	73	**44**
UR4	Initial performance — other staff	Find Query scenario 5	Time to complete	120 sec	60 sec	30 sec	15 sec	**50**
UR5	Memorability — other staff	Find Query scenario 6	Time to complete	NA	90 sec	40 sec	15 sec	**60**
UR6	User satisfaction — other staff	Questionnaire (SUMI)	Total score	NA	40	50	73	**50**
UR7	Expert performance, manager	Monitor Advisor Workload, scenario I	Time to complete	NA	50 sec	35 sec	25 sec	**30 sec**
UR8	Flexibility	Assessment by Helpline manager	Yes/No	No	No	Yes	Yes	**Yes**

Fig. 12.6   Usability specification with results of evaluation (last column)

This is a good overall usability score, and all the subscale scores are good except efficiency. We identified the SUMI questions which had contributed to the efficiency score being low, and it indicated the need for more shortcuts to eliminate keystrokes on the most commonly used tasks.

In addition to these summary results, SUMI produces results on the response to each individual question. It uses a standardization database to produce an expected pattern of responses to each question, and then analyzes how similar or different the actual responses are to those expected. In this way, it draws the evaluator's attention to questions which pinpoint weaknesses (or sometimes strengths) of the interface.

For example, the results could have been:

Q33 The organization of the menus or information lists seems quite logical.

	Y	?	N
actual:	I	2	3
expected:	4.2	0.9	0.9

This result would indicate a serious problem. Only one of our six users agrees, whereas one would expect four out of six to agree with this statement. We would follow this up by asking the users which menus they found illogical and why. Answers to questionnaire items such as this can be used to structure interviews with users.

Our usability specification table in Figure 12.6 provides a summary of how usable our GUI prototype is against our original targets.

12.4.4 Agree required redesign

We review the usability problem list, which has new entries from evaluation 3 and 'carried forward' entries from earlier evaluations. We agree to revisions which can be added into the design at little cost, but reject any where the cost would be more than an hour's effort, or which would require another cycle of prototyping and evaluation. The justification for this is that we are already achieving the planned level of some usability requirements, and are better than worst acceptable on all (Figure 12.6).

12.5   PRACTICE TIPS

12.5.1 Planning evaluations

It is important to allow sufficient time to plan and prepare for evaluations. Often it will take five times as long to prepare for an evaluation as to conduct it the first time (e.g. five hours for a one-hour session). By contrast, the preparation time for subsequent sessions using the same format is almost zero.

Do not underestimate how long it takes to recruit users and arrange suitable appointments for you to work with them. This can be extremely time consuming.

In deciding how much to do in one evaluation session, it is often best to work back from the amount of time you have with the user, to what tasks it is realistic to fit into the time. Remember you have to allow for initial welcome and instructions, and any training. Most people initially overestimate what is achievable, and then have to cut down the contents of a session.

12.5.2 Preloaded data

When evaluating prototypes which are capable of manipulating data, it is often best to populate the prototyping database with some initial data. The user is then asked to search through this data to find the relevant item, and to amend or cancel an item. For many systems this is much more realistic than the user starting with a totally empty system.

The quality and realism of the data can influence how the user responds to the evaluation, so for late evaluations which are attempting to be close to the 'real-life' situation it is worth investing some time setting up convincing data.

12.5.3 Tools to capture interaction

There are now a number of low-cost, easy-to-use software tools which you can use to capture usability evaluations. A good example is Lotus ScreenCam, which comes free with Lotus Notes 3.1, and can be used to capture all on-screen behavior and window sequences together with verbal interaction and user's comments, so it works very well with the cooperative evaluation approach. Provided your PC has a sound system, all you need to do is plug in a standard microphone and start the ScreenCam software running.

12.6   SUMMARY

This chapter has described how to evaluate a GUI prototype. Major points include the following:

- Each prototyping cycle should end with an evaluation phase.
- The objectives of evaluation are:
  - to detect usability problems;
  - to measure whether the GUI design satisfies usability requirements.
- Evaluation produces an evaluation report. This contains:
  - lists of usability problems;
  - suggested GUI design improvements;
  - measures of usability.
- Three important (and complementary) types of evaluation are:
  - review by HCI expert/heuristic evaluation;
  - user testing (including cooperative evaluation and observation);
  - survey of user attitudes and perceptions.
- Cooperative evaluation using 'thinking aloud' is a very effective and affordable way of identifying usability problems.

12.7   FURTHER READING

Monk, A., Wright, P., Haber, J. and Davenport, L. (1993) *Improving Your Human—Computer Interface: A practical technique*, Prentice Hall.
Describes 'cooperative evaluation', an evaluation technique designed for use by practitioners. Similar to the usability evaluation recommended in this chapter. The best single source of detailed guidance on how to encourage users to play the role of 'cooperative evaluator', hints on how to deal with different kinds of users, and practical tips on recording and analyzing users 'thinking-out-loud'. A manageable size (98 pages) and very readable.

Nielsen, J. (1993a) 'Iterative user-interface design', *IEEE Computer*, November, pp. 32–41.
An excellent summary of four real case-studies of iterative design with evaluation at the end of each iteration, showing how usability was substantially improved by evaluation followed by redesign.

Nielsen, J. and Mack, R.L. (1994) *Usability Inspection Methods*, John Wiley.
An excellent description of the various styles of usability inspection and evaluation.

Whiteside, J., Bennet, J. and Holtzenblat, K. (1991) 'Usability engineering: our experience and evolution', in Helander, M. (ed.), *Handbook of Human—Computer Interaction*, North Holland, chap. 36, pp. 791–817.
This paper provides a detailed and practical review of usability evaluation, ranging from checklists of possible measurable criteria for usability attributes through to the value of observing and interacting with users in their normal work context.

Hix, D. and Hartson, H.R. (1993) *Developing User Interfaces: Ensuring usability through product and process*, John Wiley.
Chapter 10 'Formative Evaluation' has a very good fifty-page practitioner level discussion of the principles and practice of performing evaluations.

Nielsen, J. (1993b) *Usability Engineering*, Academic Press.
An authoritative book on usability engineering, including substantial discussion of evaluation.

Nielsen, J. and Molich, R. (1990) 'Heuristic evaluation of user interfaces', in Chew, J.C. and Whiteside, J. (eds), *CHI '90 Conference Proceedings: Empowering People*, ACM, New York, pp. 235–241.
Nielsen's original article describing heuristic evaluation by computer science students.

Whitefield, A., Wilson, F. and Dowell, J. (1991) 'A framework for human factors evaluation', *Behavior and Technology*, vol. 10, no. 1, pp. 65–79.
A readable and comprehensive discussion of current methods of usability evaluation and a warning about common pitfalls of usability evaluations.

Ravden, S. and Johnson, G. (1989) *Evaluating Usability of Human—Computer Interfaces*, Ellis Horwood.
Chapter 3 'The Evaluation Checklist' provides an extremely comprehensive checklist on issues such as consistency, feedback, visual clarity, flexibility and control.

Gomoll, K. (1992) 'Some techniques for observing users', in Laurel, B. (ed.), *The Art of Human— Computer Interface Design*, Addison-Wesley.
A short chapter on the basic 'dos' and 'don'ts' when observing users. Includes ten steps for observing users.

Conclusion

The conclusion offers us the opportunity to re-emphasize the central themes in this book, and to end the book with some reflections on the nature and role of the GUIDE process.

Firstly, we hardly need to repeat that we see GUI design as being primarily about achieving usability; that is, about designing a user interface which fulfils the following requirements:

- Effective for real end-users to perform their actual tasks.
- Quick and easy to learn to use.
- Flexible enough to cope with minor changes in user and task circumstances.
- Satisfying and fun to use.

While usability is our central objective in GUI design, we place it in the context of usefulness (sometimes called 'utility'). You must first choose what system you are going to build, and ensure that its scope and broad functionality are genuinely appropriate and useful to the organization and people you are developing it for. There is little benefit in making the user interface wonderfully usable if you are basically building the wrong system. This issue of defining the system objectives and the high-level system design solution is not within the scope of the GUIDE process. However, if the system objectives and scope are inappropriate, this is likely to be exposed by task analysis in GUIDE, where we start asking 'How will the system help the end-user to perform their tasks?'

The usability of a system is not 'skin deep'. To achieve a highly usable system, it is usually not sufficient to have a well-designed user interface — the underlying functionality needs to be defined and organized in a way which makes it usable. One of the features of GUIDE is that it is not solely concerned with user interface design. The task analysis helps to define required system functionality, and the object modeling helps to define how system functionality can be organized in an intuitive and flexible way. In this way GUIDE can make a substantial contribution to the specification of underlying system functionality which may be implemented quite separately from the GUI (e.g. in database tables and stored procedures), in addition to being a process for designing and evaluating the user interface.

Our second general theme is that achieving usability is difficult for designers, and that the best overall approach is a philosophy of user-centered design. This involves the following:

- Paying attention to the capabilities, personal motivation, knowledge, limitations and preferences of the *people* who will actually use the system.
- Ensuring end-user participation throughout the analysis and design process.
- A process of iterative redesign, driven by feedback from prototyping and evaluating the GUI design with real users.

It is very hard for a designer to predict accurately what will be usable, without having contact with real users. One of the reasons for this is that it is almost impossible for you to put yourself 'in the user's shoes'. Many usability problems are based on user misunderstandings, and you cannot forget all you know in order to misunderstand the design in the ways that a user might.

A third theme is the role of task analysis and scenarios in defining what the user does, and the role of user object modeling in defining the 'objects in the system' which form the basis of the user's mental model. These contrasting perspectives are integrated by expressing task scenarios as actions on user objects. This combination of objects and tasks helps you to design flexible, intuitive object-based windows, and then adapt them as required to support tasks. All window design is performed in the context of an application style guide to ensure consistency.

A fourth theme is the importance of the creativity and judgment of the GUI design team. There is no 'perfect' GUI design, and no cookbook method which guarantees a good design. Just as a computer system is merely a tool for the user to achieve his or her task, a design process is no more than a tool which people in a design team use in trying to achieve their shared goal. In this case the goal is a usable (and feasible) GUI design, after spending an affordable amount of time and effort. We believe GUIDE is a good tool if *you* use it and apply it intelligently. We emphasized in Chapter 1 and we repeat here that GUIDE is highly customizable − *you* have to judge just how much time and effort to invest in each intermediate product, depending on the following:

- How difficult your GUI design assignment is (e.g. how large or complex the system, how demanding the usability requirements).
- How much time you have.
- The skills, expertise and experience you have.
- How the various GUIDE products contribute to usability in your unique situation.

Indeed, you may find GUIDE useful even if you choose not to produce any of the recommended GUIDE products (user class descriptions, usability requirement specifications, task models, user object models, etc.). As well as providing practical techniques and products, GUIDE provides a way of thinking about (and communicating about) GUI design. You may decide to ignore the standard GUIDE process and start straight off by prototyping some windows − but when it comes to discussing what a prototype window should look like you may find yourself thinking about the user's task requirements and their mental model, and justify your design choices by talking about who the typical users are and what their key usability requirements are in this situation. We are quite satisfied if reading this book has extended your vocabulary and your conceptual repertoire to include these ideas, and helped you to feel that you understand what the techniques are for and could make use of them if you wanted to. GUIDE is a mindset or orientation as much as a way of organizing a project.

Finally, there is no final answer. GUI design is a rapidly evolving field. Each year the diversity of available media becomes richer (voice, music, animation, video) and the development tools become more powerful and versatile. There is ongoing cross-fertilization between vendors, platforms and application sectors, with interaction styles which prove popular and effective in one setting 'migrating' to others and becoming *de facto* standards. In this flux of evolving technologies and conventions it is likely that the GUI design process will also continue to evolve. However, leaving the future aside, we feel that GUIDE uses the best techniques available to us now to address the challenge of this generation of software developers — there are hundreds of thousands of people who are not human factors specialists who want to know how to design usable GUIs. We hope you find this book useful, and that you experience as much interest, challenge and satisfaction in designing GUIs as we do.

GUIDE and multimedia

A1   INTRODUCTION

This appendix examines the question of whether GUIDE is applicable to the design of multimedia systems.

A2   MULTIMEDIA

The focus of this book is the design of graphical user interfaces. The detailed practical guidance and the examples discuss the kind of systems which hundreds of thousands of systems developers are designing in their day-to-day work in the mid-1990s. We have deliberately avoided the temptation to show examples of more exotic interfaces.

Yet, even as we write, technological and commercial developments are making a much richer range media available in GUI systems. This rapidly expanding area is commonly known as multimedia, and includes the following:

- Richer static images, e.g.
  - document images, such as insurance claim forms;
  - photographs;
  - maps;
  - works of art.
- Dynamic images, e.g.
  - video sequences;
  - animation;

- live television;
- teleconferencing.
- Sound, e.g.
  - voice messages;
  - voice annotation of images or documents;
  - music reproduction;
  - music composition.

As designers gain experience with multimedia, standard styles and good practice guidelines will emerge, just as they have for earlier interfaces. However, although new guidance will be needed at this specific level, we suggest that the overall philosophy and design process of GUIDE are still very applicable.

A3   APPLYING GUIDE

Our overall orientation to these systems should still be that there is a human user with task goals they are trying to achieve, and the system is a tool they use. The primary design objective is still usability.

In designing a multimedia system we should still ask the following questions:

- Who are the users?
- What are their usability requirements?
- What are the users' goals, what tasks are they performing?
- What objects in the system do the users interact with?
- What styles of presentation and interaction will be used consistently in the interface?

Having established the task model, the object model and the style guide, we still have the usability engineering cycle:

1. Design the initial interface.
2. Prototype the interface.
3. Evaluate the interface.
4. Iteratively redesign until we reach acceptable usability.

It does not change the GUIDE process that the user objects include voice mail messages, video clips, a Beethoven sonata and a Picasso painting. These objects have actions and attributes, and users perform their tasks by sequences of actions on these objects. Similarly in GUI design, the GUI consists of windows which contain views of these objects and means of manipulating them (menus, buttons, etc.)

In conclusion, the key concepts in GUIDE are applicable to multimedia, and the framework of the GUIDE process is applicable to multimedia, even though additional detailed advice will be needed on style and various design issues.

If you need this additional advice, one of the best sources is the work of Professor James Alty's group at Loughborough, which includes a set of principles and design guidelines for choice and combination of media (details below).

A4   FURTHER READING

Alty, J.L. (1993) 'Multimedia: we have the technology but do we have a methodology?', in Maurer, H. (ed.), *Proceedings of EDUMEDIA 93*, Orlando, Florida, pp. 3–10.
Principles and guidelines for selecting and combining media, including references to relevant research.

Alty, J.L. (1991) 'Multimedia – what is it and how do we exploit it?', in Diaper, D. and Winder, R. (eds), *People and Computers*, pp. 31–44, Cambridge University Press.
Keynote address to HCI 91 conference. A paper setting out major concepts for thinking clearly about good multimedia design.

Alty, J.L. and Bergan, J. (1994) 'The design of the PROMISE multimedia system and its use in a chemical plant', in Earnshaw, R. (ed.), *Multimedia Systems and Applications*, Cambridge University Press, in press.
A research report on the design and evaluation of a substantial operational multimedia interface for chemical process control.

GUIDE metamodel

The objects and relationships in GUIDE are expressed in Figure B.1 in the form of a metamodel. The diagram uses the user object modeling notation described in Chapter 7. If you are familiar with the metamodeling approach, you may find it useful to understand the different conceptual objects and the relationships between them. If you are not familiar with metamodels you may prefer to skip this appendix.

User Class is described in Chapter 5. Tasks, their subtasks and Task Scenarios are described in Chapter 6. User Objects, User Object Actions and User Object Attributes are described in Chapter 7. The metamodel also shows the following:

- User Objects have aggregation, subtyping and association relationships.
- Task Scenarios are associated to the User Object Actions they use.
- User Objects may be related to Data Model Entities, which provide stored data to support them.

Windows, Panes, Controls and Window Actions are described in Chapter 10. Windows may contain Panes, which may contain Controls. A Window Action may belong to a Control and/or a Pane, but must belong to a Window. A Window Action may invoke a Window (i.e. make it the active Window), and this is how window navigation is modeled in the metamodel.

Windows may be subtyped (the window hierarchy) and may have dependencies on other Windows.

The upper area of Figure B.1 is more abstract, dealing with Tasks and User Objects. These objects can be thought of as a model of the user's world. The lower area models the external appearance and behavior of the graphical user interface. Note how the abstract objects are mapped onto interface objects (or conversely, how the interface objects are often representations of the more abstract objects):

- A Pane usually shows a view of a User Object.
- A Control often represents a User Object Attribute.
- One (or more) Window Actions are often a way of requesting a User Object Action.
- A Task Scenario is accomplished in the interface by a Sequence of Window Actions.

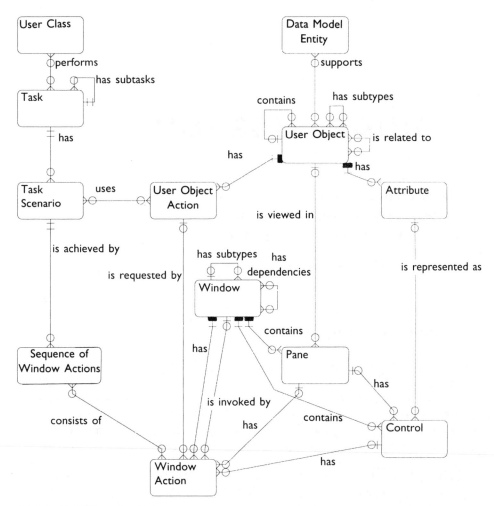

Fig. B.1   GUIDE metamodel

It is the underlying abstract model and the way it is represented in the interface which gives the interface its meaning. What does the user *mean* when he or she clicks on a button in a window? He means that he wants to perform the action on the object he is viewing in the window.

GUIDE and SSADM

CI INTRODUCTION

This appendix discusses the use of GUIDE with SSADM.

SSADM (Structured Systems Analysis and Design Method) is the standard method for analysis and design of information systems used by the British government. SSADM has been adopted by many organizations outside the government sector as an effective nonproprietary method. It has also been adopted as a standard method by a number of organizations and governments outside Britain (as far afield as Israel, Hungary and Hong Kong).

SSADM was developed before GUIs were in widespread use, and has recently been extended to cover analysis and design for GUIs. The GUI extension to SSADM is defined in a new manual *SSADM and GUI Design: A Project Manager's Guide* (1994). This document was produced by a working group of the International SSADM User's Group, and authorized by the SSADM Design Authority Board.

The SSADM/GUI project manager's guide concentrates on management-level issues, specifically on the following:

- How GUI design activities are integrated into the SSADM Structural Model (work breakdown structure).
- What GUI design products are required, and how they relate to SSADM products.

The guide does not:

- Give 'how-to' guidance on the techniques used to create the products.
- Define the notations to be used for the products.
- Give worked examples of the techniques and products.

The lead author of GUIDE was a member of the working group, with the result that GUIDE both influenced and was influenced by SSADM/GUI. As a consequence, GUIDE and SSADM/GUI are compatible and indeed highly complementary. SSADM/GUI provides a management framework for large projects. GUIDE provides precisely the practitioner-level guidance that the SSADM/GUI Project Manager's guide requires to make it complete and usable by practitioners.

C2   PLUGGING GUIDE INTO SSADM/GUI

The central recommendations of the SSADM/GUI guide are as follows:

- That GUI design should be regarded as part of the specification of the Required System, and performed in stage 3.
- That additional products are required in advance of GUI design, notably a Task Model and a Users' Conceptual Model.
- That existing products need extensions and increased emphasis, specifically on defining who the users are (User Catalogue), measurable specification of usability requirements (Requirements Catalogue), and the Application Style Guide.
- That prototyping, usability evaluation and iterative redesign are crucial for an effective GUI design process.

It can be seen that this is the same fundamental message as GUIDE. Basically SSADM/GUI defines a framework and specifies a number of additional required techniques and products (like 'sockets'); the GUIDE products and techniques plug neatly into these sockets.

Each SSADM/GUI product and technique is listed in Figure C.1, indicating the GUIDE chapter which gives practitioner-level guidance on the technique, and detailed definition and examples of the product.

C3   SSADM/GUI STRUCTURAL MODEL

How these products are integrated into an SSADM project is best illustrated by the revised SSADM/GUI structural model, reproduced from the Project Manager's Guide in Figure C.2.

SSADM/GUI technique	SSADM/GUI product	GUIDE chapter	GUIDE product
User Analysis	User Class Description	5. Users and usability requirements	User class
Usability Analysis	Usability Requirement	5. Users and usability requirements	Usability requirement
Task Modeling	Task Model	6. Task modeling	Task model
Task Scenario Definition	Task Scenario	6. Task modeling	Task scenario
Style Guide Definition	Application Style Guide	9. Style guide definition	Application style guide
User Conceptual Modeling	Users' Conceptual Model	7. User object modeling 8. Dynamic modeling	User object model Dynamic model
GUI Design	GUI Design	10. GUI design	GUI design
User Interface Prototyping	User Interface Prototype	11. GUI prototyping	GUI prototype
GUI Evaluation	Evaluation Report	12. Usability evaluation	Evaluation report

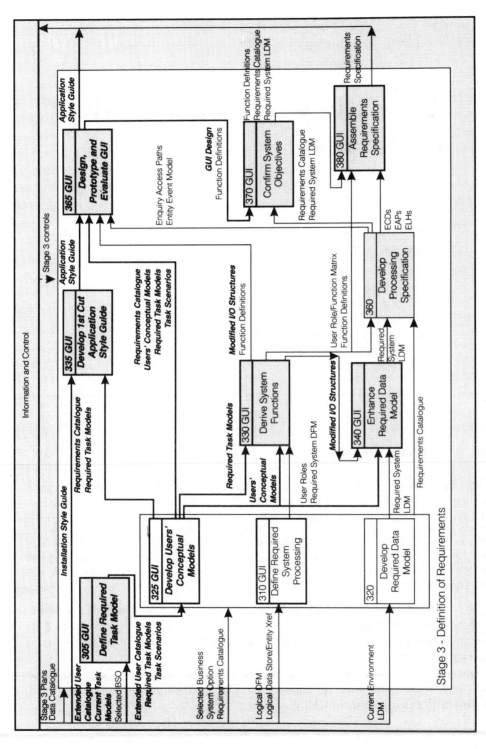

Fig. C.2   Structural Model for SSADM stage 3 showing activities for GUI design

Case study – why not just prototype?

DI INTRODUCTION

Some advocates of user-centered design suggest that prototyping and high user participation are all you need for good GUI design. Such people react to a process like GUIDE in the following way:

Why not cut out the analysis and modeling, and start prototyping on day one? The sooner you start prototyping, and the more iterations you perform, the more usable your GUI will be. If some parts of the GUI are initially not usable they will be exposed by prototyping and we'll modify them.

Real-world experience indicates that this approach can lead to serious problems. If the design team have neither GUI design skills nor a GUI design process, they are unlikely to produce a good design, no matter how much they prototype and the users participate.

This appendix consists of a brief critical review of one such system. It illustrates how prototyping and user participation may be necessary, but are certainly not sufficient to ensure a usable GUI design.

D2   BACKGROUND

The system is a management information system supporting the Helpline section of a customer support group of a software company. It provides a GUI front end to a database system holding customer queries and software problems.

The system development process involved the following:

- Very high end-user participation.
- An intimate knowledge of user tasks.
- Extensive prototyping and progressive refinement.
- Feedback from real-world operational use.
- Effective use of powerful GUI-building tools.

In this sense it represents a classic example of user-centered design. The developers were committed, and showed initiative, intelligence and design ingenuity. They were familiar with various professional GUI applications but had no training in or prior experience of GUI design, and used no defined design process.

To their credit, the system was successfully built and worked sufficiently well to be in operational use for over two years, holding 15,000 customer queries and adding a further 300 per week. It performed some tasks fast and efficiently, and provided management information that would otherwise have been impossible to obtain.

The reader will already have guessed that the system was in fact the 'existing system' in our UniSoft customer support Helpline case study. This permits various interesting comparisons to be drawn between the design created by the GUIDE process and the 'unstructured' design.

D3   CRITIQUE

The following sections in this appendix discuss the usability problems that become apparent, and the way these can be traced to the designers not addressing some of the key concerns which underpin usability.

D3.1   User classes and usability

Various people reported difficulties in use the system, saying it was 'not user-friendly' or did not enable them to achieve their goals.

Three major usability problems were identified.

System not easy to learn or intuitive to use

New staff found that it took several weeks of daily use of the system to become competent, and that it sometimes behaved in a counterintuitive way.

This reduced the effectiveness of new recruits. It also meant that the system was considered to be unsuitable for use by the company's customer support groups in other countries. The company therefore lost the business benefit of a unified worldwide customer support Helpline system for its products.

System works from perspective of only one user class

The Helpline system described in the main part of the book has six user classes, all with a legitimate interest in some of the information in the system. The previous system supported experienced Helpline advisors (who had participated in its design) to the exclusion of other user classes.

Specifically the system did not provide adequate support for the following:

- Inexperienced or infrequent Helpline advisors.
- The customer support manager.
- Salespersons and business managers.

System is inflexible

The design of the system is inflexible, in that it proved difficult to adapt it in the following respects:

- To remedy its usability defects.
- To extend it to be suitable for other user classes.
- To incorporate changing business practices (such as new procedures for quality certification).

These limitations made it difficult for the customer support manager to manage the Helpline group effectively, and made it more difficult to streamline the business process by improving information flows between the Helpline and other parts of the company.

D3.2   Task modeling

The designers had an extremely good understanding of the Helpline advisor's primary task, and the system is designed to support this well. Indeed parts of the GUI are very highly optimized to this task, and require the absolute minimum number of keystrokes and mouse clicks.

The team had (informally) used discussions of task scenarios to progressively streamline and speed up the entry of a customer query, a high-volume and time-critical task. There was, however, a problem with lack of breadth of task support. Not only were tasks of other user classes not supported, but other tasks of the Helpline advisors were not well supported.

D3.3   Style guide

The system was designed and built without a commitment to conform to any style guide. Its style is inconsistent and this makes it hard to learn and use. Although it runs under Microsoft Windows, the system is idiosyncratic — it does not look or feel like any other GUI application in the world (see Figure D.1).

The appearance is made more strikingly nonstandard by all the controls being different colors (light blue, dark blue and black and grey above, with yellow and red text) with some field prompts (e.g. Call Back) being in red.

A further comment on style is that the system is not even internally consistent — controls which look the same behave in different ways.

The representations are misleading. From using other Windows applications one might expect the icons on the left to be either objects, or subapplications (e.g. tools). In fact they are part of a menu system to pull down modal lists as part of a search process.

D3.4   User's conceptual model

The system does not enable the user to form a coherent mental model, and this causes various usability problems.

The structure of the user interface does not help the user — there is just one window, in which everything happens, and the title of the window just informs you that this is the Hotline system. It is not clear what objects there are, since none of the panes or fields have headings. Even when you know what objects there are, it is not clear which instance of an object you are dealing with. For example, although the Queries have unique reference numbers, these are not normally displayed.

Secondly, it is not clear what actions are available to the user, or which actions relate to what objects. For example, does 'SAVE' (bottom left) save a Customer, a Contact, a Query or a Bug, or all four?

Some of the objects have hidden state information, which is of interest to the user, but cannot be viewed anywhere in the user interface. (You have to interrogate the database directly using a programming tool to see this.)

Finally, some of the actions have 'clever' hidden functionality where they change the state of objects in ways which you might not expect and cannot see. For example, one important action sends a problem from the Helpline to second-line support, but there is no way in the user interface to view the effect of the action.

The effect of all this is a system where it is difficult for a user with a task goal to plan a sequence of actions in the system which will achieve that goal. In addition, users do not feel in control of their actions and lack confidence, because they are uncertain when the system will do something unpredictable that they did not intend. These are two classic symptoms of difficulties forming an adequate users' mental model.

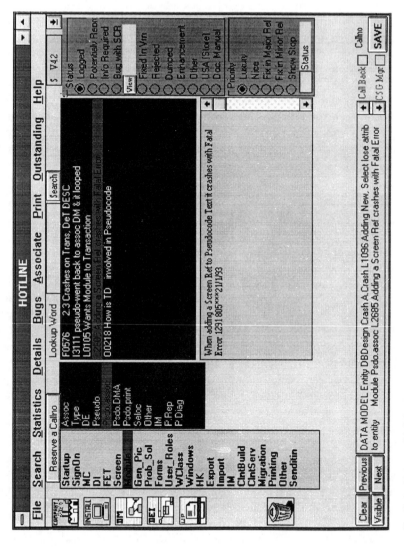

Fig. D.1 Existing Helpline system

Investigation of the system shows that this important usability problem cannot be blamed on the users. The system was designed and built without any coherent conceptual model. Even where the underlying logic is coherent, there is no attempt to make the system image guide the user towards the appropriate mental model.

D3.5   GUI design

The lack of a coherent conceptual model combines with a lack of consistent style to produce an interface in which it is very hard for the user to 'recognize' or 'guess' what controls represent or do. The absence of titles, labels, messages and help screens exacerbates these problems.

What you see here is a system designed for someone to whom it is 'obvious' what the controls mean and do, i.e. it is designed for its developers, rather than designed to be learnable and usable by a wider population of users.

Further, several of the crucial principles of user interface design have been violated − for example, the principle that the system should give the user feedback on the state of the system and the effect of actions.

D3.6   Usability evaluation

Although the GUI was prototyped extensively, it was never formally evaluated in terms of usability requirements.

Thus while the system was progressively refined and improved in the areas where it was already most usable (experienced Helpline advisors dealing with their primary task), the most serious usability defects were not addressed.

Anyone who complained about these defects was told 'this is a very fast, powerful system only suitable for experts'.

When the usability of the system was evaluated using the Software Usability Measurement Inventory (SUMI), the global usability score was 18, the lowest SUMI score we have ever seen. (This compares with a target usability score of 50 for average software, and 60 for good commercial software.)

As one might have anticipated, the Helpline advisors who had participated in the design of the software did not share other users' views of its usability. The average global usability score generated by this subset of users on the same survey was 58.

This highlights a common and important problem in GUI design and development. People who have been involved with creating a design know how it is intended to work, tend to be personally identified with it, and are inclined not to see its usability problems. One effective way to counter this tendency is to show developers videotapes of users struggling to perform simple tasks and getting stuck or lost in the user interface.

Software Usability Measurement Inventory (SUMI)

E1   INTRODUCTION

This appendix discusses the use of a standard usability questionnaire called SUMI as part of usability evaluation.

The central concern of GUIDE is to design GUI systems with high usability. But usability is a subtle, multifaceted phenomenon − it is often not obvious how usable a design is, and not obvious how to measure usability. In this situation it is very useful to have a simple, quick way of measuring users' perceptions of usability. This is what SUMI is designed to provide.

As with any measurement involving human beings, some element of caution and interpretation is required. One is not measuring usability in a direct and objective way; one is measuring the expressed perceptions of human beings. Specifically, people's responses will be influenced by various 'context' factors, such as the following:

- How experienced they are with the system.
- What tasks they perform with the system.

- Whether they associate the system with something unpleasant (such as job losses), or pleasant (such as less tedious work, or more bonuses).
- Whether they are personally identified with the system or feel 'loyal' to it for any reason.

In certain situations, people may even choose *not* to write down what they really feel, e.g. if there is some pressure on them not to be critical.

However, even allowing for influences of 'context', what users say they think and feel about using a system is some of the best evidence we have about its usability. GUIDE recommends that some form of survey of user perceptions of usability is performed as part of the GUI Evaluation process.

E2   WHY USE SUMI?

Why use SUMI, or some equivalent prepackaged usability measurement instrument?

- It is quick and easy for the end-user to complete.
- It is quick and easy for the evaluator.
- It does not require psychological expertise in formulating and piloting valid questions.
- It does not require statistical expertise in transforming or analyzing data.
- It produces a quantitative usability metric, with relevant benchmarks to compare it against.
- It produces specialized scales, measuring different aspects of usability.
- It gives indications of what types of usability problem are present in a system.

In short, it produces a useful measure of usability, and is sufficiently quick, cheap and simple to be usable by the practitioner who is not a GUI design or human factors specialist.

E3   WHAT IS SUMI?

SUMI is a psychological measuring instrument, a tool for eliciting and quantifying people's perceptions of how usable a software system is.

What exactly does SUMI consist of?

- A questionnaire with fifty statements. For each of these a user marks one of three boxes: agree, disagree or undecided. (The latter may mean 'partly agree/partly disagree' or 'not applicable'.) Examples of SUMI statements are: 'This software responds too slowly to inputs'; and 'I would recommend this software to my colleagues.'

- A floppy disk containing a statistical package which runs under Microsoft Windows on a PC. This includes:
  - a scoring system which weights the scores, and combines the scores for the different users and questions to give an overall usability score for the user interface;
  - a standardization database, which is used to compare your users' responses with the expected pattern of responses to the questions;
  - various statistical functions, such as confidence limits and statistical significance.
- A user manual which explains what to do and how to interpret the results.

E4   HOW DO YOU USE SUMI?

You identify a sample of users. This can be as small as one (SUMI will still calculate a usability score). Our experience suggests that it is possible to obtain a useful result with between five and seven users (given that perceptions inevitably vary between people). The developers of SUMI are a little more cautious, and suggest a minimum of about ten users to obtain a reasonably reliable score.

You decide what context information you wish to collect and prepare a list of questions for the cover sheet. This normally includes items such as frequency of use, length of time using software, whether formal training was received, whether manuals are accessible.

You brief your users (either verbally or by putting an introductory letter on the front explaining what you want them to do and why).

You give them a cover sheet and a SUMI form, and they mark the agree/disagree/ undecided boxes. This takes 10–20 minutes.

You type the scores into a standard word processor (12113 . . . etc.) and export it as a plain text file (ASCII). (Agree = 1, undecided = 2, disagree = 3.)

You present the file as input to the SUMI analysis package. It automatically performs the required transformations and the relevant statistical analyses, and produces a printed report with your results.

You examine the results. Example results are shown in section E5 below.

In interpreting the results, you can attempt to relate the individual user's usability scores to their context information. If you have a sufficiently large sample, you may apply further statistical techniques to establish the influence of context factors on usability scores.

You can choose to follow up the SUMI study by interviewing users and asking them further questions about their responses. For example, which functions do they think are too slow, or which menus do they think are illogical?

E5   EXAMPLE OF SUMI OUTPUT

SUMI-usability scores are standardized in such a way that 50 is the average score, with a standard deviation of 10. (In other words, most applications score between 40, which is poor, and 60, which is good.) The following are extracts from a real SUMI survey of eleven users.

> Global usability: 46
> 95% confidence limits:
> > Lower   39
> > Upper   54

In other words our best estimate of the usability score is 46, and we are 95 percent confident that the true score (allowing for sampling error) lies between 39 and 54. As the sample size increases, the confidence limits usually become closer.

Subscale scores

In addition to the global usability scale, SUMI produces five subscales which factor out user perceptions of different aspects of usability:

- *Efficiency:* Whether the user can perform tasks quickly, effectively and economically. Includes software performance and economy of keystrokes.
- *Affect:* The emotional dimension. Whether the user 'feels good, warm, happy or the opposite as a result of interacting with the software'.
- *Helpfulness:* Whether the software communicates in a helpful way and assists in problem resolution. Relates particularly to messages and help.
- *Control:* Whether the software responds in a normal, consistent and predictable way to input and commands, so that the user feels in control.
- *Learnability:* How quick and easy it is to learn how to use, and whether manuals are readable and instructive.

The scores for these subscales for the same sample were as follows:

> Efficiency   43
> Affect   59
> Helpfulness 46
> Control   47
> Learnability 65

The scores were high for Learnability and Affect (users liked the product), but low for Efficiency (in this case the users complained both about software response time and about the software being long-winded to use, with too many keystrokes).

Individual scores

SUMI outputs the usability scores for each individual user:

User	GLO	Effic	Affec	Helpf	Contr	Learn	
I	46	40	59	42	47	65	User name I
2	66	65	66	62	63	65	User name 2
etc.							

This is useful for follow-up interviews.

Consensual item analysis

SUMI compares the pattern of responses to each question (item) with the responses expected from the standardization database. Part of the report is reproduced in Figure E.1.

The goodness of fit between the observed and the expected responses is summarized using chi square. The greater this value, the more likely it is that your obtained user scores differ from the standardization database.

E6   CONTACT INFORMATION

SUMI was developed as part of a large-scale collaborative metrics project funded by the European Community (CEC ESPRIT Programme, Project 5429, Metrics for Usability Standards in Computing (MUSiC)). The questions have been extensively validated, and the standardization database contains results from over 1000 users using more than 100 application systems.

At the time of writing (1995), SUMI costs approximately $800 (IR£399 + VAT) for the standard version. A cut-down version with instructions for manual scoring (but no software) is available for academic institutions at a reduced cost of $200 (IR£99 + VAT).

It is available from:

> Mary Corbett
> Human Factors Associates Ltd
> 39 Cove Street
> Cork
> Republic of Ireland
> email: HFRG@IRUCCVAX.UCC.IE
> Tel: ++353-21-274 873
> Fax: ++353-21-274 694

Item 44   It is relatively easy to move from one part of a task to another.

Chi square value = 32.16

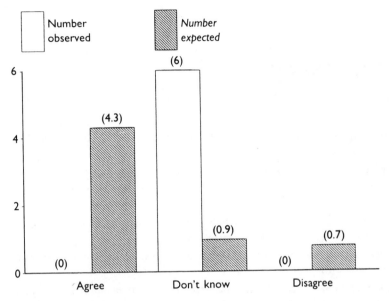

Item 22   I would not like to use this software every day.

Chi square value = 29.48

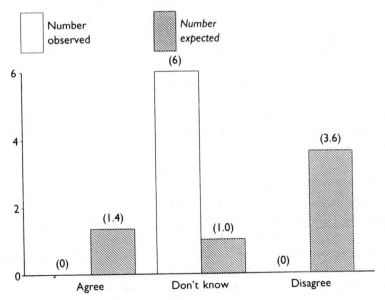

Fig. E.1   Sample SUMI consensual item analysis

Glossary

Application style guide a document which defines the agreed style consistency standards for the user interface of an application system.

Catastrophic error a situation in which a user is unable to complete a task using the GUI, or believes they have completed a task successfully when they have not.

Control see 'window control'.

Corporate style guide a document which defines the agreed user interface consistency standards for all the systems in an organization.

Data model a model of the logical data content of a system, expressed in terms of entities, relationships and attributes.

Dynamic model a model of how the behavior of an object depends on (and affects) its state.

Environment style guide a document which defines the consistency standards for a specific GUI environment (e.g. Microsoft Windows, Apple Macintosh).

GUIDE the Graphical User Interface Design and Evaluation process described in this book.

Helpline the name of the system used as a case study example in this book.

Incremental development a way of organizing design and development in which the planned system is partitioned into a number of increments, which are prioritized and developed one at a time.

Iterative design an approach to design in which an initial design is revised several times in response to feedback.

Mental model a model (of a computer system) in someone's mind. Mental models are usually incomplete and may be inaccurate, but are very important for users to understand and predict system behavior.

Menu a list of actions (or objects) from which the user can select.

Process the way in which an activity is performed.

Product something which is produced by a process.

Prototyping the process of developing and interacting with a partial version of a system in order to gain user feedback and evaluate usability.

Scenario-based prototyping a form of prototyping where the depth and breadth of the prototype is determined by the requirements of a few scenarios.

SUMI Software Usability Measurement Inventory, a standardized questionnaire for measuring usability (see Appendix E).

Task model   a diagram and supporting text showing the hierarchic structure of a user task.

Task scenario   a specific example of a task and how it is performed.

Usability   the extent to which a computer system is easy to learn and effective to use. Usability depends on who the user is and what the task is.

Usability engineering   a technique for achieving usability by evaluating an initial design against predefined measurable usability requirements, and redesigning where necessary.

Usability problem   some aspect of the system which is a problem for usability, e.g. something which frustrates or confuses the user, or fails to meet a usability requirement.

Usability requirement   a statement of how usable the system is required to be, including how this will be measured or tested.

User-centered design   an approach to systems design in which the system is adapted to the activities, requirements and preferences of the end-user.

User class   a group of users who have a similar pattern of use and usability requirements.

User object   an object the user thinks is in the system.

User object action   an action the user can perform on an 'object in the system'.

User object model   a model of the objects the user thinks are in the system, including their attributes, relationships and the actions the user can perform on them.

Window   an area of the screen with a well-defined boundary (usually rectangular), which is used as the primary unit of GUI design.

Window action   an action that the user can perform on the user interface, such as selecting a menu item or pressing a push-button.

Window control   a visible object through which the user communicates with the system. Examples include push-button, check-box, scrollable list.

Window hierarchy   a diagram showing how the standard types of window in a system are related to each other. The hierarchy forms part of the application style guide.

Window navigation diagram   a diagram showing how users can navigate from one window to another.

Bibliography

Andriole, S.J. (1991) *Rapid Application Prototyping: The storyboard approach to user requirements analysis*, McGraw-Hill.

Apple (1987) *Human Interface Guidelines: The Apple desktop interface*, Addison-Wesley.

Booth, P. (1990) *Introduction to Human–Computer Interaction*, Laurence Earlbaum.

Browne, D. (1994) *Structured User-interface Design for Interaction Optimisation (STUDIO)*, Prentice Hall.

Coad, P. and Yourdon, E. (1991) *Object Oriented Analysis*, Prentice Hall.

Diaper, D. (1989) *Task Analysis for Human–Computer Interaction*, Ellis Horwood.

Gilb, T. (1988) *Principles of Software Engineering Management*, Addison-Wesley.

Gomoll, K. (1992) 'Some techniques for observing users', in Laurel, B. (ed.), *The Art of Human–Computer Interface Design*, Addison-Wesley.

Gould, J.D., Boies, J.J., Levy, S., Richards, J.T. and Schoonard, J. (1990) 'The 1984 Olympic message system: a test of behavioural principles of system design', in Preece, H. and Keller, L. (eds), *Human–Computer Interaction*, Prentice Hall.

Green, T.R.G. and Benyon, D. (1991) 'Describing information artifacts with cognitive dimensions and structure maps', in Diaper, D. and Hammond, N.V. (eds), *Proceedings of HCI '91: Usability now*, Cambridge University Press.

GUI Guidelines (1993) Corporate Computing Inc., Sausalito, Calif.

Harel, D. (1987) 'Statecharts: a visual formalism for complex systems', *Science of Computer Programming*, vol. 8, pp. 237–274.

Hix, D. and Hartson, H.R. (1993) *Developing User Interfaces: Ensuring usability through product and process*, John Wiley.

HUFIT Planning, Analysis and Specification Toolset (1990) HUSAT, University of Loughborough, UK.

IBM (1991) *Systems Application Architecture: Common user access guide to user interface design* (document number SC34-4289-00), IBM Publications.

International SSADM Users' Group (1993) *SSADM and GUI Design: A project manager's guide*, HMSO, London.

Laurel, B. (ed.) (1990) *The Art of Human–Computer Interface Design*, Addison-Wesley.

Microsoft (1992) *The Windows Interface: An application design guide*, Microsoft Press.

Monk, A., Wright, P., Haber, J. and Davenport, L. (1993) *Improving Your Human–Computer Interface: A practical technique*, Prentice Hall.

Nielsen, J. (ed.) (1989) *Coordinating User Interfaces for Consistency*, Academic Press.

Nielsen, J. (1993) *Usability Engineering*, Academic Press.

Nielsen, J. (1993) 'Iterative user-interface design', *IEEE Computer*, November, pp. 32–41.

Nielsen, J. and Mack, R.L. (1994) *Usability Inspection Methods*, John Wiley.

Nielsen, J. and Molich, R. (1990) 'Heuristic evaluation of user interfaces', in Chew, J.C. and Whiteside, J. (eds), *CHI '90 Conference Proceedings: Empowering people*, ACM, New York, pp. 235–41.

Norman, D. (1988) *The Psychology of Everyday Things*, Basic Books.

Norman, D. and Draper, S. (eds) (1986) *User-centered System Design: New perspectives on human–computer interaction*, Laurence Earlbaum.

Open University (1990) *A Guide to Usability*.

Open University (1990) *Human–Computer Interaction. Unit 4 Knowledge and Action: Mental models in HCI*, Course PMT 607, Open University, Walton Hall, Milton Keynes, UK.

OSF (1991) *OSF/Motif Style Guide*, revision 1.1, Prentice Hall.

Ould, M.A. (1990) *Strategies for Software Engineering*, John Wiley.

Potosnak, K. (1989) 'Mental models: helping users understand software', *IEEE Software*, September.

Ravden, S. and Johnson, G. (1989) *Evaluating Usability of Human–Computer Interfaces*, Ellis Horwood.

Rettig, M. (1994) 'Prototyping for tiny fingers', *Communications of the ACM*, vol. 37, no. 4.

Rubinstein, R. and Hersh, H. (1984) *The Human Factor*, Digital Press.

Rumbaugh, J., Blaha, M., Premerlani, W., Eddy, F. and Lorenson, W. (1993) *Object Oriented Modelling and Design*, Prentice Hall.

Shackel, B. (1990) 'Human factors and usability', pp. 27–41 in Preece, J. and Keller, L. (eds), *Human–Computer Interaction*, Prentice Hall.

Shneiderman, B. (1992) *Designing the User Interface: Strategies for effective human–computer interaction*, Addison-Wesley.

Smith, S.L. and Mosier, J.N. (1986) 'Guidelines for designing user interface software', Report MTR-10090, Esd-Tr-86-278, Mitre Corporation, Bedford, Mass.

Wagner, A. (1992) 'Prototyping: a day in the life of an interface designer', in Laurel, B. (ed.), *The Art of Human–Computer Interaction*, Addison-Wesley.

Walsh, P. (1989) 'Analysis for task object modelling (ATOM): towards a method of integrating task analysis with Jackson System Development for user interface software design', in Diaper, D. (ed.), *Task Analysis for Human–Computer Interaction*, Ellis Horwood.

Whitefield, A., Wilson, F. and Dowell, J. (1991) 'A framework for human factors evaluation', *Behavior and Technology*, vol. 10, no. 1, pp. 65–79.

Whiteside, J., Bennet, J. and Holtzenblat, K. (1991) 'Usability engineering: our experience and evolution', in Helander, M. (ed.), *Handbook of Human–Computer Interaction*, North Holland, chap. 36, pp. 791–817.

Index